972.95053 B273v

Vieques, the Navy, and Puerto Rican Politics

New Directions in Puerto Rican Studies

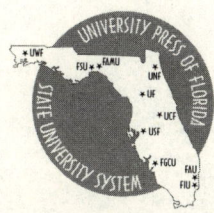

Florida A&M University, Tallahassee
Florida Atlantic University, Boca Raton
Florida Gulf Coast University, Ft. Myers
Florida International University, Miami
Florida State University, Tallahassee
University of Central Florida, Orlando
University of Florida, Gainesville
University of North Florida, Jacksonville
University of South Florida, Tampa
University of West Florida, Pensacola

New Directions in Puerto Rican Studies
Edited by Félix V. Matos Rodríguez

This series focuses on the diasporic experience in the United States and on the economic, political, cultural, and social aspects of life on the island of Puerto Rico. Of particular interest are manuscripts about the interplay between Puerto Rican and Latin identities, racial identity and racism, art history, nationalism and identity, migration and transnationalism, politics in the United States, the militarization of Puerto Rico, sexuality and gender, culture studies, and environmental issues.

Vieques, the Navy, and Puerto Rican Politics

Amílcar Antonio Barreto

University Press of Florida
Gainesville · Tallahassee · Tampa · Boca Raton
Pensacola · Orlando · Miami · Jacksonville · Ft. Myers

```
972.95053 B273v

Barreto, Amílcar Antonio.

Vieques, the Navy, and
 Puerto Rican politics
```

Copyright 2002 by Amílcar Antonio Barreto
Printed in the United States of America on acid-free,
TCF (totally chlorine-free) paper
All rights reserved

07 06 05 04 03 02   6 5 4 3 2 1

Library of Congress Cataloging-in-Publication Data
Barreto, Amílcar Antonio.
Vieques, the Navy, and Puerto Rican politics / Amílcar Antonio
Barreto.
p. cm.—(New directions in Puerto Rican studies)
Includes bibliographical references and index.
ISBN 0-8130-2472-2 (cloth: alk. paper)
1. Puerto Rico—Politics and government—1952. 2. Puerto Ricans
—United States—Politics and government. 3. Vieques Island (P.R.)
—History, Military. 4. United States. Navy—Maneuvers—Puerto
Rico—Vieques Island. 5. United States. Marine Corps—Maneuvers—
Puerto Rico—Vieques Island. I. Title. II. Series.
F1976 .B373 2002
972.9505'3—dc21   2002020001

The University Press of Florida is the scholarly publishing agency
for the State University System of Florida, comprising Florida A&M
University, Florida Atlantic University, Florida Gulf Coast University,
Florida International University, Florida State University, University
of Central Florida, University of Florida, University of North Florida,
University of South Florida, and University of West Florida.

University Press of Florida
15 Northwest 15th Street
Gainesville, FL 32611-2079
http://www.upf.com

To my grandmother, Ana Delia Castro Molina

Contents

List of Maps ix

List of Tables xi

Foreword by Félix V. Matos Rodríguez xiii

Acknowledgments xv

Abbreviations xvii

Introduction 1

1. Settlement and Fortifications 6

2. Target Practice 21

3. The Canonization of David Sanes 37

4. Clemency and Consensus 53

5. Politics in El Barrio 71

6. Transnational Identities 86

7. A New Era 98

Notes 105

Bibliography 127

Index 161

Maps

Map 1.1. Puerto Rico and U.S. Virgin Islands   9

Map 2.1. Vieques   25

Tables

3.1. Opinion on the U.S. Military Presence in Puerto Rico, August 1999   51

3.2. Opinion on the Transfer of the Southern Command to Puerto Rico, August 1999   52

4.1. Opinion on the U.S. Military Presence in Puerto Rico, June 2000   65

Foreword

It is a fairly common assertion these days that the struggle to have the U.S. Navy cease its use of the island of Vieques as a training and target-practice facility has changed the face of Puerto Rican politics. Many point to the development of a so-called consensus on the issue that has united people of different political, ideological, and religious backgrounds. Still, while speculation has been abundant, more serious analysis of the long-term implications of the politics around Vieques has been lacking.

Amílcar Barreto's book provides a deeper level of analysis by probing how the Vieques situation has altered not just Puerto Rican politics on the island but also in the United States. The mobilization against the U.S. Navy has also changed, according to Barreto, the Puerto Rican political landscape in the U.S. and the way in which Puerto Rican and mainland politics intersect. Barreto describes how, for example, Puerto Rican political leaders in New York City have made the Vieques crusade a local issue, developing strategic alliances with other Latinos, African Americans, and other civil rights forces. Both in Puerto Rico and in the United States, support for the Vieques cause has been turned into a decisive feature of Puerto Rican cultural and national identity. Barreto carefully explores the historical and political forces behind this development and also documents the ironic tale of the role of U.S. armed forces and federal agencies in helping to fuel an increasing evolution of Puerto Rican identity.

One of the most innovative features of this book is the systematic linkage of political events in Puerto Rico with political and social developments in its diasporic communities. Barreto documents, for example, a new assertiveness and engagement by Puerto Rican politicians in the United States related to issues affecting Puerto Rico, particularly regarding its status and economic development. Politicians in Puerto Rico are usually uncomfortable with such engagement but have learned how to manipulate it for local political gain. Finally, Barreto's book also provides one of the first academic analyses of the politics behind President Clinton's controversial release of Puerto Rican political prisoners, highlighting the importance of island-mainland coalitions in this process.

As this book goes to press, the final outcome of the Vieques struggle is still uncertain. On the political arena, it is clear that the resolution or lack thereof of the Vieques situation will have a significant impact on the governor's race in Puerto Rico in 2004. Furthermore, Vieques is also bound to play a major role in the alliances of Puerto Rican elected officials in the United States. From the vantage point of civilian society, the campaign against the U.S. Navy's presence in Vieques has transformed the way that coalitions and mobilization occur among the so-called new social actors—such as environmental, grassroots, pacifist, labor, and religious groups—in Puerto Rico. The legacy of this transformation still remains to be seen.

This is the first book published in the series New Directions in Puerto Rican Studies, a collaborative venture between the University Press of Florida and the Center for Puerto Rican Studies. I cannot think of a better book to launch the series than Barreto's. I hope readers enjoy it and learn from it as much as I did.

Félix V. Matos Rodríguez
Series Editor

Acknowledgments

As a child of the "borderlands," I was made aware of the importance of cultural identities and their fluidity. Most of these identities took on special meanings, an almost sacrosanct significance, in particular places. In the mid-1970s our family resided in San Antonio, Texas. There I recall the reverence expressed, especially by Anglos, upon entering the Alamo. Its basic function as a house of worship continued. However, the dogma being affirmed was secular in nature. An old Spanish mission was transformed into a sanctuary of Texan identity.

Though raised in the United States, I understood that my parents' hometown of Lares also held special significance. On occasional visits to Puerto Rico, we made several stops in Lares to spend time with a rather large extended family. Looking at it now, it is hard to imagine that the charming plaza facing Lares's Catholic church was the focal point of an insurrection against the Spanish Crown in the nineteenth century. Perhaps the one place where this imagery came alive more than any other was my grandfather's ice-cream parlor across the street from the plaza. Salvador "Yinyo" Barreto did not just own a small business, he administered a minishrine and museum to the Grito de Lares and *puertorriqueñidad*. Here, too, I saw an ideal finding expression and special significance in a particular locality. I was reminded here that nationalism is a principle inherently obsessed with territoriality.

Years later I had the opportunity to visit another area before it attained a semimythical significance. In the early 1980s my uncle Ferdinand Quiñones took my brother Carlos and me to my first sojourn to Vieques. At the time I could not have imagined that this town, the neglected stone in the Puerto Rican edifice, would become the cornerstone of such an impressive pan-Puerto Rican movement. The signs, nonetheless, were there for anyone paying attention. I could not forget the image of a T-shirt prominently displayed in a souvenir shop. In big, bold letters it simply said, "*¡Fuera la Marina!*" (Navy get out!). That slogan was generally associated with independence supporters. And yet, as in all Puerto Rican towns, the overwhelming majority of Vieques residents supported either pro-Commonwealth or pro-statehood politicians. I remember conversations where people on the main island dismissed the community's pleas, claiming that all Vieques residents were closet independence supporters. Times have certainly changed. The events of April 19, 1999, drew me back to Vieques and served as a catalyst for this book.

Writing entails both ideas and a great deal of support. I was very fortunate to have friends, relatives, and colleagues provide me with an abundant supply of both. I would like to thank the Office of the Provost at Northeastern University for funding this project and giving me the time off to carry out this undertaking. I am grateful to assistance I received from the librarians and staff at Northeastern University; the Universidad del Sagrado Corazón in Santurce, Puerto Rico; and the Office of the Resident Commissioner in San Juan, Puerto Rico. But I am particularly indebted to the extraordinary help provided by the librarians at the Centro de Estudios Puertorriqueños at Hunter College, City University of New York.

While in New York City and San Juan, several dear friends and family members helped me out in numerous ways. I deeply appreciate the assistance of Olga Barreto, Joan and Robert Brand, Maud Duquella, Aida and Ferdinand Quiñones, and Luis Tulier. At the Political Science Department at Northeastern, I was fortunate to have the aid of Barbara Chin and Janet-Louise Joseph. Also, I would like to thank my morale boosters in the Political Science Department and the Program in Latino, Latin American, and Caribbean Studies at Northeastern. I thank my colleagues Christopher Bosso, Luis Falcón, Robert Gilbert, Robert Hall, Matthew Hunt, Constance Rose, Eva Thorne, Bonnie TuSmith, and Alan West-Durán. To my dear friend Ana Yolanda Ramos-Zayas at Rutgers University, *gracias mil* for all the support and advice. I also benefited from some wonderful suggestions from Katherine McCaffrey at John Jay College, Vieques activist Robert Rabin, and Bonnie Urciuoli at Hamilton College. I am deeply indebted to James Jennings at Tufts University and Félix Matos Rodríguez, director of the Centro de Estudios Puertorriqueños, and an anonymous reviewer for their critiques of an earlier draft of this manuscript. I would also like to thank Robert Burchfield for copyediting this work.

Finally, I would like to close by thanking one of my greatest supporters and one of the most special persons in my life, my grandmother, Ana Delia Castro Molina. As a former teacher and elementary school principal, she was a firm believer in a solid education and tough love. There are military academies that could take pointers from her (*¡fuego!*). Little did I realize that I would follow in her footsteps and teach. Through thick and thin she has always been there for me, and it is to her that I dedicate this book. *¡Gracias abuelita!*

Abbreviations

AFL	American Federation of Labor
AFWTF	Atlantic Fleet Weapons Training Facility
CPRDV	Comité Pro Rescate y Desarrollo de Vieques
EMA	Eastern Maneuver Area
FALN	Fuerzas Armadas de Liberación Nacional
FBI	Federal Bureau of Investigation
FMLN	Frente Farabundo Marti para la Liberación Nacional
FUPI	Federación Universitaria Pro Independencia
MINP	Movimiento Izquierdista Nacional Puertorriqueño
MOU	Memorandum of Understanding
MPI	Movimiento Pro Independencia
NAF	Naval Ammunition Facility
NATO	North Atlantic Treaty Organization
NMIP	Nuevo Movimiento Independentista Puertorriqueño
OEA	Office of Economic Adjustment
PAC	Political Action Committee
PIP	Partido Independentista Puertorriqueño
PNP	Partido Nuevo Progresista
PPD	Partido Popular Democrático
PRSU	Puerto Rican Student Union
PSP	Partido Socialista Puertorriqueño
ROTHR	Relocatable over the Horizon Radar
SNCC	Student Nonviolent Coordinating Committee
SOUTHCOM	United States Southern Command
UPT	Unificación Puertorriqueña Tripartita

Introduction

Boriquén—as its aboriginal inhabitants called their homeland—is celebrated for sand and sun. Tourists may see Puerto Rico as a haven from the frosty clutches of the northern latitudes, but this island is also a colonial outpost and a garrison from which two global empires extended their might into the Caribbean. The mass extinction of most colonial jurisdictions and the ensuing nativity of independent states remain one of the great hallmarks of the twentieth century. Yet at the dawn of the twenty-first-century Puerto Rico holds the distinction as the most populous colonial dependency. For the past five centuries Puerto Rico, the scenic tropical island, has also been a fortress.

Military landholdings run from one end of Puerto Rico to the other, but of the seventy-eight municipalities, none has become as intimately associated with the armed forces and debates over civil-military relations as has Vieques. Its shores are strewn with the remains of bullet casings, bomb fragments, and the refuse of war. Portions of Vieques were transformed into an environmental nightmare and a health hazard to those who call this place home. For years armed forces from the United States and its North Atlantic allies have employed Vieques for target practice and a staging ground for naval exercises. Its location in the northeastern corner of the Caribbean made this islet a coveted strategic locale. Of course, a windfall for the military became a disaster for Vieques residents—*viequenses*. The island's fate has been determined by military planners and administrators in distant capitals oftentimes indifferent to the plight of its inhabitants.

While still a Spanish colony, the Crown periodically dispatched troops from the main island of Puerto Rico to restore order in Vieques. They were not ordered in to protect the local populace so much as they were sent to protect Spain's territorial claims. Metropolitan powers were always concerned with the fate of their landholdings, less so over Puerto Rico's residents. Since the end of the 1898 Spanish-American War, Vieques has been

Washington's responsibility. Cries for help were ignored in San Juan as often as they were disregarded in Madrid or Washington. Mainstream politicians on the main island shamelessly, and with alarming frequency, sacrificed *viequense* interests to curry favors from the metropolitan capital, which is why Vieques residents often refer to themselves as the *colonia de la colonia* (the colony's colony).

For years local residents protested naval activities on their home islet. The U.S. Navy's use of Vieques for target practice devastated their livelihoods, physical health, and emotional well-being. Among the few who joined the *viequenses* to bring attention to their cause were environmentalists, social progressives, church activists, and Puerto Rican independence supporters. Protestors blocked entrances to military installations. Sympathizers published editorials and wrote to Washington. Decade after decade their calls were largely ignored. Like a dormant volcano that erupted with little warning, Vieques's plight became Puerto Rico's cause célèbre. Beyond the confines of the West Indies, Puerto Ricans living in New York, Chicago, Hartford, Boston, and other American cities joined their Caribbean brothers and sisters in words and protest. This book will explore the evolution of civil-military relations in Vieques and their impact on the transformation of ethnic identity on the island and the U.S. mainland. Vieques marks a new chapter in Puerto Rican history—the ascent of a more fervent cultural nationalism and ethnic identity.

The most recent wave of protests were triggered by the death of a *viequense* civilian killed during military exercises. Yet the conflict between locals and the armed forces has a rather long history. Chapter 1 delves into Vieques's role in the defense of its original colonial ruler—Spain. Throughout the first three centuries of Madrid's rule over Vieques, an administrative adjunct of the neighboring island of Puerto Rico, little was done in the way of development until other powers in the region displayed an interest in colonization. The earliest significant fortifications of Vieques in the nineteenth century inadvertently coincided with the emergence and evolution of a distinctive Puerto Rican identity—one that differentiated between *puertorriqueños* (Puerto Ricans) and European-born Spaniards.

This identity survived Puerto Rico's occupation by the United States and manifested itself in various forms. One of these expressions was the emergence of a more resolute variant of Puerto Rican autonomism and separatism. Nationalism, in particular its pro-independence alternative, was viewed by federal administrators less as a consequence of U.S. rule than a challenge to it. In the 1930s Washington's military plans in Puerto

Rico were premised on the suppression of this nationalism and in particular the squashing of one of its most memorable leaders—Pedro Albizu Campos. The image of Albizu Campos and his words of defiance find resonance in the slogans of modern-day protests.

Nineteenth-century military planners coveted Puerto Rico for its strategic location. At the dawn of the Second World War that value increased further. Chapter 2 focuses on this period, when the U.S. Navy purchased most of Vieques and forcibly relocated half its population. The quest to reoccupy former civilian lands became a hallmark of the Vieques struggle. Another dimension to the movement was added in the 1970s when the navy began using Vieques for military war games with live shells. Throughout the second half of the twentieth century these activities were justified in the name of the Cold War antagonisms between the United States and its rival, the Soviet Union.

Little was done about the military's activities until April 19, 1999. On that day, two navy planes flew off course and dropped their explosive consignment near a group of civilians. David Sanes Rodríguez, who died in that incident, became a martyr to the Vieques movement. Chapter 3 probes the myriad activists who decided to defy Washington openly by setting up an encampment on navy-owned beaches used for war games. A clear majority of all Puerto Ricans insisted that the navy should halt its bombing runs over Vieques and that the military should withdraw, conveying its landholdings to the municipality of Vieques. Many activists were pleasantly surprised when the island's pro-statehood ruling party, usually an apologist for U.S. military actions in the region, sided with the protestors and insisted that the navy put an immediate end to its bombing runs. Nationalism was now revealing itself in all quarters. What were Washington policy-makers to make of this display?

In the midst of the Vieques crusade, the demilitarization movement was linked to the release of a group of Puerto Rican political prisoners incarcerated in the 1980s. Their harsh sentences, many argued, were related less to their alleged activities and more to their connection with the Puerto Rican independence movement. Chapter 4 looks at President Bill Clinton's decision to offer them conditional clemency. The concurrence of these two movements—the release of the prisoners and the end to bombing in Vieques—equipped the navy's supporters with rhetorical ammunition. In their minds, the independence movement was behind both causes. They failed to realize the depths to which ordinary Puerto Ricans, even those unaffiliated with the independence cause, believed that the two issues were representative of injustices perpetrated against the Puerto Rican people.

Indeed, in the Vieques crusade, the traditional political parties played only minor roles. Instead, an array of civil, labor, and religious organizations took charge.

The involvement of mainland Puerto Ricans was as important as the activism of Puerto Rican islanders. The fifth chapter describes the persistent participation of large numbers of activists and ordinary citizens in the plight of Vieques and challenges previously held assumptions that mainland Puerto Ricans constitute an apolitical community. Throughout the conflict, mainland Puerto Rican community leaders and elected officials were in the vanguard of a movement determined to stand up against social injustice. Their involvement in defense of Vieques residents marked a new assertiveness of mainland Puerto Ricans in federal affairs. It also speaks volumes about the endurance of a distinctive Puerto Rican identity in the United States and its connection to the course of civil-military relations in Vieques. The articulation of a more assertive Puerto Rican nationalism on the U.S. mainland is derived from Puerto Rican interactions with American society. This defiant expression of cultural nationalism owes much to the historic struggles of African Americans. Racism and socioeconomic marginalization remain part and parcel of the urban experience of a racialized community.

Outside the standard parameters of public policy, the Vieques crisis highlights the evolving nature of Puerto Rican identity. Chapter 6 links the Caribbean and mainland branches of Puerto Rican nationalism. Articulated in different manners on the mainland and in the Caribbean, Puerto Rican identity, channeled through the Vieques crisis, took on a new and more assertive dimension. For years the separatist branch of Puerto Rican nationalism could rejoice in having one spot where it could celebrate and express its hopes and aspirations—the western town of Lares. The military's activities in Vieques, coupled with popular outrage over David Sanes's death, fertilized a new sociocultural terrain. Puerto Rican cultural nationalism, a more extensive variant than its separatist companion, now had its own sacrosanct site on the beaches of Vieques.

While stable at any given time, over the long run ethnic boundaries represent a shifting battlefield where rival claimants contest one another in an effort to characterize and redefine their group's parameters vis-à-vis others. Crises provide golden opportunities to agitate previously existing boundaries and rearticulate group identities. The recent Vieques movement is one such example. A host of social, cultural, religious, and political actors from Puerto Rico and the U.S. mainland contributed to this process. Vieques became a focal point of Puerto Rican transnationalism.

Disagreements over Vieques policy mask discrepancies over rival sociocultural myths. While Washington interpreted the Vieques conflict in terms of national security, Puerto Ricans construed it as the latest in a series of sociopolitical injustices, an issue of human rights, a patent expression of colonialism, and a blatant expression of disdain by federal officials toward their people. Beyond the standard confines of civil-military relations, the tensions between the U.S. government and Puerto Ricans represent the latest chapter in the progression of a cultural identity that refused to capitulate.

1

Settlement and Fortifications

In examining the current crisis in Vieques, one needs to understand the source of this conflict. Contemporary activists reach back into history when outlining Vieques's grievances and the indifference of its largest landholder—the U.S. Navy. At times indifference has bordered on hostility. In this chapter I examine some key milestones in Vieques's history under Spanish and American suzerainty. The contemporary dilemma over Vieques's fate has been marked by geography and the ambitions of military planners, as was the case with the neighboring island of Puerto Rico. Vieques's destiny was shaped by longitude and latitude, by the surrounding Atlantic and Caribbean trade routes, and by the ambitions of empire builders in Europe and North America.

Spanish Conquest and Settlement

Struggles among the major colonial empires from the sixteenth through the twentieth centuries highlight the importance of geography in international conflict. Localities were coveted for their natural resources, their potential as markets for metropolitan goods, and the strategic advantages they provided. Spain plundered Mexico and Peru for their deposits of precious metals. India became a major market for goods manufactured in the United Kingdom. Meanwhile, both Spain and Great Britain scuffled over Gibraltar—the gatekeeper to the western Mediterranean. Puerto Rico was the easternmost island in the Greater Antilles. Along with Cuba, Puerto Rico commercially and militarily linked Spain with the gold and silver mines of Mexico and Peru.[1] To lose either of these strategic islands to competitors jeopardized Spain's dominance in continental Latin America.

Fate sandwiched Vieques between the main island of Puerto Rico to its west and the U.S. Virgin Islands of St. Thomas and St. John to its east. Vieques is roughly twenty miles long and four and a half miles wide at its widest point. With a surface area of approximately fifty-one square miles, Vieques is twice as large as the island of Manhattan. While it administratively belongs to Puerto Rico, Vieques could be regarded, geographically, as one of the Virgin Islands.[2] Its current name derives from its indigenous name, "*Bieque*," literally "little island." This explains the island's Spanish nickname, *la Isla Nena*.[3]

Europeans first sighted Vieques during Columbus's second voyage to the Americas in 1493. Neighboring Puerto Rico was conquered and settled by Spain in a few years, but the Spanish Crown paid scant attention to Vieques until rivals showed interest in this real estate. By the middle of the seventeenth century England occupied Tortola—today part of the British Virgin Islands—and set its sights on expanding westward into Vieques.[4] In 1689 Puerto Rico's governor, Don Gaspar Martínez, sent an expedition of Spanish troops to expel three hundred English settlers on Crab Island—the British name for Vieques.[5] Three decades later Spanish troops left San Juan harbor to dislodge yet another group of British settlers.[6] By the mid-1750s Spain was obliged to oust English colonizers from Crab Island once again.[7] Its nearby garrisons in San Juan apparently had little deterrent effect on British regional expansionism. Despite the island's vulnerability to foreign incursion, Madrid deliberated over Vieques's fate until the early 1800s.[8] By then Madrid could no longer ignore the territorial ambitions of both its American and European competitors. Furthermore, Vieques could also serve as a pirate haven or a staging point for launching insurrections in Puerto Rico and possibly Cuba.

Early in the nineteenth century Spain's continental colonies were engrossed in rebellion. Napoleon's 1810 invasion of Iberia served as a catalyst for revolutionary activism throughout Spanish-speaking Latin America.[9] Simón Bolívar was in the process of spreading a new political order throughout northern and western South America. Though there is no documented evidence of his arrival, popular legend claims that in 1816 Bolívar was in Vieques bent on spreading his insurgency to the Spanish-speaking Antilles.[10] Reportedly, Bolívar entered Vieques through St. Thomas, but improved relations between Spain and the United Kingdom eliminated Vieques as a possible platform for launching an insurrection in Puerto Rico.[11] Regardless of his possible visit, Puerto Rico would not join the Bolivarian insurgency. Its relatively small size, compared to Spain's possessions in Central and South America, facilitated colonial domination over Puerto Rico. Additionally, the migration of Spanish monarchists from continental Latin America to the Antilles injected a conservative community into this insular society.

Vieques's fate was also shaped by the geopolitical strategies of the United States. This young republic was demarcating the West Indies as part of its sphere of influence. In 1789 Alexander Hamilton wrote about the importance of the West Indies in *The Federalist Papers*: "By a steady adherence to the Union, we may hope, erelong, to become the arbiter of Europe in America, and to be able to incline the balance of European competitions in this part of the world as our interest may dictate."[12] In Thomas Jefferson's administration, there were policy-makers who openly longed to add Caribbean islands to their territorial wish list, especially Cuba.[13] Jefferson and John Quincy Adams, among others, opposed independence for Spain's Caribbean islands, hoping that one day they would become American possessions.[14] The boundaries between the United States and nearby European colonies were delineated by treaty. Nonetheless, in the mid-1800s Alexis de Tocqueville predicted that these accords would not stand in the way of American expansion.[15]

In April 1823 U.S. Secretary of State John Quincy Adams sent an emissary to King Fernando VII expressing American concerns over the status of Spanish Cuba and Puerto Rico. Secretary Adams responded to rumors that Spain might transfer these islands to the French. Adams's letter, issued only months before President James Madison went before Congress and announced what later became known as the Monroe Doctrine, reaffirmed the administration's viewpoint that the United States opposed the transfer of these islands to any other European power.[16]

Presupposing that settlement would preserve Spanish authority in the region, Puerto Rico's governor, Don Miguel de la Torre, sought the assistance of Vieques's largest landholder, Don Teófilo Jaime José María Leguillou.[17] Its smaller neighbor, the islet of Culebra, remained unsettled until 1880.[18] Though he was French, Leguillou has been regarded as Vieques's "founding father."[19] His fortunes were sustained by the slave labor that toiled in his cane fields. Leguillou's arrival on Vieques coincided with Denmark's claims on Vieques, given the island's proximity to the neighboring Danish colonies of St. Croix and St. Thomas.[20] Leguillou was appointed its first governor.[21] Vieques retained its own governor until 1843, when it became one of Puerto Rico's municipalities.[22] Its status as a Puerto Rican municipality remained unaffected by U.S. rule.

Puerto Rico's governor, Rafael Aristegui, established a military garrison on Vieques in 1844 and began the construction of a permanent citadel locally known as the Fortín.[23] His successor, Don Juan Prim y Prats, expanded the fortifications despite contrary orders from Madrid. Spain was reluctant to invest in additional military infrastructure until the island's

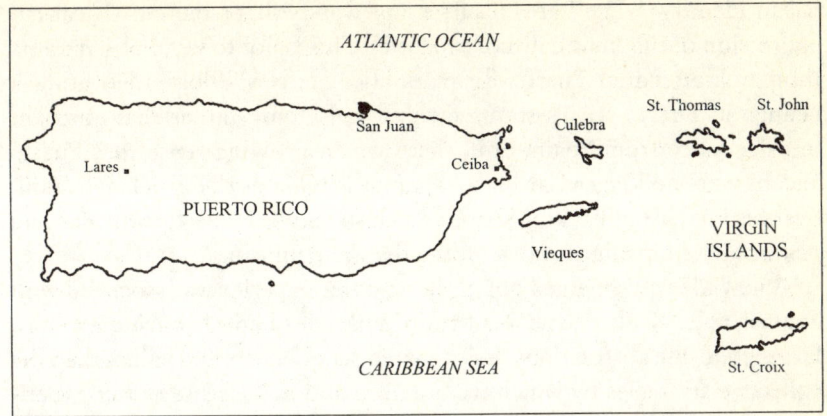

sovereignty was settled and recognized by the neighboring colonial states. For disobeying orders, Prim y Prats was relieved of the governorship on September 4, 1848. Ironically the garrisons that cost the governor his post helped secure Spain's claims over Vieques.[24]

Politics and Identity in the late 1800s

As noted earlier, Spanish authorities were constantly concerned with the territorial ambitions of their colonial rivals and the spread of revolutionary ideals from the new sovereign states in Latin America to Cuba and Puerto Rico. Suspicions of subversive activity led Spanish authorities to crack down swiftly and harshly on the regime's opponents. The most notorious period of political persecution was the *compontes* of 1887—a campaign of repression whereby autonomists were accused of secretly plotting independence. This local reign of terror was headed by Governor Romualdo Palacio González.[25] Spanish conservatives justified their actions on account of earlier insurgencies, such as the 1868 Grito de Lares rebellion in Puerto Rico. Whereas the Lares uprising was quickly crushed, its contemporaneous rebellion in Cuba, the 1868 Grito de Yara, ignited a decade-long insurgency.[26] In the aftermath of that insurgency, bitterness toward the Crown ripened, particularly among black Cubans, leaving promises of increased autonomy disregarded and suspect.[27] These upheavals served notice that islanders—Cuban and Puerto Rican—no longer considered themselves Spanish.

Vieques's political reintegration with Puerto Rico in the second half of the nineteenth century coincided with the evolution of a distinctive Puerto

Rican identity.[28] The Lares insurrection was perhaps the most clear-cut expression of that new collective identity. This is not to say that separatist thought dominated Puerto Rican political circles. Most advocating a change in Puerto Rico's status favored autonomy rather than outright independence from Spain. Still, there was a growing sense that Puerto Ricans were no longer Caribbean Spaniards but a distinctive people. Politics was increasingly taking shape as a clash between *puertorriqueños* and *peninsulares* (Spaniards born on the Iberian peninsula).[29]

A new identity emerged out of the negative experiences associated with Spanish rule. "Culture and identity are a parade of anachronistic symbols, larger-than-life abstractions, less a shared set of beliefs and values than the collective strategies by which we organize and make sense of our experience, a complex yet tightly integrated construction in a state of perpetual flux."[30] Ethnogenesis, the creation of a new ethnic identity, is an elite-driven process.[31] It is usually led by a segment of the local intelligentsia who utilize the media and social networks to disseminate their nationalist aspirations first among a select elite core and secondarily to the masses.[32] The construction of such collective allegiances is a deliberate process.[33] Their formation within a given society is almost always unevenly distributed between urban and rural, intellectual and the less learned, elite and pleb.[34]

If successful, the members of this new collectivity will see themselves as members of an extended family. This applies regardless of whether the identity being created brings together members of society's dominant group or one or more of its subalterns.[35] The creation of a new ethnic or national identity is frequently one of the responses of an emerging elite confronted by discrimination or frustrated by its lack of socioeconomic ascendancy.[36] In Puerto Rico, as in the rest of Latin America, this process was led by island-born whites—the criollos (Creoles)—who felt the sting of ostracism and prejudice doled out by *peninsulares*.[37] Criollos glorified the *gran familia puertorriqueña* (the great Puerto Rican family) as the unifying myth linking all islanders and peninsular Spaniards.[38]

Cultural markers are selected in order distinguish group members from outsiders, and these traits are highlighted as evidence of the group's distinctiveness.[39] Ethnic groups may be discernible on the basis of numerous traits, but the process of defining ethnic boundaries usually centers on only a few.[40] Ultimately, the traits selected to objectify the new national identity reflect the interests of the ethnic mythmakers.[41] In Puerto Rico, resentment toward Spaniards opened the door for criollos to invent a new identity positioning the center of their cultural universe in the Caribbean rather than in Europe. Ethnogenesis may be an elite-driven process, but it cannot succeed without the cooperation of society's rank and file, which explains why ethnic and national identities are grounded in society's "popular culture."[42] Criollo elites, particularly intellectuals, situated this new identity in the island's white highlands rather than on the more racially heterogeneous coasts.[43]

> Originally, the distinguishing features of a view of national identity—the *jíbaro*'s white skin, Spanish culture, materially impoverished lifestyle, preference for political autonomy if not neutrality, and patriarchal masculinity—were defined, legitimized, and romanticized by discrete members of the elite for their own class purposes. Eventually, broad acceptance of the jíbaro by all classes came to represent not only a legitimation of a sense of Puerto Rican-ness, which all Puerto Ricans discursively shared, but also a form for contestation of the legitimacy of the North American colonial project and the corresponding colonial identity it assigned to Puerto Ricans.[44]

The highland peasant, or *jíbaro*, was transformed into the paradigmatic Puerto Rican.[45] Such a definition inevitably marginalized black and racially mixed Puerto Ricans.[46] Yet the popularity of the *jíbaro* myth provided future activists with a potent political weapon. The defense of nonindustrial forms of production—agriculture, fishing, and the manufacture of handmade arts and crafts—was tantamount to safeguarding *puertorriqueñidad*.[47] Over time other ethnic mythmakers extolled *puertorriqueñidad*, though defining it differently than their predecessors. Twentieth-century Puerto Rican identity would have to take into account a new cultural matrix, one where the United States now played a significant role.

The American Invasion

Vieques's fortunes were tied to the main island—Spanish Puerto Rico became the U.S. territory of Porto Rico. The United States had a keen interest in attaining Puerto Rico long before the Spanish-American War. Federal officials were eager to take possession of this Spanish dependency that could serve as a military outpost and, secondarily, a market for American-produced goods.[48] "Military control of the Caribbean, as well as of the Atlantic and Pacific approaches to the United States, might be imperatively necessary to render the continental homeland of the American people invulnerable to external pressure and armed aggression. That idea in one form or another was historically one of the foundation stones of American diplomacy. It was the very essence of the Monroe Doctrine."[49] Regional military ambitions were supplemented with economic motivations. Indeed, many economic analysts at the time were convinced territorial expansion ensured secure markets for surplus production and alleviated the depression of the 1890s.[50]

One of the leading proponents of American overseas expansion in the late nineteenth century was Admiral Alfred Thayer Mahan, who exerted great influence over Theodore Roosevelt and the influential Republican senator from Massachusetts, Henry Cabot Lodge.[51] Great Britain served as Mahan's inspiration and model for the construction of an overseas American empire. For Mahan, the construction of a Central American canal, along with the acquisition of bases and the naval personnel to defend it, was a vital strategic objective.[52] In 1880 Mahan insisted that "to control at the Isthmus we must have a very large Navy—and must begin to build as soon as the first spade full of earth is turned at Panama."[53] It was not only important for the United States to construct such a canal, he insisted, but imperative that the country own it outright.[54]

The sinking of the battleship *Maine* in Havana's harbor served as the rationalization for the U.S. occupation of Spain's overseas colonies in the Atlantic and Pacific: Cuba, Guam, the Philippines, and Puerto Rico. In the course of the Spanish-American War, the U.S. Navy blockaded Puerto Rico. The main island was invaded on July 25, 1898, but Vieques was not occupied until September 10 of that year. Cut off from Spanish supplies, Vieques residents went hungry. Throughout the blockade of Vieques, rumors abounded that American forces would reduce the town to ashes and massacre the civilian population.[55] U.S. military officials were apparently unaware that the cannons in Vieques's fortress were unusable. At the time of their surrender, the 104 Spanish troops on Vieques—of which 13 were hospitalized—were armed only with hand weapons.[56]

By the end of 1898 the American Empire stretched from the Caribbean to the South China Sea and raised the country to the status of a world power.[57] American expansion prevented another power, Germany, from establishing a foothold in the region.[58] Puerto Rico, at the apex of the Greater and Lesser Antilles, became "the cornerstone of the U.S. strategic-military structure in the Caribbean."[59] Over the course of the twentieth century its value to defense planners continued to increase. "Because of the small size of Puerto Rico, the military has been able to dominate its civilian life from the very beginning of Spanish settlement. Time has only increased the island's military value and the determination of the military to keep it as a strategic base. Civil life is necessarily carried on in the shadow of military installation."[60]

The motivations behind the 1898 invasion still haunt efforts by the defense establishment and its supporters to recast the past in an effort to depict contemporary civil-military relations in a more positive light. Assessments of U.S. intentions in the 1898 conflict are influenced by the numerous military interventions in the Caribbean region, particularly Washington's involvement in Panama's partition from Colombia in 1903.[61] Judgments of American objectives in the Spanish-American War are also shaped by the total disregard showed toward Puerto Rico's incumbent civilian government.

At the time of the invasion Puerto Ricans were governed under a constitution conferred by the Spanish parliament—the 1897 Charter of Autonomy.[62] That pact left military matters in the hands of the Crown-appointed governor-general, while civil legislation was the responsibility of the local parliament. Spain relinquished its right to unilaterally amend its constitutional relationship with Puerto Rico. The charter stated plainly that "it shall not be amended except by virtue of a law and upon the petition of the insular parliament."[63] Overall, it granted *puertorriqueños* a substantial level of autonomy. José Trías Monge described the charter as "the most advanced document of any Caribbean colony until after the Second World War," and it marked the apex of Puerto Rican autonomy.[64] Washington became Puerto Rico's new colonial ruler without consulting the insular legislature or the island's inhabitants.[65] With the signing of the 1898 Treaty of Paris, Puerto Rico's sovereignty was conveyed to the United States without local input and without guarantees as to the island's final status.[66]

Puerto Rico's transfer of sovereignty may seem odd given the U.S.'s legendary veneration of democracy, individual liberties, and egalitarianism.[67] Still, it has been argued that the glorification of liberty and democracy early in U.S. history was less an expression of cosmopolitanism than a rhetorical device to distinguish American colonials from the British.[68] As one historian remarked, "American nationalism has often been circumscribed by implicit or explicit racial limitations that belied its universalistic promises."[69] From the perspective of the island's new rulers, Puerto Ricans, regardless of class membership, were nonwhite, and their assumed racial inferiority made them ineligible to govern themselves.[70] "Racialist constructions of Anglo-Saxon superiority were central ideological rationalizations for denying Puerto Ricans a decisive role in their own society."[71] Such a cultural construct—the relegation of the new colonial subjects as racialized, hence permanent, others—had an enduring impact on the course of U.S.–Puerto Rican relations. "Nationalism, by equating loyalty to the state with membership in the nation, transforms by definition members of national minorities into enemies of the state."[72] Federal policy-makers coveted the land of Puerto Rico but did not hold its populace in the same regard.

Puerto Ricans were eventually accorded a limited degree of autonomy with the establishment of the Commonwealth in 1952. However, even one of the architects of that political document underscores that this is still a colonial status.[73] Commonwealth status founders and their supporters have attempted to disseminate a new mythology painting the United States of the late 1800s as "a forgetful, kindly giant who by a trick of fate found itself unexpected with an empire on its hands."[74] This version of events is hard for some to accept when taking into account the less-than-generous public comments expressed by federal officials and prominent individuals.

Alfred Thayer Mahan, the architect of American expansion in the Caribbean basin, believed in the superiority of whites. That racial prejudice carried over to the inhabitants of the country's new colonial possessions. "The American officers of the navy and army are the best possible guardians you can give to these dependencies which have come to us under the treaty of peace. We have the opportunity of bestowing upon them a beneficence which they have never known. The officers of the army and navy are better qualified to deal with these subject races than men engaged in the hard fight of ordinary existence."[75]

Classifying a group as a "subject race" implies that it is the duty of self-anointed superiors to rule over their inferiors. Such a negative attitude toward the new colonials was not unique to Mahan or high-ranking American officials. As Edward Said has pointed out, "human societies, at least the more advanced cultures, have rarely offered the individual anything but imperialism, racism, and ethnocentrism for dealing with 'other' cultures."[76]

In the first years of U.S. rule, the federal government established a commission, headed by Henry Carroll, to make recommendations on the island's future. Assumptions of American racial and cultural superiority over Puerto Ricans were explicitly outlined in the commission's report,[77] which recommended the cultural assimilation of the island's inhabitants. Since the inception of the United States, its political elites viewed the cultural and linguistic incorporation of European immigrants into American society as a necessity.[78] National cohesion required a new identity, which was facilitated through the celebration of common public rituals such as the Fourth of July and Thanksgiving Day.[79] In keeping with this counsel, American presidents embarked on a half-century-long program to forcibly assimilate Puerto Ricans.[80] Indeed, President Franklin D. Roosevelt wrote in 1937: "It is an indispensable part of American policy that the coming generation of American citizens in Puerto Rico grow up with complete facility in the English tongue. It is the language of our nation. Only through the acquisition of this language will Puerto Rican Americans secure a better understanding of American ideals and principles."[81]

Americanization was undertaken, supposedly, for the insular community's benefit. President Roosevelt commented in 1934 that "the people in Puerto Rico and the Virgin Islands, and the Canal Zone and Hawaii, no matter what their racial origin may have been, are still our fellow citizens, and as such we have a very distinct responsibility for them as long as the American flag floats over them."[82] It was the duty of the United States to promote culture shift among its new colonials regardless of their racial differences.

Federal policies and attitudes toward the nation's new subjects were paradoxical. Washington insisted that Puerto Ricans discard the cultural traits distinguishing them from mainstream white society. Linguistic defection is a common first step in the integration—whether voluntary or involuntary—of subalterns into the larger society.[83] Still, even when they acquired these traits, Puerto Ricans were regarded as outsiders. As Walker Connor noted, "ethnic problems in the United States have not been primarily characterized by minorities resisting assimilation, but rather by the unwillingness of the dominant group to permit assimilation at the tempo desired by the minorities."[84] Federal officials neglected to take into account the islanders' preexisting identity as *puertorriqueños*. What government officials failed to see, others saw clearly. A traveler observed in the 1910s: "at the heart the Porto Rican is a Porto Rican first, last, and all the time, and to his credit be it said, for our colonial policies are far from perfection, and we have much to learn."[85]

Unfavorable perceptions of Puerto Ricans were far from the exclusive purview of the executive branch. Supreme Court Justice Henry Brown referred to Puerto Rico and the other recently conquered overseas territories as lands "inhabited by alien races."[86] Few were as frank about their bigotry as Tennessee Senator William Bate. In 1900 this former Confederate soldier referred to Puerto Rico and the Philippines as a "heterogeneous mass of mongrels."[87] Negative assessments of Puerto Ricans help explain why virtually none of the children of American bureaucrats or soldiers born in Puerto Rico in the early twentieth century identified themselves as Puerto Rican.[88]

The military government in Puerto Rico (1898–1900) was replaced by a congressionally imposed charter—the Foraker Act (1900). Under the Foraker Act, the governor was appointed by the U.S. president, who also appointed the members of the Executive Council—a body acting both as the governor's Cabinet and the upper chamber of the territorial legislature.[89] Despite the prior existence of a civilian government under the 1897 Charter of Autonomy, islanders' electoral rights were restricted to selecting lawmakers in the lower house of the bicameral legislature and municipal-level officers. In theory, Americans were appointed to top positions in the insular administration in order to tutor islanders in democratic governance. In practice, these proconsuls created highly centralized regimes that reinforced a social hierarchy of metropolitans above their Caribbean charges.[90] Tutelage was necessary from the U.S. perspective because the "[s]ubject races did not have it in them to know what was good for them."[91]

Most federally appointed governors were ignorant of island affairs prior to assuming their post. Few spoke Spanish. Many appointments were merely payback for political favors.[92] Governors were appointed under the Foraker Act and the Jones Act of 1917. Federal appointment of the insular governorship remained until the Jones Act was amended in 1947.[93] The Jones Act also imposed U.S. citizenship on the island's populace.[94] Federal control of the local executive certainly gave Washington policy-makers a freer hand in carrying out their military designs.

Following the war with Spain, the federal government procured several military sites around San Juan and Culebra.[95] Spain's citadels in Old San Juan—San Cristóbal and El Morro—fell under the jurisdiction of the War Department. Despite the historic Fortín, Vieques remained a largely agricultural society, economically dominated by sugar cane cultivation. Its relative prosperity was such that workers from neighboring islands, including the main island of Puerto Rico, migrated to Vieques to cut cane.[96] This state of affairs changed in the 1930s as defense strategists began making preparations for the Second World War. Thousands of Puerto Ricans served in the military, largely through conscription. In the 1930s jobs were scarce and welcomed in an impoverished society, but preparations for the war would also entail the loss of homes and thousands of livelihoods in Vieques. The same federal regime that gave with one hand took with the other. As Alpheurs Verrill commented in the second decade of the twentieth century: "One cannot blame the Porto Ricans if they chafe more or less under American rule; we have taken much from their lives, and while we have given a great deal in some ways, yet we leave much to be desired in others."[97]

Albizu Campos and the Nationalists

In the first few years of American rule, military analysts were already pointing out the strategic importance of Vieques and Culebra.[98] Priorities elsewhere put Vieques on the back burner until the 1930s, when federal officials began preparing for the pending conflict in Europe. For years the U.S. Navy conducted occasional operations on the island of Culebra. Starting in 1936 Culebra became a regular site for naval target practice.[99] Renewed activities on Culebra focused attention on neighboring Vieques.

Before plans to expand military operations on Vieques could be implemented, policy-makers would have to contend with local resistance. Vieques had its share of troubles and even a few episodes of labor-related violence. Sugar cane workers throughout Puerto Rico staged numerous strikes in 1915 and 1916 protesting deplorable working conditions and low wages.[100] In the course of the 1915 protests, police killed several strikers in front of the Vieques town hall. One author referred to those killed in 1915 as the "first martyrs in the struggle of the people of Vieques."[101] In addition to labor union activism, military planners were also concerned with independence advocates. Syndicalist and separatist leaders found that their fortunes were inversely related to the fate of the economy.

Though small compared to its continental counterparts, there was an independence movement in Puerto Rico in the nineteenth century. The event most frequently cited as its debut was the 1868 Grito de Lares rebellion. While this uprising failed to achieve its political goals, it served subsequent generations of Puerto Rican separatists as a pivotal and defining moment. Although the 1868 rebellion was led by Ramón Emeterio Betances, the individual most responsible for popularizing September 23, the Grito's anniversary, in nationalist folklore and commemoration was his twentieth-century heir, Pedro Albizu Campos. This Harvard-educated lawyer was the president of the Partido Nacionalista (Nationalist Party) in the 1930s, and he tenaciously opposed the American military's presence in Puerto Rico.[102]

Conceived while the island was still under Spanish tutelage, Puerto Rican nationalism persisted well into the American era. Although most nationalists were, and remain, autonomists rather than separatists, there has always been a persistent core of islanders determined to see their homeland break its colonial bonds.[103] Albizu Campos's impact on island nationalism far surpassed his, and his party's, electoral appeal.[104] He insisted on the immediate independence of his homeland and the withdrawal of all U.S. military forces.[105]

Pedro Albizu Campos was but one nationalist leader. A far more troublesome concern for American officials was the ongoing separatist movement in the Philippines. Early in their occupation of the Philippines, American forces battled Emilio Aguinaldo in an attempt to thwart his drive to establish a sovereign archipelagan state. Though Albizu Campos's movement did not pose the same threat to U.S. rule in Puerto Rico, American officials based in San Juan were nonetheless alarmed at the specter of the Sakdal uprising in the Tagalog provinces of the Philippines in 1935.[106] From 1941 until 1946 Rexford Tugwell was the governor of Puerto Rico. Referring to his predecessor, Guy Swope, and the connection between military base development and the Nationalist Party Tugwell said: "For these *Nacionalistas* were, if not communists, at least allied with them in the common purpose of causing disorder; and they were well educated in terrorist tactics. As the national defense work went on and the interest of the United States in Puerto Rico as a base became greater, he [Swope] foresaw grave trouble which would be precipitated by an intolerant military and end in widespread incidents."[107]

In 1930 Albizu Campos's Nationalist Party convened an assembly in Vieques.[108] An enlarged military role for Vieques had yet to be announced. Still, for Albizu Campos, the withdrawal of U.S. forces was an indispensable step in the struggle for Puerto Rico's independence.[109] Tensions mounted between the American regime and the Nationalist Party in the 1930s. Several violent clashes between authorities and members of the Nationalist Party in the mid-1930s culminated in the assassination of Colonel Francis E. Riggs, the island's chief of police. In response, Albizu Campos was convicted of conspiring to overthrow the U.S. government in Puerto Rico in 1936.[110]

Albizu Campos's incarceration left a political void filled by the charismatic Luis Muñoz Marín. Both the Roosevelt and Truman administrations considered him a moderate leader with whom they could negotiate a continuing U.S. presence on the island—one that would satisfy federal interests, heavily laced with military objectives, and the pent-up frustrations of tens of thousands of Puerto Ricans. As one observer commented in the 1940s:

We have heard the fabulous profits made by sugar interests in Puerto Rico, but has that profit to a small group of investors balanced the cost to the American taxpayer, to our prestige in international affairs, and above all to our democratic conscience? What are our responsibilities to ourselves, to the Puerto Rican people, and to humanity? Military considerations are certainly counter-balanced by the bitter anti-American feeling on the island which supplies excellent material to the anti-American publicists throughout Latin America and the rest of the world. Would it not be far cheaper to pay the Puerto Rican people a yearly rental for army and navy bases than to contribute to their upkeep as we have been doing in recent years, while at the same time supplying political ammunition to those who are not too friendly to the United States and the American way of life?[111]

Muñoz Marín's political party, the Partido Popular Democrático (PPD) (Popular Democratic Party), was founded in 1938 and spearheaded the creation of the Commonwealth status. In the eight years following its founding, the PPD united both autonomists and separatists. Throughout the 1940s the Populares, as members of the party are still known, succeeded in channeling Puerto Rican nationalism from support for independence to espousal of autonomy in one guise or another.[112] At the time, this alliance between separatists and autonomists concerned American officials. As Governor Tugwell wrote: "Mr. Swope indicated to me that he had found he could trust Muñoz, that he believed him to be a high-minded man; but that he was, nevertheless, profoundly concerned with his followers. They would, he felt, push their party further and further into anti-Americanism."[113] This predicament was eliminated in 1946 when Muñoz Marín declared that his party would not support independence; thus, he expelled *independentistas* from his party.[114] These dissidents, under the leadership of Gilberto Concepción de Gracia, organized the Partido Independentista Puertorriqueño (PIP) (Puerto Rican Independence Party).

The fiery Pedro Albizu Campos, behind bars in the federal penitentiary in Atlanta, no longer posed a problem for the federal government. Yet his persecution and prosecution by federal authorities had an enduring impact on the role of culture and Puerto Rico's independence movement. Contemporary independence leaders such as the social democratic Rubén Berríos Martínez and the Marxist Juan Mari Bras extol Pedro Albizu Campos as the founder of modern Puerto Rican national identity.[115]

"Albizu refined and popularized national sentiment in Puerto Rico like no one else, before or after him; and until the present there has not been another voice in this country like his."[116] Throughout the twentieth century Pedro Albizu Campos became an icon shaping the discourse on cultural authenticity.[117]

Albizu Campos's vehement opposition to the American forces helped to link the connection between separatism and the drive to oust the U.S. military. That connection solidified even further thanks to the continuing campaign for the island's demilitarization, led by various parties and organizations directly affiliated with the independence movement. Albizu Campos's legacy, combined with the impending Cold War, aided American apologists in their rhetorical crusade. Those supporting demilitarization were *independentistas*; hence they were subversives and possibly agents of Cuba and the Soviet Union. In only four decades Puerto Ricans went from being an "obedient," "moral," and "law-abiding" community, in the view of Henry Carroll, to a people showing clear signs of discontent with their assigned station.[118] The struggle to demilitarize Puerto Rico, with or without much popular support in different periods, always found separatists at its forefront.

The new ethnic boundaries also laid the groundwork for the progression of tensions between the people of Vieques and the U.S. armed forces. While they may have been unaware in the 1930s and 1940s, Pentagon planners resolving to maintain U.S. military operations in Vieques became key players in a cultural conflict between Puerto Rico and the United States—a discord with serious implications for U.S.–Puerto Rican political relations. Patriotic folklore in the United States asserts that loyal Americans should always support the armed forces. Unquestioned commitment to the U.S. armed forces took on a distinctly contradictory meaning in Puerto Rico. To support the navy's activities in Vieques would be articulated as tantamount to supporting social injustice and cultural betrayal. The cultural divide between Puerto Ricans and Americans expanded to include incongruent assessments of national security needs and human rights.

2

Target Practice

Responding to a looming global conflict, Franklin Roosevelt's administration planned to build a Caribbean base on the order of Pearl Harbor in eastern Puerto Rico. The Roosevelt Roads base would encompass portions of Ceiba, on the main island, and the island municipalities of Culebra and Vieques. Most of Vieques was purchased by the U.S. military and much of its civilian population relocated, despite strong local objections. While many *viequenses* were ejected from their homes in the 1940s, their worst fears were not realized until the 1970s. A prolonged civil disobedience campaign convinced the Pentagon to stop using Culebra for target practice. Instead, the defense establishment opted to use Vieques for that purpose. Over the last quarter century Vieques residents and sympathizers from abroad advocated the end of naval bombing and the return of military landholdings to civilian use. Opponents and proponents of the military's policies engaged in continual struggle for the sympathies of the Puerto Rican public. An unnerving question that never disappeared was whether the U.S. Navy would have persisted in its operations were the local population not Puerto Rican. Civil-military relations in Vieques could not escape the "Puerto Rican factor." On the mainland, Puerto Ricans were a marginalized minority. In the Caribbean, this island remained a U.S. colonial outpost.

Navy Expropriations on Vieques

German expansionism in the late 1930s alarmed the United States and its European allies. Adolf Hitler's invasion and subsequent annexation of Austria persuaded the United States to enlarge its armed forces. In May 1938 Congress passed the Vinson Bill providing for a 20 percent increase in the number of existing naval vessels and military aircraft.[1] In addition to their concerns over Germany's territorial ambitions in continental Europe, Allied leaders were also concerned with the Nazi regime's designs on

British and French possessions in the West Indies and possibly the Panama Canal.[2] By the summer of 1938 Charles Edison, acting secretary of the navy, appointed a commission to review the country's maritime defense needs. The commission, headed by Rear Admiral Arthur J. Hepburn, prioritized several base construction and expansion projects. Four out of the five projects deemed "of immediate strategic importance" were in the Pacific. The only locale assigned such a high priority in the Atlantic was Puerto Rico.[3]

American and British government representatives negotiated a "Destroyers for Bases" agreement in September 1940 in the hopes of preventing a German takeover of the Caribbean. The United Kingdom received fifty destroyers from the United States; in exchange, the U.S. government secured the right to build bases in several British possessions—mostly in the Caribbean.[4] In addition, the Roosevelt administration wanted to construct a large base on American property. Military planners had in mind a naval complex in Puerto Rico on the order of Pearl Harbor in the territory of Hawaii. This expansion allowed the army airmen to build a base on an island described as the most important U.S. possession in the Antillean chain.[5] As a result, San Juan's Isla Grande was transformed into a major military airfield, as was Punta Borinquen in the northwestern city of Aguadilla.[6]

American defense strategists were deeply concerned with the lack of dry docks between Charleston, South Carolina, and the Panama Canal Zone. San Juan harbor was already used by civilian and military vessels. Furthermore, the construction of a wartime dry dock required a sizeable parcel of land. The military's solution was the construction of a major fleet base at Roosevelt Roads in eastern Puerto Rico. The base would provide anchorage, docking, fuel, and repair services for 60 percent of the Atlantic Fleet.[7] Were the United Kingdom invaded, this Puerto Rican base would serve as a refuge for the Royal Navy.

The importance of this base was such that in February 1938 President Roosevelt, accompanied by Admiral William D. Leahy, personally came to observe military exercises in the waters of the Vieques Passage, the proposed site for this megabase.[8] Such a gesture is noteworthy given that U.S. presidents rarely visit Puerto Rico. The following year Roosevelt nominated Leahy to be governor of Puerto Rico to replace Major General Blanton Winship—one of the island's most unpopular governors. Admiral Leahy was appointed to the post, in large measure, to oversee the creation of this base.[9] His task was simplified when the territorial legislature transferred public lands in Culebra to the navy in 1939.[10]

Around the same time Governor Leahy took office, the U.S. Navy acquired the several plantations in Vieques. The largest, the Benítez estates, had been purchased in the late 1930s by Juan Angel Tió.[11] For years this sugar plantation suffered serious financial difficulties. During the Great Depression the federal Agricultural Adjustment Administration imposed severe sugar quotas in an attempt to reduce the glut on the domestic market. These quotas applied to Puerto Rico, a U.S. territory. Moreover, the plantation managers had to contend with new federal labor guidelines instituting an eight-hour workday. These factors drove the plantation out of business, and the land was assigned to the Bank of Nova Scotia.[12] In 1941 the military began its Vieques expropriations.

Through condemnation—seizing of private property for public use through eminent domain—the military took Tió's 10,209-acre Playa Grande plantation, compensating him $379,300 for his loss. The Eastern Sugar Associates were paid $423,000 for their 7,940-acre Esperanza estates. The federal government took 1,000 acres from the Benítez and Rieckehoff families and another 2,000 acres from a hundred smaller landholders. In all, the navy confiscated 21,100 acres in the early 1940s for $1,041,500. A few years later the navy took another 4,340 acres from the Puerto Rican government and several private owners, paying them $520,400.[13] From that point on, the U.S. military became the largest landholder on Vieques.

Ironically, the U.S. military, the same institution that fostered land reform in Japan and Korea following World War II, amassed large landholdings in Puerto Rico, dispossessing thousands of landless peasants in Vieques.[14] "Vieques was a perfect spot to practice war, and, with Puerto Rican residents not allowed to vote in national elections, political fallout would be minimal."[15] It is often assumed that adjoining communities reap tangible benefits from their proximity to military bases. Certainly that was not the case for Vieques residents. The War Department had no intention of becoming a landlord to thousands of sugar cane cutters and their families. Long-term residents on plantation grounds felt a sense of belonging. Of course, this sentiment had no legal weight. These residents were forced to move to other parts of Vieques, the main island of Puerto Rico, or St. Croix in the U.S. Virgin Islands.[16]

Military sources estimated that their acquisitions forced the relocation of 4,350 to 5,000 residents, or 40 to 50 percent of Vieques's population.[17] Families that resettled on other parts of Vieques found they were prevented from attaining legal title to their new homes. Without titles, the military could readily relocate them yet again. Despite owning three-quarters of Vieques, the navy aspired to secure the entire island. Vieques residents lived with the perpetual fear the military would ultimately transplant the entire civilian population, and this preoccupation greatly influenced their local identity. "Anti-military activists have viewed the usurpation of island land as the original atrocity committed by the Navy against the Viequense people, the source of communal outrage against the military."[18] Pedro Albizu Campos, the leader of the Nationalist Party, reserved some particularly stinging words for the U.S. military's actions: "In Vieques, the government of the United States is performing the vivisection of our nation. Vieques' society is dying, extinguishing itself before the cold, deliberate, and intentional attack of the United States government."[19]

By 1943 Allied commanders were encouraged by their victories in North Africa and Sicily. While German submarines continued to pose a threat to Allied shipping in the Caribbean, it was becoming clear that the West Indies would not become the next major battleground in the war. In addition, naval planners realized that concentrating operations in one immense base, such as Pearl Harbor, carried far too many risks.[20] Thus, American military planners modified their priorities and scaled back their construction plans at Roosevelt Roads. *Viequenses* hoped that the erection of a proposed sea wall linking eastern Puerto Rico with western Vieques would employ hundreds of locals. The proposed fourteen-mile breakwater would have provided sheltered anchorage for the Atlantic Fleet. However, the project came to a halt in August 1943, and it was never completed.[21] As Secretary of the Navy Edward Hidalgo would tell a congressional committee in 1980, unemployment on Vieques was not the responsibility of the U.S. armed forces; after all, "we are not a social organization."[22] The expropriation of the Benítez plantation, like the destruction of Solomon's Temple in Jerusalem by the Romans in the first century, spelled the beginning of a new chapter in Vieques's history—the onset of the Vieques diaspora.

By 1945 World War II was winding down, and Britain's navy was safe in its own territorial waters. This global conflict and the United Kingdom's need for an Atlantic safe harbor justified the navy's land purchases on Vieques and the ensuing forced relocation of almost half the *viequense* population. Naval planners found a new mission for Vieques. The military linked its properties on Vieques, Culebra, and Ceiba to form a single complex, Roosevelt Roads Naval Station.[23] Officially the navy owns five major plots of land on Vieques, but they are usually referred to as the western and eastern properties.[24] Western Vieques is dominated by the Naval

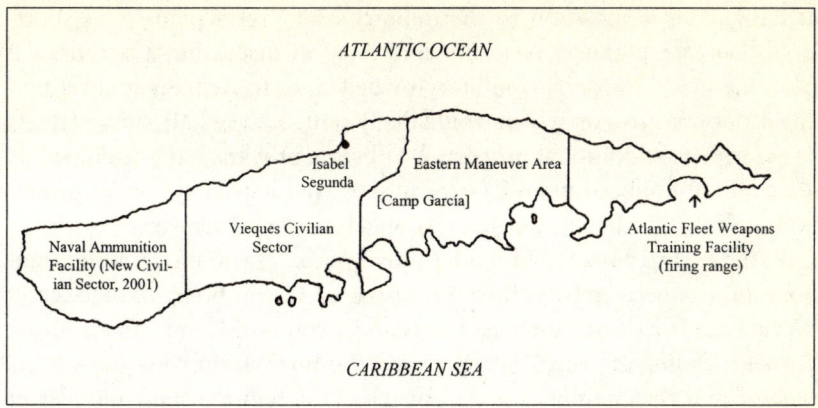

Ammunition Facility (NAF). Eastern Vieques is divided into two zones: the Eastern Maneuver Area (EMA) and the Atlantic Fleet Weapons Training Facility (AFWTF).[25]

With the close of World War II, the Cold War served as a rationale for the navy's landholdings on Vieques. That justification found renewed vigor in the wake of the 1962 Cuban Missile Crisis.[26] "[T]he uncertain status of Guantánamo and the prospective loss of military installations in Panama by the year 2000 meant that the Puerto Rican installations, especially Roosevelt Roads, had become more important than ever in protecting the sea lanes between the Venezuelan oil fields and the refineries of the Gulf Coast as well as the Atlantic sea routes north of Puerto Rico sailed by oil tankers from Saudi Arabia too large for Suez."[27]

In response to these new circumstances, Roosevelt Roads was redesignated as a naval operating base. Its new mission was to serve as a training center, a fuel depot for the Atlantic Fleet, and the center of the Atlantic Fleet's guided missile operations.[28] Safeguarding commerce on the high seas was one of the fleet's top responsibilities. Without a doubt the most important commodity passing through this area was petroleum.[29] Thus, Puerto Rico played a key role in safeguarding U.S. interests in the Atlantic zone, while U.S. interests in the Caribbean and Central America were safeguarded by the U.S. military installations in Panama, the headquarters for the U.S. Southern Command (SOUTHCOM).[30]

Though its influence with the armed forces may have been limited, the Puerto Rican government did attempt to persuade the defense strategists to return military lands back to Vieques's civilian population. In 1944 the Navy acquiesced, opting to lease some of its land to Puerto Rico's government for agricultural rehabilitation. As it turned out, this measure, aimed at dampening opposition to the military's long-term plans, was short-lived. Defense planners were not interested in discussing a withdrawal from Vieques. Transferring military-owned lands to civilians could stimulate economic growth, which would likely stall, or even halt, future efforts to expropriate additional property.[31] Subsequently, the navy rescinded its lease and announced plans to expropriate even more land on Vieques.[32] Still, political leaders in San Juan assigned Vieques a very low priority.

In the early 1940s PPD founder Luis Muñoz Marín unreservedly supported the American war effort. He also used the outbreak of the Second World War to justify moving the island's status dilemma to the back burner.[33] Following the 1940 elections, Muñoz Marín took his seat as senator and the chamber's president. His PPD had the same number of seats in the House of Representatives as the Republican-Socialist coalition. The PPD was able to secure a House majority by forging an alliance with a small party with three seats—the Unificación Puertorriqueña Tripartita (UPT) (Tripartite Puerto Rican Unification). Senator Muñoz Marín could ill afford to alienate the *independentistas* in his own party, which included Senators Francisco Susoni and Vicente Géigel Polanco. By postponing a resolution of the status question, Muñoz Marín bought himself time to fortify his position within his newly formed party prior to a showdown with the PPD's separatist faction.[34]

Populares were not alone in looking for federal support. Statehood supporters were always eager to display their loyalty to the United States and its military objectives.[35] Indeed, in the 1940s Puerto Rico's statehood movement increasingly engaged in anti-independence and anti-Communist rhetoric, despite the movement's long-established coalition with the island's labor movement and the Socialist Party.[36] Marginalized in the wake of the PPD's virtual monopoly on power in the 1940s and 1950s, the statehood movement found its fortunes changing significantly in the 1960s. Puerto Rico's growing economic dependence on the United States would hamper calls for greater autonomy or independence, leaving fertile terrain for the statehood movement.[37] As Gordon Lewis said with caustic flair, "Puerto Rico, in brief, is the kept woman of the United States, with all the attendant fringe benefits of that status."[38]

Vieques after World War II

American military bases on Puerto Rico represented a key component in the U.S. Cold War regional strategy. Puerto Rico, it was thought, had to remain under American jurisdiction in one form or another in order to assure the continued existence of these bases. Still, Puerto Ricans agitated for a change in status. In the short term, the PPD's leadership supported amending the Jones Act to allow for direct gubernatorial elections. In the long run, Muñoz Marín sought to replace the Jones Act with a more "autonomist" regime. President Harry Truman agreed to these changes and in 1946 appointed Jesús T. Piñero to the island's governorship. The following year Congress passed the Elective Governor Act, and in 1948 Muñoz Marín won Puerto Rico's first gubernatorial election.[39] From his new post, Muñoz Marín lobbied Washington for a new constitution. The military, one of the acknowledged "power elite," would play an important role in shaping the outcome of this congressional process.[40]

In January 1948 Senator Hugh M. Butler, the author of the Elective Governor Act and the future author of the bill creating the Commonwealth constitution, embarked on a fact-finding trip to Puerto Rico. During his stay, the senator was given a tour of Vieques by high-ranking naval officials. This trip coincided with a new round of civilian resettlements. Military planners wanted to enlarge their holdings in Vieques to train American troops. Admiral Daniel E. Barbey recommended that Vieques could also be used to train troops from other countries in the Americas. Puerto Rico's government took financial responsibility for relocating these families since the navy claimed it lacked the financial resources to do so. Nonetheless, the navy was allocated the funds to expropriate additional tracts of land, and territorial expansion sandwiched civilians in central Vieques.[41] An islet of sugar cane was transformed into training grounds for the U.S. military and its allies.

Puerto Rico in general and Vieques in particular played important roles in American foreign policy throughout the Cold War. Vieques was used extensively for training during the wars in Korea and Vietnam. Before dropping napalm on the forests and people of Indochina, the U.S. military tested the defoliant on El Yunque rain forest on the main island of Puerto Rico.[42] Vieques was also used as a training facility in several noteworthy episodes in Latin America: the overthrow of Guatemalan President Jacobo Arbenz in 1954, the Cuban Bay of Pigs operation in 1961, the invasion of the Dominican Republic in 1965, the overthrow of Chilean President Salvador Allende in 1973, the invasion of Grenada in 1983, and the invasion of Panama in 1989. In the 1980s the United States used Puerto Rico to train the Contras fighting Nicaragua's Sandinista government, as well as members of El Salvador's armed forces in their war against the Farabundo Marti National Liberation Front (FMLN).[43] Roosevelt Roads Naval Station served as a stopover for the British Royal Navy in the 1982 Malvinas/

Falklands War between Argentina and the United Kingdom.[44] During the early 1990s, American troops trained in Vieques to prepare for war in the Persian Gulf.[45] The American invasion of Puerto Rico in 1898 was prompted by its military promise. A century later that potential was ardently harvested.

Debates over military activities in Vieques have also been caught up in discussions over the Roosevelt Roads base's role in nuclear warfare. Allegations have proliferated for years that the U.S. Navy stores nuclear weapons at Roosevelt Roads.[46] The Pentagon insists, however, that no nuclear arms are permanently maintained in Puerto Rico.[47] How is Puerto Rico affected by the 1967 Treaty of Tlateloco that forbade the use, testing, production, or storage of nuclear weapons in Latin America? The multilateral accord specifically excludes the continental United States and its territorial waters, but not its territorial possessions in Latin America.[48] Contrary to the text of this document, the United States refuses to include Puerto Rico in the treaty's definition of Latin America.[49] As a territory, Puerto Rico counts as a domestic jurisdiction for some matters, while for others it is excluded.[50]

Whether as a training facility or as part of a nuclear storage facility, the navy used its existing operations as a pretext to widen its ownership of Vieques. In 1960 the House Armed Services Committee studied the possibility of allocating additional funds for the purpose of procuring additional lands on Vieques. Subsequently it was revealed that the proposed civilian expulsion from Vieques would even include the island's deceased. The so-called Dracula Plan was designed to sever any emotional ties to the land by transferring Vieques's deceased to St. Croix in the U.S. Virgin Islands.[51] Governor Muñoz Marín wrote to President John F. Kennedy asking for his intervention in this matter, and the plan was never implemented.[52]

Since the navy already owned three-quarters of Vieques, the acquisition of additional land would spell the end of civilian occupancy and would require relocating the remaining inhabitants to the Virgin Islands or the main island of Puerto Rico. While the navy was not authorized to increase its property holdings on Vieques, it punished *viequenses* indirectly by retarding their economic growth. Puerto Rico's government approved a project, outlined by the Woolnor Corporation in 1960, to build a large resort on Commonwealth-owned lands. In order to build such a tourist complex, authorities would have had to enlarge Vieques's airstrip. The navy refused to cede any land for the airport. Additionally, the navy refused to give Woolnor assurances that it would not try to expropriate the resort itself at some future date. As Katherine McCaffrey noted, "the Navy demonstrated its latent hostility toward the civilian population, and its belief that any type of economic development threatened its interests."[53] Cut off from their traditional occupations as sugar cane cutters, many Vieques residents turned to fishing.

Outside of institutional concerns, there were also problems with individual servicemen. These incidents embittered an already tense relationship with civilians. In 1953 Pepe Christian, a seventy-year-old storekeeper, was killed and his seventy-three-year-old friend was seriously injured by a group of Marines angered by the proprietor's refusal to sell them more alcohol. A military hearing later acquitted the two Marines charged with his death. There was also an incident in 1959 where nineteen locals were injured by a group of soldiers who raided a private party.[54] Inebriated military personnel harassed local women and vandalized homes.[55] While not well publicized, locals claimed there were frequent fights between *viequenses* and military personnel.[56]

Off-duty servicemen have been known to cause trouble in many off-base communities. Yet island residents were enraged that local police totally ignored their grievances. This implicit impunity, coupled with government-imposed economic stagnation and the continual threat of further expropriation, sensitized *viequenses* to their predicament as a bona fide colony of, ironically, a democracy. "Democratic rule may be a necessary but not a sufficient condition for the respect of human rights."[57]

From Culebra to Vieques

In the 1960s the only locals protesting against the military with equal conviction as the *viequenses* were their neighbors, the *culebrenses*. During that decade Culebra was used for target practice. Resentment toward the U.S. armed forces grew with the thunder of each bomb, as the military purchased more land and as the livelihood of Culebra residents was threatened by navy restrictions on fishing in the area.[58] In 1967 the Asociación de Pescadores de Culebra (Culebra Fishermen Association) petitioned Puerto Rico's legislature to appeal to Washington on their behalf. The following year a group from Culebra wrote directly to the White House and Congress asking for a cessation to all military exercises. In a symbolic act of defiance, the Culebra Municipal Assembly declared the U.S. Navy non grata in their town.[59]

In the early 1970s local residents were joined by outside organizations interested in seeing the military withdraw from Culebra, including two separatist parties, the Partido Independentista Puertorriqueño (PIP) and the Partido Socialista Puertorriqueño (PSP) (Puerto Rican Socialist Party). Separatist movements in Puerto Rico have long been organizational havens for middle-class intellectuals.[60] The intelligentsia has customarily provided the leadership of peace and ecological movements in other settings.[61] Joining the PIP and PSP were several progressive evangelical organizations. Culebra activists did not trust Governor Luis A. Ferré. Ferré, the founder of the pro-statehood Partido Nuevo Progresista (PNP) (New Progressive Party), had a cozy relationship with President Richard Nixon. The governor accepted a conditional agreement with the Nixon administration to transfer all of Culebra to the armed forces.[62]

Succumbing to years of constant local pressure, the federal government finally agreed to stop shelling Culebra in 1971.[63] Culebra's relief, however, became Vieques's nightmare. The navy did not stop military exercises in the region; it merely shifted them from one portion of the Roosevelt Roads base, Culebra, to another, Vieques. As Rear Admiral Arthur Knoizen, commander of the U.S. Naval Forces in the Caribbean, put it:

> The [Roosevelt Roads] complex allows "one stop" training for an individual unit, a task force, or an entire fleet. It is the only complex where naval tactics, including air strike, air defense, electronic warfare, amphibious landings and maneuvers, submarine operations and anti-submarine operations can be conducted simultaneously.... Of course, there are other training areas where one or two evolutions can be performed simultaneously, but nowhere else can we do them all at one place.[64]

Vieques was also, Secretary of the Navy Edward Hidalgo claimed, imperative to U.S. security interests, which is exactly what the armed forces had said about Culebra.[65] The defense establishment knows there are rarely any repercussions to its Vieques operations. As Raymond Carr commented: "To the Navy the bombardment of Vieques is part of a greater scheme of things: the effective defense of the West by an efficient Navy. The Navy admits that the training is being conducted in an area where local protests will have no direct repercussions in Congress. It is this that fires the indignation of Puerto Ricans: the Navy is treating Puerto Ricans, citizens of the United States, as it would not dare to treat the citizens on the mainland."[66] In the 1980s and 1990s the Pentagon came up with another rationale for its Vieques operations—its role on the frontline of the "War on Drugs."[67]

In response to these changing circumstances, community activists mobilized. One early and short-lived group was Viequenses Unidos (Vieques Islanders United). Its demise has been attributed, in part, to the organization's desire to distance itself from traditional nonlocal groups, particularly those affiliated with the Puerto Rican Left.[68] A local organization with greater staying power was the Asociación de Pescadores (Vieques Fishermen's Association). Expulsion from farming and other agricultural work infused in many fishermen a vigorous sense of determination.[69] Fishing came to represent not just a way of life but a sign of economic self-determination and a symbol of resistance. The successes of fishermen associations in Vieques and other coastal towns in Puerto Rico depended on avoiding direct entanglements with island partisan politics.[70] "In a highly charged and politically divisive colonial setting . . . the image of the fisherman allows islanders to express local grievances in terms that are 'authentic,' i.e., untainted by a broader political agenda."[71] Unity among Puerto Rico's various fishermen associations was also key to their long-term goals.[72]

In 1978 locals organized under the banner of the Cruzada Pro Rescate de Vieques (Crusade to Rescue Vieques)—an organization aimed at demilitarizing Vieques and not just at defending the rights of fishermen. On February 6, 1978, a small civilian flotilla sailed into military waters to protest the navy's restrictions on fishing for the duration of thirty-day training exercises. For a time military and *viequense* roles switched. The mini-armada prevented the armed forces from carrying out their mission.[73] The following spring twenty-one individuals were arrested for trespassing. They were holding an ecumenical service on a stretch of coast normally used to stage amphibious landings. Eleven of the twenty-one were imprisoned. While in a federal penitentiary in Tallahassee, Florida, one of them—Angel Rodríguez Cristóbal—died under what have been described as "suspicious circumstances."[74] In retaliation, the Macheteros (Machete Wielders), a revolutionary pro-independence organization, attacked a navy bus, killing two servicemen.[75]

Antinavy protests were also faced with pronavy activities. Countering the Fishermen's Association were the Navy League and the Vanguardia Pro-Navy—two organizations with strong ties to the armed forces.[76] In an attempt to sway the loyalties of local residents, the military and its supporters in the league and the Vanguardia sponsored a host of social, sports, and cultural activities. This was their soft sell in their battle with the protestors. On the other hand, there was also the hard sell, which focused on attempts to discredit protestors. Navy supporters viewed theirs as a patriotic mission in defense of American values and U.S. rule in Puerto Rico.

Before Congress, Robert Kuhn—president of the Vieques Navy League, a former Marine, and an expatriate American living in Vieques— referred to the protestors as a small clique of leftists and unpatriotic outsiders. In a Cold War tirade, he blasted the influence of teachers in Vieques who sympathized with the Fisherman's Association. "The Vieques high school and to a lesser extent the lower schools have an abnormally high percentage of separatist teachers who actually attempt to subjugate the students with anti-Navy and anti-American propaganda while extolling the virtues of life in Cuba and the Soviet Union."[77] Admiral Arthur Knoizen also tried to dismiss the protestors as a loud minority sponsored by subversive outside agitators.[78] Such comments repoliticized the debate over the military's role in Vieques and often had the opposite of the intended effect.[79] Rather than view *independentistas* as unwanted outsiders, many *viequenses* saw them as partners in a common quest.

The congressional committee investigating the navy's training facilities on Vieques in the early 1980s recommended that the Pentagon find an alternative site. House Armed Services Committee chair Ronald Dellums chastised the way in which the armed forces handled relations with Vieques' civilian community. As he put it, "Insensitivity has been the hallmark of the Navy's approach, resulting in legal action and protests."[80] Still, political instability in the Caribbean and Central America was used to back the military's argument.[81]

The Fortín Accord

President Ronald Reagan's tenure during the 1980s marked one of the most intense chapters in the Cold War rivalry between the United States and the Soviet Union. Minimalistic in his view of many complex issues, Reagan attributed upheavals and social unrest south of the Río Grande, in one fashion or another, to the Communist menace emanating from Moscow and Havana. To offset this influence, Washington spent lavish sums on Central America and the Caribbean. Most of these funds were not spent on economic development but on providing arms to regimes embracing Reagan's staunch anti-Communist philosophy. Still, there was an economic component to his regional master plan—the Caribbean Basin Initiative. Political leaders in San Juan went along with this plan in the hopes of stimulating the Puerto Rican economy.[82]

Pressure from Congress, combined with a lawsuit filed by the Puerto Rican pro-statehood governor, Carlos Romero-Barceló, convinced the navy to open negotiations on Vieques's future. The end result was the 1983 "Memorandum of Understanding Regarding the Island of Vieques," also known as the Fortín Accord, signed by Governor Romero-Barceló and Secretary of the Navy James Goodrich. The accord stipulated that "the Navy recognizes its obligation to be a good neighbor to the people of Vieques and will continue to strive to improve the welfare of the island's people."[83] The governor gambled on Puerto Rico's strategic value to the United States. "Romero's strategy was based on the undeniable fact that the United States has important economic and military interests in Puerto Rico and that it is willing to pay a high price to retain the territory."[84]

One of the top priorities outlined in the agreement was the navy's commitment to find civilian industries willing to locate plants on Vieques. The navy made no commitment to withdraw from Vieques. In exchange for a promise to improve economic conditions on Vieques, the Romero-Barceló administration agreed to terminate its lawsuit. At the time, many viewed the navy's signature as victory for the people of Vieques.[85] Those cheering this understanding forgot one important point: the U.S. Navy's commitment to improving Vieques's economic development was institutional self-interest designed to prolong the use of this island as a bombing range.[86]

Responsibility for formulating a Vieques economic policy belonged to the Defense Department's Office of Economic Adjustment (OEA). The OEA developed a "Top Ten" program whereby the navy invited the chief executives of its ten largest contractors to inspect Vieques.[87] Among the ten were General Electric, General Dynamics, Grumman Aerospace, Lockheed, McDonnell Douglas, and United Technologies. These businesses were lured to Vieques by its high unemployment rate and Puerto Rico's prized tax benefits. Those attending this Vieques field trip were rewarded with a reception at the home of Vice President George Bush.[88] Rather than demilitarize Vieques, the Fortín Accord was designed to militarize the *viequense* civilian sector.

Any company that contemplated establishing a production facility on Vieques had to contend with several major problems. Water and sewage facilities on the island were limited, and the main aquifers in Vieques were under the military's property.[89] There were also additional transportation costs since goods traveling between the United States and Vieques had to pass through the larger ports on the main island of Puerto Rico. Once in Puerto Rico, commodities destined for Vieques had to take a detour. Before opening the Roosevelt Roads base, ships took a nine-mile route between Vieques and the main island; after its construction, all commerce was rerouted along a new eighteen-mile course. In the end, few followed the navy's lead. Within a few years, Dandie, South Bronx Greenhouse, and Vieques Graphics closed their Vieques operations. Dandie and South Bronx Greenhouse were tainted with allegations of corruption.[90] Many *viequenses* saw these closings as still more failed promises.

To make matters worse, tensions were growing between *viequenses* and a small community of mainlanders. "The North Americans gave a face to the feelings of displacement Viequenses experienced."[91] Wealthy Americans, many with connections to the armed forces, build vacation homes in Vieques. Eventually some became full-time residents. These expatriate Americans were vehement in their defense of the navy.[92] When all was said and done, the *viequense* community found itself with no improvement in its employment condition, the navy still owned most of their island, the bombing runs over their island continued, and a wealthy expatriate community was buying up what little private land was left.

A Close Call

Throughout the 1980s the Pentagon successfully thwarted efforts to abandon Vieques or stop using it for military exercises. Nor did the end of the Cold War alter the island's status. Whether under a Republican or Democratic administration, Vieques was still coveted by the military establishment. In addition, President Clinton was in no mood to further antagonize his relationship with the armed forces. The Clinton administration addressed three major social issues in the military: sexual harassment, women in combat roles, and whether gays and lesbians could openly serve in uniform. Of these three, the debate over gays and lesbians in the military was by far the most contentious, igniting the wrath of military leaders and socially conservative legislators.[93] Clinton failed to convince the military that his "Don't Ask, Don't Tell" policy was akin to the racial desegregation of the armed services in 1948. Vehement opposition to this policy filtered all the way down to the lowest ranks in the armed services.[94] Given that Clinton sought rapport with the Pentagon, he decided that if the armed services felt strongly about holding on to Vieques, the White House would not stand in the way.

Less than a year into his presidency, Clinton faced his first crisis over Vieques. In March 1993 a group of *viequenses* wrote to Secretary of Defense Les Aspin, asking him to close the military's installations. Among the signatories was a new organization, the Comité Pro Rescate y Desarrollo de Vieques (CPRDV) (Committee for the Rescue and Development of Vieques).⁹⁵ Their petitions were largely ignored until the fall of that year. On October 24, 1993, the community of Santa María was jolted by a powerful explosion.⁹⁶ *Viequenses* had heard bombs going off before, but this time a navy fighter accidentally dropped several quarter-ton bombs six miles off course. They detonated only a mile from a populated sector.

The October 1993 bombing stimulated renewed interest in the Vieques controversy. This close call galvanized local activists in Vieques, in San Juan, and their supporters in the United States. The culmination of these efforts was a series of congressional hearings on Vieques's future. Vieques community activists wondered how they and their cause would be received by Congress. As Gordon Lewis suggested: "With the exception of a few friendly congressmen, the general congressional attitude to Puerto Rico is a mixture of ignorance, disdain, and irritation, which sees the territory as a subdivision of the nation that receives more benefits than most senators and representatives believe it is entitled to, without paying, by means of federal taxes, any of the price of the status it enjoys."⁹⁷

The House Subcommittee on Insular and International Affairs conducted a series of hearings in Washington and Vieques. Under the provisions of H.R. 3831—also known as the Vieques Lands Transfer Act of 1994—the federal government would convey to the island's municipal government the eight thousand–acre Naval Ammunition Facility (NAF) in the west.⁹⁸ The bill was introduced by Resident Commissioner Carlos Romero-Barceló, who as governor had signed the 1983 Fortín Accord.⁹⁹ Reiterating its support for U.S. defense policy, the Puerto Rican government officially endorsed this proposal. Transferring the navy's western properties would not solve every problem in Vieques, Romero-Barceló argued, but it would improve navy-*viequense* relations.¹⁰⁰

Speaking in opposition to H.R. 3831 was Rear Admiral Ernest E. Christensen. Vieques-trained U.S. troops were deployed to Bosnia, Haiti, Kuwait, Somalia, and elsewhere. The admiral maintained that U.S. national defense interests outweighed those of the *viequenses*. Lack of economic development on Vieques, according to Admiral Christensen, was not the navy's failure to live up to the 1983 Fortín Accord but rather was due to the costs associated with doing business on an islet physically disconnected from the main island of Puerto Rico.¹⁰¹

The House subcommittee referred H.R. 3831 to the full committee in 1995. However, the proposed transfer of the NAF to the Municipality of Vieques was never voted on by either the full House or Senate. Despite a near miss with a cluster of quarter-ton bombs, Congress assigned Vieques a low priority. In Puerto Rico, Governor Pedro Rosselló had other priorities. In the mid-1990s the territorial governor was adamant about privatizing publicly owned corporations and strongly supported new educational policies promoting the English language. With a Republican majority in Congress, these measures were designed to foster congressional support for a federally sponsored status referendum or plebiscite in Puerto Rico.[102] In the past, statehood advocates played up Puerto Rico's role in U.S. military affairs in an effort to link American defense strategies to Puerto Rico's continued relationship with the United States.[103] They argued that this relationship could only be guaranteed with a permanent union.[104] Though Governor Rosselló wanted to focus on promoting Puerto Rican statehood in Congress, subsequent events obliged him to concentrate on Vieques.

3

The Canonization of David Sanes

Despite demonstrations, letters to the Commonwealth and federal governments, and occasional acts of civil disobedience, few outside Puerto Rico were aware that a controversy existed over Vieques. For most Puerto Rican administrations, the military's use of Vieques for target practice and war games was simply the price paid for maintaining a steady stream of economic assistance from the U.S. government. For naval planners along the Potomac, it was business as usual in these tepid waters west of the Virgin Islands. Civil-military relations took a sharp turn for the worse in the spring of 1999.

In the course of the spring 1999 training exercises, two navy fighters dropped their ordnance. As in 1993, the planes flew off course; this time, however, one of the bombs dropped on Vieques killed a civilian security guard, David Sanes Rodríguez. For years local fishermen, environmentalists, and independence activists warned the military that such a calamity was not only possible but also likely. As infuriating as the death itself was the military's frigid indifference to it. Puerto Rico was soaked in a new wave of nationalist fervor, but this nationalism was not a call for independence from the United States. It was an act of "self-empowerment."[1] Sanes's death tore a severe rift in Puerto Rican–American relations and cast an ominous shadow over Washington's rule in this Caribbean island.

The 1998 Plebiscite and Its Aftermath

In 1998 Puerto Rico commemorated the centennial of the Spanish-American War and the hundredth anniversary of U.S. rule. For Governor Pedro Rosselló, a statehood proponent, this was an occasion to celebrate. In contrast, others looked upon this moment to mourn the invasion and the loss of autonomy and to protest U.S. policies. On July 25, 1998, these conflicting viewpoints converged. In the southern town of Guánica—site of the 1898 landing of U.S. troops—those proposing statehood exalted

U.S. dominion, while independence supporters remonstrated against the American occupation of Puerto Rico. Commonwealth supporters gathered on the grounds of El Morro castle in Old San Juan to commemorate the forty-sixth anniversary of the 1952 constitution. The same day was mythologized in three entirely divergent ways.

Governor Rosselló used this assembly to announce the celebration of a status plebiscite. Rosselló eagerly sought congressional backing for such a federally sponsored referendum or plebiscite. Each time it was proposed, the measure died before reaching the president's desk. In July 1998 the governor believed that his movement had a chance to win a plurality, and possibly a majority, in this special election. Rosselló was convinced that his party had recovered from its 1993 plebiscitory defeat in which Commonwealth status won 48 percent of the electorate's support, while 46 percent of the voters favored statehood. Breaking with tradition in 1998, the Rosselló administration opted to define the status alternatives itself rather than rely on parties to define their respective status preferences. Furthermore, another ballot choice was added, "Associated Republic" status. This constitutional arrangement rested somewhere between outright independence and the status quo. Presumably such an alternative would divide Commonwealth supporters. For the first time a fifth option was offered: *ninguna de las anteriores* (none of the above).

As an opposition party, the PPD could not prevent the government from holding a plebiscite. Outraged that the Commonwealth was defined as a "colonial" status, the PPD asked its membership to vote for the fifth option. The government was surprised to discover that a majority of the island's electorate cast their votes for *ninguna de las anteriores*. According to the "radical" statehooders: "The statehood strategy of the PNP was rejected in the plebiscite. The statehood movement has arrived at a maximum point of saturation."[2] Popular Democrats savored their second plebiscitory victory of the decade, but it was only a partial victory.[3] Commonwealth, it turned out, was more popular than the party defending it.

Half of those who usually supported independence instead voted *ninguna de las anteriores*. A bruised PIP sought to reevaluate its political strategies and establish "lines of communication" with other pro-independence organizations.[4] Some of these groups were concerned less with status plebiscites than with the fate of a dozen Puerto Rican prisoners.[5] Federal authorities had indicted these individuals for their involvement in various terrorist activities on the U.S. mainland in the late 1970s and early 1980s. Statehood leaders resoundingly opposed their release, since these acts were carried out in the name of Puerto Rican independence.[6]

The first months of 1999 brought little relief to an administration smothered in allegations of corruption. During the 1988–92 term, Rosselló was the health director for the municipality of San Juan, and Yamil Kouri was his adviser. When Rosselló was elected governor in 1992, Kouri became an adviser on health reform issues. In 1993 PIP Representative David Noriega Rodríguez began investigating allegations that federal funds earmarked for an AIDS hospital were misappropriated. Given a PNP majority, Noriega found major impediments to an in-depth investigation into one of their own. Unsatisfied with the legislature's investigation, Noriega presented his evidence to federal investigators—an astonishing act for a lawmaker committed to the island's independence from the United States.[7]

While federal prosecutors tried Kouri, the public's attention turned to a governor under investigation for allegedly misappropriating $250,000 in federal funds.[8] Rosselló's PNP was not the only party accused of placing its hand in the proverbial cookie jar, but most of those accused of involvement in the AIDS hospital case had strong connections to the ruling party and the incumbent administration.[9] Noriega suggested this federal probe would eventually involve many others.[10] Public opinion polls reported that Rosselló would lose to San Juan Mayor Sila María Calderón, the PPD's 2000 gubernatorial candidate. According to the same March 1999 survey, were another status plebiscite held, Commonwealth would receive 7 percent more votes than statehood.[11]

Political attention was focused on the unfolding events in the federal courthouse, not on the situation in Vieques. In the first days of 1999 dozens of Vieques and Culebra residents protested in front of the Fortaleza, the governor's residence, to criticize the poor ferry service between the main island and their island municipalities. Transportation problems inflicted numerous personal hardships and eroded the economic vitality of their communities.[12] These difficulties were exacerbated by the navy's presence in Vieques, since the armed forces restricted commercial navigation between the main island and the navy-owned lands of western Vieques. *Viequense* moral resolve was bolstered by a human rights award from the National Council of Churches honoring their peaceful efforts to demilitarize their community.[13] Perhaps one day Vieques might put an end to naval bombings in their home as had Hawaiians on the island of Kaho'olawe in the early 1990s.

Protests and political pressure succeeded in demilitarizing Kaho'olawe, the smallest of Hawaii's eight major islands.[14] The U.S. Navy's Pacific Fleet used Kaho'olawe as a bombing range from 1953 to 1990. The demilitarization of Kaho'olawe was a focal point of political activism for Hawaiian nationalists, who regarded this a sacred place.[15] Paralleling Vieques, the local peace movement was spearheaded by fishermen starting in the mid-1970s.[16] Foreshadowing events in Vieques, popular support for their cause ballooned following the deaths of Project Kaho'olawe Ohana activists George Helm and Kimo Mitchell in 1990.[17]

On October 22, 1990, President George Bush ordered an end to the bombings in Hawaii.[18] Rumors persist that this decision was connected to the upcoming November 1990 elections. Republican Representative Patricia Saiki was locked in a tight race to unseat incumbent Democratic Senator Daniel K. Akaka.[19] At a fund-raising dinner for Saiki, President Bush said: "And just this week I directed the Secretary of Defense to discontinue the island's [Kaho'olawe] use as a weapons range, effective immediately. And if that is good, give some credit to Pat Saiki."[20] Three years later President Clinton signed a bill returning Kaho'olawe to the state of Hawaii.[21] The federal government earmarked hundreds of millions of dollars to clean up this island in an attempt to restore it to its prebombing conditions.[22] Despite the Defense Department's insistence that Kaho'olawe was unique and "the only place for the kind of training we need to perform,"[23] the navy moved the Pacific Fleet's training to California's San Clemente Island.

Hawaii's good fortune seemed very far from Vieques early in 1999. Local leader Carlos Ventura charged that federal and Commonwealth agents were harassing local fishermen.[24] These law enforcement agents were investigating a row between the navy and local fishermen on Mother's Day in 1997. In addition to feeling beleaguered, *viequenses* also suffered severe economic hardships. General Electric announced that it was laying off most of its workforce at its plant in Vieques—the town's last manufacturing facility. Community leader Alba Encarnación described this announcement as a mortal blow.[25] Economic development was assigned a low priority both by the federal and Commonwealth governments. Encarnación exclaimed: "We are prisoners of the Navy and slaves of Puerto Rico. We are the lamb that has been sacrificed so that the big island lives comfortably."[26]

Adding to this gloomy scenario was the realization that the transfer of the U.S. Southern Command from Panama to Puerto Rico could increase naval activity in the area.[27] Military spokespersons claimed that the transfer of the Southern Command represented a net gain for Puerto Rico, injecting $100 million into the local economy.[28] Community activist Robert Rabin countered that the military projects in Vieques—such as the construction of a radar to detect regional drug trafficking—posed an environmental hazard.[29] A 1997 study revealed that from 1985 to 1989 the risk of cancer on Vieques was almost 27 percent higher than on the main island.[30]

Conditions on Vieques deteriorated to the point where Senator Roger Iglesias introduced a resolution in the Puerto Rican legislature asking the navy to immediately halt its activities on that island.[31] Such a move was out of character for a lawmaker from the pro-statehood PNP—a party that hardly ever criticized the U.S. military. While the territorial legislature looked into these cancer rates, the navy continued its war games in Vieques.[32] Expressing outrage over the continued bombing, PIP representative Víctor García San Inocencio exhorted all Puerto Ricans to join efforts to demilitarize Vieques, claiming that the time to do so had come.[33] Three months later Puerto Ricans heeded his call to action.

April 19, 1999

Few Puerto Ricans were aware that the aircraft carrier USS *John F. Kennedy* was conducting war games in the Vieques Passage. On April 19, 1999, two FA-18 Hornets were cleared to take off from the *Kennedy* with orders to release two 500-pound Mark 82 bombs on Vieques. However, the pilots flew off course, and their payloads detonated near an observation post on Camp García.[34] This time, four civilians were wounded and a security guard, David Sanes Rodríguez, was killed. For years Vieques residents feared that something like this could happen. After all, a *viequense* was killed in the early 1940s when he touched an explosive lying on the ground.[35] More recently, in 1993, another navy sortie dropped several quarter-ton bombs off their intended mark. For a traumatized community, this incident represented a tragic episode of déjà vu.

Civilian tragedies, both subtle and gross, were nothing new to the people of Vieques. Neither was the military's insensitive response. The following day the navy suspended its operations in the area and promised an investigation.[36] However, no civilians would be invited to investigate the matter.[37] To many, this decision gave the appearance of a whitewash or cover-up. Unlike previous civilian-military conflicts, *viequenses* would not allow the spring 1999 incident to be swept under the rug. April 19, 1999, represented for *viequenses*, and all *puertorriqueños*, the veritable "straw that broke the camel's back."[38]

Wasting little time, independence advocates rapidly and vociferously condemned the fatality. Only a week before David Sanes's death the PIP had called for the navy's immediate withdrawal and the economic development of Vieques.[39] Unlike most previous conflicts between civilian *viequenses* and the military, after Sanes's death Puerto Ricans of all political stripes joined the demilitarization chorus.[40] On the U.S. mainland, ethnic Puerto Ricans also reacted with outrage. Representative Luis Gutiérrez of Illinois immediately called for a congressional hearing, and Representative José Serrano of New York asked the White House and the Defense Department to draw up plans to withdraw from Vieques. Governor Rosselló informed President Clinton that the Puerto Rican legislature passed a resolution requesting that the navy stop using live shells on Vieques.[41] The PIP claimed that this gesture was "too little and too late."[42] Its leaders insisted that until the navy departed, *viequenses* remained at risk for another calamity, as exemplified by the American bombing of the Chinese embassy in Belgrade only weeks after Sanes's death.[43]

Protests erupted on Vieques along with solidarity rallies organized by Puerto Rican communities in the United States. April 19, 1999, marked the start of a new stage in Vieques history and the course of civil-military relations in Puerto Rico, as well as a more public manifestation of Puerto Rican cultural nationalism on the main island and the U.S. mainland. The first organized protest of the new era began in front of the Vieques town hall two days after Sanes's death.[44] A major departure from earlier periods was the active, intense, and persistent participation of non-Vieques residents. Vieques, the marginalized municipality, took the political center stage.

Senator Rubén Berríos Martínez, a veteran of the 1970s protests over Culebra, announced that his independence party would set up an encampment on the navy's bombing range and remain there until the armed forces left or he was imprisoned.[45] To honor the memory of David Sanes Rodríguez, the beach serving as ground zero for the 1999–2000 protests, known as the Bahía de Carruchos (Conch Shells Bay), was unofficially renamed Monte David (Mount David).[46] The senator asked, "Is the United States willing to risk a Caribbean Quebec or a tropical Northern Ireland?"[47] In order to find out, Berríos Martínez opted "to make Puerto Rico into a gigantic classroom and transform its actions for peace in Vieques into lessons of affirmation and national consciousness raising."[48] *Independentistas* saw this crisis not only as a fight for demilitarization but also an opportunity to openly challenge the island's colonial status, refortify the parameters of Puerto Rican identity vis-à-vis the United States, and kindle a more assertive cultural nationalism.

For decades *viequenses* had protested naval practices without mass support on the main island. As with peace movements in Europe, the media's hunger for ratings often led them to play up the most controversial aspects of a protest, portraying protestors in a negative light.[49] Past demonstrations, even if led by local activists, were linked to the independence movement. In 1999 the Vieques encampments on navy property expanded far beyond independence supporters.[50] There were camps operated by several local families, students from the University of Puerto Rico, veterans, teachers, intellectuals from the Congreso Nacional Hostosiano (Hostosian National Congress), labor activists, the Roman Catholic Church, and the Evangelical Council.[51] From the start, antimilitary protestors agreed on a common strategy centered on passive resistance and civil disobedience.[52]

The civilian occupation created numerous problems for the Pentagon and the Commonwealth government. Defense Department officials decided to suspend their spring 1999 war games. Still, Secretary of the Navy Richard Danzig warned that Vieques's coastlines were laced with unexploded ordnance and hence unsafe.[53] Federal authorities were eager to have the Commonwealth take responsibility for arresting the protestors. Governor Rosselló was stuck between trying to appease local opinion, which favored the military's withdrawal, and attempting to placate the federal government. The navy was eager to resume its Vieques maneuvers before completing its investigation of Sanes's death.[54] Another dilemma for the Rosselló administration was the timing of the Vieques tragedy, which coincided with the start of congressional deliberations over Puerto Rico's status.[55]

Unlike Governor Carlos Romero-Barceló in the early 1980s, Rosselló refused to file a lawsuit against the military. Instead, he announced the creation of a working group to study the matter. Among those invited were die-hard separatists, such as Socialist leader Juan Mari Bras, and a group opposing the navy's activities for years—the Comité Pro Rescate y Desarrollo de Vieques (CPRDV) (Committee for the Rescue and Development of Vieques).[56] This organization was founded by community leaders in 1983 in response to a naval mishap; an FA-18 Hornet missed its target and dropped several bombs near civilian settlements.[57] In addition to calling upon political and community activists, the governor also asked for the input of religious leaders. For years many progressive clerics—the majority members of mainline Protestant denominations—played a major role in the Vieques campaign. A surprising turn of events was the participation of one of Puerto Rico's most conservative organizations—the Roman Catholic Church.

The Nationalization of the Catholic Church

Among those long involved in publicizing the plight of *viequenses* were socially progressive Protestant churches. In cases where the religious are involved in conflict resolution, one cannot dissociate morality and theology from the larger social and political context.[58] Severino Rivera Morales, an activist in the Methodist Church, felt a "Christian" obligation to protect Vieques's environment and his people. Some of the activist clerics were pleased that their presence lent the cause greater respect and moral fortitude and subtracted from the movement's reputation as an *independentista*-led cause.[59] After April 19 they were out in force, but now they were joined by several Catholic clerics.

Under Spanish sovereignty, Roman Catholicism was the sole authorized faith. Despite the fusion of the Catholic Church and the Spanish state, Puerto Rico's Catholic Church was unofficially divided into two categories. One was a theologically orthodox Catholicism followed by the island's upper classes and intimately associated with the Crown. Puerto Rico's grassroots or popular Catholicism, in contrast, embraced the so-called cult of saints and borrowed components from the island's indigenous legacy and African spirituality.[60] Madrid's colonial administrators often discovered that their grip on Puerto Rican society, outside the confines of the major urban centers, was precarious at best.[61] With a decentralized authority structure, many priests saw this grassroots Catholicism as a threat to their power.[62] After 1898 Rome transferred Puerto Rico's Spanish bishops, replacing them with American prelates.

Throughout much of the twentieth century Puerto Rican Roman Catholicism was a conservative, Irish-dominated institution more interested in instilling religious orthodoxy than in social activism.[63] The advent of American rule introduced an array of new spiritual alternatives. Large sectors of Puerto Rican society found evangelical Protestant churches more sympathetic to their social and spiritual needs.[64] In response to the void created by the suppression of the popular Church, they turned to Protestantism, particularly Pentecostalism.[65]

Social and political activism was a well-entrenched practice among many churches in the United States, especially black and mainline Protestants churches. Protestant churches took the lead in an array of movements—from abolition, temperance, moral reform in the nineteenth and early twentieth centuries to the antiwar movement of the 1960s and civil rights movement of the 1950s and 1960s.[66] Protestantism, a faith representing cultural assimilation and Americanization early in the twentieth century, was Puerto Ricanized, in terms of its local clergy, in relatively short order. Free of the constraints of an American-led hierarchy, Puerto Rican Protestantism was free to champion *puertorriqueñidad*.

One high-ranking Catholic cleric who consistently sided with the Vieques movement was Alvaro Corrada del Río, bishop of Caguas, whose diocese included Vieques. Bishop Corrada blessed an icon of Our Lady of Carmen, the patron saint of fishermen, on the protestors' encampments in the summer of 1999.[67] In contrast, the island's prelate, Cardinal Luis Aponte Martínez, did not play a major role in the Vieques movement. Early in 1999 Puerto Ricans were notified that the cardinal would step down as archbishop of San Juan to be replaced by Roberto González Nieves—a mainland-born Puerto Rican who served as the auxiliary bishop of Boston and bishop of Corpus Christi, Texas.

Most of González Nieves's priesthood was spent in New York City, particularly the Bronx.[68] Though born in Elizabeth, New Jersey, the new archbishop passionately identified with Puerto Rico.[69] He claimed that all Puerto Ricans, whether on the island or on the U.S. mainland, represented one people with one "spiritual reality"; Puerto Rican identity, he remarked, was anchored in Latin America and not in United States.[70] His first homily as archbishop fell on Mother's Day, and he used this opportunity to set a new tone for his ecclesiastical administration.[71]

> True I was not born on Puerto Rican soil, but I dare say that yes I was born in Puerto Rico. National identity does not depend on place of birth alone, that which could be a completely accidental event. Puerto Rican identity is found in the heart and runs through the veins; it is what we affectionately and with pride call *the plantain stain*. It is a spiritual reality that affects the way to perceive, judge, and cultivate life—from here the concept of *culture*—in solidarity with a people that lives out its humanity in accordance with a unique and particular tradition that is propelled towards a common destiny loyal to its historic roots.[72]

While distancing himself from party politics Archbishop González Nieves acknowledged that *"the promotion of the church's social teachings will be an inseparable dimension of our evangelizing vocation."*[73] Indeed, as a young priest he worked on community housing issues and served as a community organizer for the United Farm Workers.[74] He maintained: "It [the parish] can be an oasis of hope within a conflict-ridden social situation and a light which sheds meaning on the social order."[75] His words resonated like music to the ears of progressives and cultural nationalists.[76]

"These statements indicate that it appears that the Catholic Church is willing to express itself and behave like the true national religion of Puerto Ricans."[77] This marked a new and more assertive stage in the social activism of the Roman Catholic Church in Puerto Rico.

The vast majority of Puerto Ricans are cultural nationalists.[78] The last nationalist leader who attempted to infuse nationalism with a distinctly religious flavor was Albizu Campos in the 1930s. For strategic reasons, ethnic mythmakers rejected Albizu Campos's fervent Catholicism while they embraced other aspects of his nationalism.[79] However, Archbishop González Nieves was not attempting to fuse Catholicism with separatist nationalism but with the more all-encompassing cultural nationalism deeply entrenched in Puerto Rican society. Church involvement in the Vieques crisis made it more difficult to dismiss protestors as marginal extremists. Interdenominational cooperation also provided the entire undertaking a greater degree of legitimacy.

Rosselló's Agenda

Governor Pedro Rosselló decided to present the federal government with the will of the Puerto Rican people by way of a special commission. Heading this commission was Secretary of State Norma Burgos. Another prominent PNP participant was Manuela Santiago, mayor of Vieques. Among those not affiliated with the ruling party were San Juan mayor Sila María Calderón and Archbishop González Nieves.[80] One well-known leader who would not join this commission was Senator Rubén Berríos Martínez, who was camped out on the beaches of Vieques. At this point he refused to speculate on why the administration convened such a commission.[81] Nonetheless, *independentistas* were pleasantly surprised to find a pro-statehood governor appointing such a diverse commission.[82]

Senator Berríos's participation in the Vieques protests was becoming an embarrassment to the pro-statehood administration. Senate president Charlie Rodríguez criticized his colleague's legislative absences.[83] PNP Senator Sergio Peña Clos warned Berríos that these absences were grounds for possible expulsion from the legislature.[84] Still, PNP Senator Ramón Rivera Cruz defended Berríos's right to peaceful expression.[85] In May the Senate president was walking on the beaches of Vieques alongside Berríos.[86] By June Charlie Rodríguez excused his *independentista* colleague for the remainder of the legislative session.[87] The decision to excuse Senator Berríos demonstrated the popularity of the PIP leader's acts of civil disobedience.

For years independence supporters championed the demilitarization of Vieques and Culebra. If separatists were seen as pro-*viequense*, those on the opposite end of the ideological continuum, annexationists or statehood supporters, were often viewed as promilitary. In 1999 Romero-Barceló, who as governor signed the Fortín Accord with the U.S. Navy in 1983, was now Puerto Rico's resident commissioner. He criticized the navy for failing to live up to the 1983 accord.[88] Still, he refused to demand the navy's withdrawal from Vieques, citing the island's importance to U.S. national defense interests.[89] Romero-Barceló declined to join the efforts of another Puerto Rican in the U.S. House of Representatives who advocated Vieques's demilitarization—Luis Gutiérrez, representing Illinois' fourth congressional district.[90]

The PNP's strong association with the U.S. military was likely a major factor in the party's poor showing in public opinion polls. The PPD led the PNP by seventeen percentage points.[91] Public opinion was unlikely to swing in the government's favor given the navy's plans to resume its war games around Vieques by the end of June.[92] The Rosselló administration now refused to rule out filing a case in federal court to block these maneuvers.[93] The governor was unable to satisfy both public opinion and the military.

In June 1999 Rosselló announced that he would not seek a third term as governor.[94] Governor Rosselló had other options. He was an early supporter of Al Gore, and rumors abounded that a future Gore administration might appoint Rosselló to a Cabinet post.[95] Others suggested that the governor's decision not to run again was influenced by the growing federal investigation into the AIDS Institute scandal.[96] In light of the allegations about the institute, the gay rights organization Act Up counseled the Gore campaign to review its association with Puerto Rico's governor.[97]

The Pentagon was keen on recommencing battle drills since the USS *Kennedy* needed further training before its scheduled arrival in the Adriatic.[98] This was the same vessel that launched the aircraft that killed David Sanes Rodríguez. American naval personnel were using the waters off the Puerto Rico coast to prepare for their Balkan missions. Rumors circulated that the decision to suspend naval exercises and review the military's operations in Vieques were tied to Hillary Rodham Clinton's senatorial aspirations.[99] It was known that the First Lady was interested in running for the New York Senate seat being vacated by Daniel Patrick Moynihan. To win this seat, she would need the support of the state's Puerto Rican community.

Citing Vieques's importance to U.S. national security President Clinton asked Secretary of Defense Richard Cohen to name a special panel to evaluate the situation.[100] Various Vieques community leaders voiced skepticism about this federal panel.[101] Their cynicism centered on the ostensibly pronavy bias of the panel membership. One member was a former representative, Lee Hamilton; two were retired officers, Marine Corps General Richard Neal and Admiral Diego Hernández; and the panel chair was Frank Rush, a Defense Department undersecretary.[102] Norma Burgos, the Commonwealth's secretary of state, expressed her disappointment with this panel—a rarity for an official in a pro-statehood administration.[103] Her willingness to question her party's unquestioning devotion to federal views led to her marginalization within the PNP.

The White House tried to assure all concerned that this panel did not have a promilitary bias. Federal officials pointed out that no navy personnel were on the panel and that Admiral Hernández was Puerto Rican.[104] Still, as one activist remarked: "The Navy's foremost attribute throughout all of these years has been to lie and at least here no one believes a word they say."[105] Subsequently, it was revealed that the navy had been diverting water from the Río Blanco de Naguabo gratis for years and without the mandatory authorization of the Commonwealth government.[106] Two weeks later Marine Corps officials disclosed that they had dropped napalm on Vieques in 1992.[107] These incidents convinced many that the armed forces conducted its affairs as if Puerto Rico were its private fiefdom.

For years navy reports categorically denied that their operations had any negative impacts on Vieques's ecology.[108] However, distrust was fueled by the revelation that some of the shells dropped on Vieques contained uranium.[109] Depleted uranium enables shells to pierce armor.[110] Still a navy spokesperson insisted that there was no evidence that the depleted uranium contributed to the high rates of cancer on Vieques.[111] Such assurances were rather remarkable given that the armed forces warns soldiers against prolonged exposure to depleted uranium.[112] The navy insisted that the radioactive substances used on the munitions in Vieques contained only "reduced uranium."[113] Revelations that the military was far from honest with the Puerto Rican people, coupled with revelations that the navy veiled some of its activities, seriously undermined its efforts to earn the trust of *puertorriqueños*.

When persuasion failed, strong-arm tactics were employed. Pentagon officials were well aware that Puerto Rico was extremely dependent on federal funds for its fiscal well-being. A leaked navy report indicated that Puerto Rico's federal funds were threatened unless military maneuvers resumed on Vieques.¹¹⁴ This was not the first time the armed forces used federal transfers to silence their critics. During a congressional hearing in 1980, Admiral Knoizen was asked whether the navy would remain if it could no long bomb Vieques. He responded: "In all probability we would remain in Puerto Rico, but in a much lesser fashion than we are now."¹¹⁵ Were the navy to pull out of Puerto Rico, no municipality would feel its economic impact greater than Ceiba—the operational epicenter for Roosevelt Roads. Gerardo Cruz, Ceiba's mayor, was worried about just such a scenario. Nevertheless he said: "There is no doubt we would be affected a great deal if the navy left Vieques, but if I had to choose I prefer defending *viequense* lives."¹¹⁶

Paralleling the work of the presidential panel in Washington was a Commonwealth government panel operating in San Juan. In early July 1999 the governor's special panel on Vieques announced its findings. Governor Rosselló announced that he accepted its recommendations, including the military's withdrawal from Vieques and the transfer of navy-owned lands to the municipality's civilian population.¹¹⁷ The panel's very formation strained relations with Romero-Barceló.¹¹⁸ To no one's surprise, the navy called the report "distorted"and insisted that Vieques was the only place on the East Coast where one could carry out military exercises with live ordnance.¹¹⁹ Of course, the military had said similar things about Culebra and Hawaii's Kaho'olawe.

The fact that a pro-statehood governor was willing to oppose military policy openly led some to speculate whether there was a fundamental shift in Puerto Rican politics. In contrast to the statehood movement of the first two-thirds of the twentieth century, the *estadistas* (statehood supporters) of the last third were more culturally nationalistic.¹²⁰ Indeed, Romero-Barceló adamantly maintained that "*neither our language nor our culture is negotiable.*"¹²¹ Contrasting with earlier generations of statehood leaders, the new generation was willing to label the current Commonwealth status as a "colony." In effect, Romero-Barceló accused the federal government of perpetuating colonialism by maintaining the status quo. By the 1990s a new bloc of "radical statehooders" continued this attack on the status quo though employing a postmodernist analytical framework.¹²² Some suggested that these radical statehooders were little more than the same old movement draped in a new frock.¹²³ Yet the tone set by this new annexationist undercurrent opened the doors for the administration to criticize federal policy in a manner often associated with the Left and *independentistas*.

The armed forces spent the last weeks of the summer of 1999 trying to mend fences while maintaining its resolve. A navy report issued in early August 1999 blamed Sanes's death on the pilot and the ground control officer.[124] Sanes's family was outraged at the navy's earlier insinuation that Sanes himself may have been partially responsible for his death.[125] No one was surprised that the names of these two individuals were not released. Still, the navy demonstrated its aspiration to remain in Vieques. Years earlier the military announced plans to build a large radar system on Vieques.[126] The Relocatable-Over-The-Horizon-Radar (ROTHR) was designed to monitor narcotraffic in Latin America. In August 1999 the navy announced it was awarding the Raytheon Corporation a $112.6 million contract to build and install the device.[127]

The Vieques issue was now attracting significant attention. The United Nations was holding hearings on Puerto Rico's status. Julio Muriente, president of the Nuevo Movimiento Independentista Puertorriqueño (NMIP) (New Puerto Rican Independence Movement) submitted a copy of the Commonwealth government's Vieques Commission Report to the U.N.'s Decolonization Committee.[128] Governor Rosselló also spoke before this body. Much to his dismay, this U.N. committee approved a resolution favoring Puerto Rico's right to free determination, the navy's withdrawal from Vieques, and freedom for the Puerto Rican political prisoners.[129] Unlike the celebrated Security Council, the United States has no permanent seat or veto in this committee.

Vieques, a headache for Washington, proved to be just the issue to revitalize the PIP.[130] While the PIP praised Governor Rosselló's special commission on Vieques, it was not about to let down its guard.[131] The party would continue with its acts of civil disobedience until the navy left Vieques.[132] This decision even had the blessing of the municipality's PNP mayor.[133] The report's acceptance animated Vieques supporters, who organized a protest outside the main gates of the Roosevelt Roads base in Ceiba. Despite strong reservations from key pro-statehood leaders about attending such an event, several prominent PNP members participated in the protest.[134] The "Todo Puerto Rico con Vieques" (All Puerto Rico with Vieques) rally, held July 4, attracted fifty thousand supporters.[135] One could not help but notice the symbolism of holding such a large assembly calling on the U.S. government to withdraw its military operations from an American territory on the anniversary of the country's independence. David Sanes Rodríguez was canonized as a martyr to the Puerto Rican cause. His death served as a catalyst for a new and more communal cultural nationalism.

Public Opinion of the Military

In the summer of 1999 public opinion surveys showed that most Puerto Rican voters saw crime, drugs, unemployment, health, AIDS, and corruption as more important problems than the perennial status dilemma.[136] This is consistent with other studies showing public interest for matters other than the status question.[137] Yet the status debate has long been the centerpiece of island politics.[138] Analyses indicate that status preferences remain the most significant determinant of how the average citizen votes.[139] In 1999 Puerto Ricans were still deeply divided on this question: 43 percent supported the status quo, 34 percent favored statehood, and 6 percent wanted independence.[140] When asked to assess the impact of U.S. military presence in Puerto Rico, the public was also deeply divided.

Apologists for the U.S. military could no longer paint credible scenarios in Cold War hues. David Sanes's passing marked the first time since the Vietnam War that so many Puerto Ricans viewed the American armed forces in a destructive light. About 37 percent viewed the military's role as positive; 36 percent said it was negative. The partisan breakdown was rather illuminating. A majority of statehood supporters gave the military high marks. Still, among all the other sectors—independence supporters, Commonwealth advocates, and those not affiliated with any status preference—a majority or plurality viewed the military less favorably (see Table 3.1). Partisan leanings also impacted support for the Southern Command's presence in Puerto Rico (see Table 3.2). Here again, the only ideological faction sanctioning this military relocation was statehood supporters. Outside of *estadistas*, Puerto Ricans were reaching a political consensus.

Table 3.1. Opinion on the U.S. Military Presence in Puerto Rico, August 1999 (percent)

Party	Status Preference	Positive	Negative
PNP	Statehood	54	23
PPD	Commonwealth	29	45
PIP	Independence	6	74
Nonaffiliated	(none)	28	37

Source: "Lo bueno," 5.

Table 3.2. Opinion on the Transfer of the Southern Command to Puerto Rico, August 1999 (percent)

Party	Status Preference	Positive	Negative
PNP	Statehood	49	29
PPD	Commonwealth	20	55
PIP	Independence	6	86
Nonaffiliated	(none)	20	39

Source: "Lo bueno," 6.

Despite the persistent division of status politics, most Puerto Ricans were united around one political issue for the first time in ages. Around 73 percent of all Puerto Ricans wanted the navy to pull out from Vieques.[141]

> Puerto Ricans, perhaps without fully realizing it, are telling the United States: Vieques is our territory, not your, Americans. . . . It is possible that from now on things between the United States and Puerto Rico will never go back to being the same. What is interesting about this Vieques issue is that Puerto Ricans reacted the same as any Latin American: they jumped with indignation upon feeling that another country, another government, another one different from me, was appropriating its territory.[142]

Consequently, Washington would levy subtle, and not so subtle, pressure on the Puerto Rican government to sanction the resumption of military exercises. Federal officials clearly were not seeking "permission." Local acquiescence was merely a fig leaf sought to justify federal actions. A proposal to release a group of Puerto Ricans indicted for conspiracy to commit politically motivated acts of violence—the *presos políticos* (political prisoners)—suddenly found new life. Those in the Vieques struggle insisted their release should not deter the demilitarization mission.[143] The complex web of Vieques, political prisoners, human rights, and cultural identity became even more entangled.

4

Clemency and Consensus

In the 1980s several organizations campaigned to free a number of political prisoners connected to the independence cause. To many Puerto Ricans, their prolonged confinement was an issue of human rights rather than national security. To certain *independentistas*, the prisoners were heroes in the tradition of Pedro Albizu Campos. The campaign for their release echoed an earlier crusade to free a group of Puerto Rican nationalists jailed in the 1950s for revolutionary activities. Progressive political activists insisted that the fate of these detainees and the crisis in Vieques were rooted in the same basic problem. Both derived from Puerto Rico's colonial relationship with the United States. The politics displayed in numerous rallies and demonstrations for the prisoners and Vieques were manifestations not of separatism but of cultural nationalism. Still, such public displays alarmed those who advocated statehood. For them, even temperate parades of Puerto Rican ethnic pride were potentially harmful to their goal of eventual admission into the Union.

Politics and Clemency

In the 1990s the group Pro Libertad conducted a grassroots crusade seeking the release of fifteen individuals arrested between 1980 and 1986.[1] Most were charged with seditious conspiracy for their alleged involvement in several acts of terrorism attributed to the Fuerzas Armadas de Liberación Nacional (FALN) (Armed Forces of National Liberation) or the Macheteros in the 1970s and 1980s.[2] Though small in terms of numbers of members, Puerto Rican revolutionary organizations were responsible for almost half of the terrorist acts on the U.S. mainland in the late 1970s.[3] The FALN claimed responsibility for more than a hundred bombings in the mid-1970s to the early 1980s. The Macheteros were best known for a 1981 attack on Muñiz Air National Guard Base in Carolina,

Puerto Rico, and the 1983 Wells Fargo heist in Hartford, Connecticut.[4] Their sentences ranged from 35 to 105 years.

As one activist noted: "They've spent more time in prison than many child molesters, rapists and murderers."[5] Former Puerto Rican governor Rafael Hernández Colón commented that "the Puerto Rican prisoners have already served three times the average served by common criminals for more serious offenses. This disproportionate duration of incarceration is what makes them prisoners for purely political reasons."[6] Representative José Serrano surmised that these sentences were designed not only to punish these individuals but also strike fear into the hearts of *independentistas*.[7] Notables such as New York's late Cardinal John O'Connor, former President Jimmy Carter, and South African Archbishop Desmond Tutu added their names to the list asking the Clinton administration to review the prisoners' sentences.[8] Mainland Puerto Rican politicians and political activists played a key role in redefining these individuals within ethnic communities as "political prisoners," rather than as "terrorists," and amassing popular support for their release.[9]

Federal officials were searching for a way to improve relations with Puerto Ricans following the April 19 tragedy and the news, less than a month later, that an unexploded torpedo was located near a populated area.[10] An August 1999 rally in Puerto Rico calling for the prisoners' release and a halt to the navy's activities in Vieques drew 150,000 participants.[11] However, beyond concerns over insular Puerto Ricans was an interest in conciliating mainland *puertorriqueños*. New York City Council member José Rivera for years had advocated the prisoners' release.[12] Renewed interest in their possible release, he contended, was connected to the political aspirations of First Lady Hillary Rodham Clinton and Vice President Al Gore.[13] In a close election, the electoral fates of Senate candidate Rodham Clinton and presidential candidate Gore could hinge on support from New York State's sizeable Puerto Rican community. This may explain why the vice president announced his support for the navy's withdrawal from Vieques more than a year before the 2000 elections.[14]

In August the White House announced that it would offer eleven of the fifteen prisoners immediate freedom and reduce the sentences of two others.[15] Far and away the most controversial condition on clemency President Clinton imposed was the proviso that the former prisoners could not associate with anyone with a criminal record.[16] In effect, they were barred from meeting with one another. Governor Rosselló applauded Clinton's move.[17] Though initially upset with their release, Resident Commissioner

Romero-Barceló eventually defended the president's actions on humanitarian grounds.[18] Others, such as José Rivera, favored an unconditional release but believed it was important that the *presos políticos* join the struggle for Vieques.[19]

President Clinton defended his decision to grant conditional clemency based on the harshness of their original sentences.[20] Elizam Escobar, Ricardo Jiménez, Adolfo Matos, Dylcia Noemí Pagán, Alicia Rodríguez, Ida Luz Rodríguez, Luis Rosa, Carmen Valentín, Alberto Rodríguez, Alejandrina Torres, and Edwin Cortés were immediately released. Oscar López Rivera refused to accept the clemency offer. Though he would still serve five years more years in prison, Juan Enrique Segarra accepted the offer. Clinton did not offer clemency to Carlos Alberto Torres. Another prisoner, Antonio Camacho Negrón, freed in 1998 and arrested three weeks later for failing to report to his parole officer, had his $100,000 fine commuted.[21] The former prisoners' arrival in Puerto Rico turned into a festive homecoming.[22]

Not all observers agreed that their release would benefit the First Lady. Former Clinton adviser Dick Morris suggested that the clemency issue could hurt Rodham Clinton's electoral prospects.[23] By supporting their release, she could be portrayed by her opponents as lenient toward criminals. Rodham Clinton insisted that her husband did not consult her before freeing the prisoners,[24] and she withdrew her support for the prisoners' release.[25] Council member Rivera denounced her decision.[26] Nonetheless, Dennis Rivera, the labor leader heading Local 1199 and representing 150,000 New York City health workers, still supported her.[27] This Senate candidate would have to perform a delicate balancing act, attempting to appease Puerto Ricans and placating others who opposed clemency.

In response to the White House's decision, the president's adversaries went on the offensive. House Majority leader Dick Armey accused Clinton of putting politics before the country's affairs and insisted on a congressional censure.[28] New York City Mayor Rudolph Giuliani questioned the clemency's timing and demanded that the Justice Department release its confidential report on the prisoners.[29] At that time, most pundits assumed Giuliani would stand as Rodham Clinton's main rival for the U.S. Senate seat. The president, claiming executive privilege, refused to make public any of these documents.[30] Anthony Senft, a New York police officer wounded in an FALN bombing, described the president's clemency offer as "repulsive."[31] Richard Pastorella, another officer wounded in an FALN attack, accused the president of "pandering to the Hispanic community on behalf of his wife."[32] Ironically, by granting clemency the president lost significant leverage with Congress on the Vieques issue.[33] Time may reveal whether the president was aware of this fallout or even if he was counting on it.

In the fall of 1999 President Clinton faced the same angry legislature that impeached him only a few months earlier. Texas Senator Phil Gramm accused the president of "playing New York politics." Gramm's colleague from Alabama, Jeff Sessions, labeled Clinton's action "one of the greatest miscarriages of justice I have seen in our country." Representative Thomas Reynolds of New York called the act "a very real threat to the safety and security of the American people." Comments from these Republican lawmakers also put Puerto Rican members of the Congress on the defensive. Representative José Serrano tried to put the clemency issue into the larger context of federal-territorial relations. Serrano insisted that this was an "act of national reconciliation." Representative Nydia Velázquez charged others with attempting to impair Rodham Clinton's senatorial campaign.[34] In the end, the House voted overwhelmingly to censure the chief executive.[35] Yet Senate Majority Leader Trent Lott was perplexed by the more than seventy House members who voted "present" rather than vote for or against the measure.[36]

In the midst of the Senate debate on a presidential censure, the Vieques issue resurfaced. Oklahoma's senator James Inhofe chastised Attorney General Janet Reno for not sending federal marshals to remove the Vieques protestors.[37] If the navy could not train in Vieques, perhaps Congress might consider retaliating by downsizing the Roosevelt Roads base.

> It is true that the people and the citizens of the island of Puerto Rico would like to have this range deactivated. But they also at the same time want to keep our facilities that are so significant in making contributions to their economies, such as Roosevelt Roads. As chairman of the Readiness Subcommittee of the Senate Committee on Armed Services, I went out and told them I am going to do everything within my power—if they deactivate this range; and are successful in doing this, through the White House and the President's efforts—to do what we can to move those functions that take place in Roosevelt Roads, to deactivate that and bring those back to various installations in the United States that are only partially utilized.[38]

Senator Lott also threatened Puerto Rico with a cut in federal aid unless the navy resumed its training.[39] Rosselló went on the counteroffensive, stating that the Mississippi senator "has been prejudiced with other Hispanic matters."⁴⁰ Despite such threats, Governor Rosselló's working group on Vieques insisted on a naval departure.⁴¹ By linking the clemency issue with civil-military policy, lawmakers, by design or default, refortified the sociocultural divide between Puerto Ricans and Americans.

The Clinton Plan

A week after Congress registered its opposition to Clinton's clemency decision, the presidential panel on Vieques rendered its verdict. The panel recommended that the navy should reduce its exercises in Vieques from 180 to 140 days per year and cease its bombing activities after five years.⁴² It would be left up to the navy to find an alternative site. Governor Rosselló insisted that the proposed reduction of bombing days was unacceptable.⁴³ He did point out, however, that at least this federal report advocated the navy's eventual withdrawal.⁴⁴ Community activists Robert Rabin and Alba Encarnación called the offer of a $27 million economic aid package an affront.⁴⁵ Hillary Rodham Clinton also expressed her disappointment with the panel's recommendations, but she refused to challenge the administration directly by visiting the protestors on Vieques.⁴⁶

A recurring question was how this persistent defiance of federal authority would affect Puerto Rico's image in the United States. More to the point, members of the ruling PNP were concerned with how this glaring display of cultural nationalism would affect their plans to drum up congressional support for statehood. One statehood proponent argued these incidents would build support for the movement.⁴⁷ Others were not persuaded by that argument. PNP Senator Sergio Peña Clos warned, "At this moment statehood is very battered on account of nationalism."⁴⁸ Governor Rosselló and House Speaker Edison Misla Aldarondo called on statehood backers to repair Puerto Rico's image in Washington.⁴⁹ Though the island's independence movement was small, its mere existence made amassing federal support for annexation problematic at best. As Jorge Ramos claimed:

> The U.S. Senate does not have the slightest intention of discussing the possibility of making Puerto Rico the 51st state. Vieques is the excuse they were searching for [for] the longest time. And in Puerto Rico, neither statehood nor the current Commonwealth have [sic] enough votes to amply win in a plebiscite. So, perhaps what we are seeing is how Puerto Rico is becoming an independent state by *default*. That is, faced with the impossibility of choosing, clearly and without doubt, statehood or commonwealth, Puerto Ricans are be-

ing left with—though a majority do not want it—the only available alternative: involuntary independence.[50]

Rosselló maintained that nationalism was not increasing; instead we were witnessing a growing "Puerto Ricanist sentiment."[51] Paradoxically, his comments came on the same day as the Grito de Lares celebration—September 23. Every year *independentistas* convene in this western highland town to commemorate an unsuccessful revolt against the Spanish Crown and celebrate Puerto Rican ethnic pride. Organizers dedicated the 1999 Grito to the demilitarization of Vieques. This turned out to be the largest Lares gathering in two decades.[52] Fearing the possibility of coming into contact with one another, a violation of their clemency, the recently released prisoners opted to stay away from Lares or Vieques.[53] To counter the perception of an escalation of nationalism, PNP Senator Orlando Parga proposed holding a "Pro American March."[54] Still, his party was uncertain about supporting this march or even the civil disobedience campaign in Vieques.[55] Uncertainty about nationalism did not hamper Congress.

In October 1999 the Senate Armed Services Committee decided to hold hearings on Vieques. They were animated from the start. Representative José Serrano told John Warner, the senator chairing these hearings, that his decision to exclude the PIP from the hearings was unjust, antidemocratic, and insensitive.[56] Warner made it clear he would resist the navy's withdrawal from Vieques and the return of this military property to civilians.[57] The Virginia lawmaker had close connections to the armed forces and military-related industries. Warner received more campaign donations from political action committees (PACs) than any other congressional candidate in 1996—over $1.5 million. Of that sum, more than $250,000 came from defense industry PACs or individuals connected to those companies.[58] Like many others in Congress, Senator Warner failed to heed President Dwight D. Eisenhower's admonition, uttered decades earlier, about the dangers of expanding commercial interests in the defense establishment. Eisenhower warned: "In the councils of government, we must guard against the acquisition of unwarranted influence, whether sought or unsought, by the military-industrial complex."[59] Peace in Vieques meant the navy was spending less on ammunition and other implements of war, leading to a decline in defense-industry profits.

Governor Rosselló insisted that *viequenses* would have to be consulted.[60] In the early 1980s federal lawmakers were convinced that a referendum in Vieques would bode well for the navy.[61] How would voters respond were a referendum held in 1999? A survey revealed that 56 percent of Puerto Rican islanders wanted the navy to withdraw completely from Vieques; 80 percent of *viequenses* favored that option. While 58 percent of Puerto Ricans thought the navy's departure in two or three years was unacceptable, 83 percent of *viequenses* found it objectionable. Would the navy's departure from Vieques affect relations with the United States? A bare majority of Puerto Ricans, 51 percent, said no, compared to 80 percent of Vieques islanders. When asked whether they supported a continuation of the civil disobedience campaign, 56 percent of Puerto Ricans said yes while 76 percent of *viequenses* answered in the affirmative.[62] Those camping out in the navy's firing range were encouraged by such signs of popular support. Indeed, some were so adamant about remaining on the beaches surrounding Monte David that they refused to evacuate the area even as Hurricane Lenny passed through the northeastern Caribbean.[63]

Despite objections from Puerto Rico's governor and resident commissioner, President Clinton announced the resumption of naval exercises in Vieques with inert ammunition beginning in the spring of 2000.[64] In keeping with his panel's recommendation, the navy would remain in Vieques for up to five years while the number of training days would decrease from 180 to 90 days. As an economic incentive, Vieques would receive $40 million from the federal treasury.[65] As far as Representative Luis Gutiérrez was concerned, the White House was simply selling out Vieques to the Pentagon and its congressional guardians.[66] When the chips were down, the White House valued the navy's interests far above the will of Puerto Ricans.

Clinton's decision left many Puerto Ricans wondering to what degree they could count on the benevolence of the federal government. Soon many questioned to what degree they could even count on Washington's honesty. Trust in federal institutions diminished with Federal Bureau of Investigation (FBI) Director Louis Freeh's disclosure that the FBI had persecuted *independentistas* for decades.[67] Federal officials began monitoring Puerto Ricans for their political beliefs immediately following the Spanish-American War.[68] Freeh subsequently turned over to Representative Serrano thousands of documents on federal surveillance of *independentistas*, and he said Serrano should expect an additional two million documents.[69] Federal persecution of Puerto Ricans for their political beliefs, especially *independentistas,* was an integral part of the century-plus relationship between the United States and *puertorriqueños*. As Representative Serrano noted: "We cannot deny the fact that the FBI files are part of our history, though it's an ugly topic."[70] Later it was discovered that despite Freeh's apology, the FBI set up undercover observers at pro-independence rallies such as the Grito de Lares.[71] Apparently, old habits are hard to break.

Public disclosures also shed an uncomplimentary light on the Commonwealth government. On behalf of the territorial government, Governor Rosselló apologized for the persecution of *independentistas*.[72] It was also revealed that the Commonwealth's Office of Police Intelligence maintained daily contact and strong links with the FBI regarding "subversives."[73] In the end, Rosselló commended academics and pro-independence leaders for revealing the existence of these files and recommended that the insular government compensate the victims of persecution.[74] Perhaps David Sanes's death marked a new period of political cooperation.[75] Others still questioned how long this harmony would endure.

Bombing Resumes

Early in 2000 Puerto Rican public attention was focused on the second series of federal trials involving the AIDS Institute. Rumors abounded that prominent political figures—such as the PNP's former vice house speaker José Granados Navedo—would be implicated.[76] Administration critics suggested that the ruling party might use Vieques to divert attention away from accusations of administration corruption and to promote statehood in Washington.[77] PIP leader Rubén Berríos also saw a connection between Vieques and Puerto Rico's status.[78] President Clinton laid most of blame for the crisis on a lack of congressional will to confront Puerto Rico's final status and noncompliance with the 1983 Fortín Accord.[79] Representative Don Young of Alaska made it clear that congressional status deliberations would have to wait until the Vieques matter was resolved.[80]

In his last State of the Commonwealth address on January 31, Governor Rosselló announced that he accepted the White House plan.[81] Exalting the plan's benefits, he underscored that President Clinton would ask Congress to transfer the western portions of the island to the Vieques municipal government for civilian use.[82] Plans were under way to hold a referendum on the federal proposal, but it would be limited to Vieques. Two choices would not appear on the ballot: a "no bombing" option and a "none of the above" alternative.[83] Governor Rosselló and his party had introduced the "none of the above" alternative in the 1998 status plebiscite, and it was this very option that caused his administration the greatest embarrassment. In response, an outraged PIP delegation walked out of the governor's address.[84] The Independence Party accused the governor of betrayal and promised to make Vieques a major campaign issue.[85] Governor Rosselló's decision thrust aside the warning by social progressives within his movement, the so-called radical statehooders, to steer clear of alliances with a stateside organization as conservative as the military.[86]

The White House denied that it was sacrificing Vieques in order to promote Puerto Rican statehood.[87] Nonetheless, soon after Rosselló agreed to the plan, Clinton began prodding Congress to tackle the status impasse.[88] Since Rosselló was negotiating with a lame duck president, there was no guarantee that Congress would sign on to Clinton's plan or that a future commander-in-chief would abide by it.[89] Rosselló's endorsement of this federal plan seemed sufficient to ease the ire of congressional Republicans.[90] Even Senator Inhofe, who months earlier threatened to cut Puerto Rico's financial aid, now sounded more conciliatory: "I hope that the people of Vieques—who have earned the gratitude of the American people for what their island has contributed to national defense—will see the extraordinary benefits that the navy is offering in exchange for allowing the continuation of training with live munitions, which will serve to protect liberty and democracy around the world."[91]

Just how did *viequenses* feel about this accord and the way in which it was negotiated? A February 2000 survey showed that Vieques islanders overwhelmingly believed that this scheme protected the navy (93 percent), that it violated the government's promise of *ni una bomba más* (not one more bomb) (82 percent), and that the protestors should remain on their island municipality (79 percent). When it came to the accord itself, 55 percent supported the navy's departure in three years, while 29 percent wanted the armed forces to leave immediately, though this option would not appear on the governor's proposed referendum.[92] Vieques residents differentiated between the navy's presence in Vieques and the military's bombing of their municipality.

The survey also revealed how *viequenses* judged various leaders. Were the elections held then, around 41 percent would support Sila María Calderón, the PPD's gubernatorial candidate; 25 percent would vote for PIP leader Rubén Berríos; and 16 percent favored the PNP candidate, Carlos Pesquera.[93] This represented a significant shift of partisan preferences, given the PNP's 1996 victory in this municipality by almost 4 percent.[94] Overall, Vieques residents gave high marks to Rubén Berríos, Archbishop González, Bishop Corrada, and community leaders Carlos

Ventura and Alba Encarnación.[95] The PNP leadership and President Clinton received failing marks by a wide margin.

V*iequenses* also accorded high marks to cleric activists. Church participation in the protests lent an air of moral authority to the civil disobedience campaign and fortified the civic and social components of the cultural nationalism on display. Clerics, peace activists, and community organizations stood at the vanguard of the Vieques crusade, joining, and at times overshadowing, the traditional front-line role played by pro-independence political parties. Church involvement in the Vieques crisis, both Protestant and Catholic, made it more difficult for the federal and Commonwealth governments to justify an agreement that bypassed the community leadership in Vieques and the input of other political and civic organizations.

Traditionally the Catholic Church was associated with a rather conservative brand of politics. Under Spanish rule the Catholic Church supported the Crown, which rewarded the Church of Rome with a monopoly over institutional religious life. Following the Spanish-American War, the pope replaced Spanish bishops with Americans who eagerly embraced the federal government's Americanization policies. In the early 1960s the island's top Catholic leaders were deeply embroiled in partisan politics. Archbishop Davis of San Juan and Bishop McManus of Ponce locked horns with Governor Luis Muñoz Marín over his administration's sterilization policies, lack of state funding for religious activities, and religious instruction in public schools. Their incongruent principles led to the emergence of a religiously based party—the Partido Acción Cristiana (Christian Action Party)—and benefited the political fortunes of Muñoz Marín's primary rival, the statehood leader Luis A. Ferré.[96]

Church support of the Vieques cause turned the old battle lines around 180 degrees. Statehood leaders were now criticizing the Catholic Church for its involvement in political matters, and the PPD was defending it.[97] PNP Representative José Núñez wrote to the Vatican asking the pontiff to reprimand the island's Catholic leadership.[98] Whereas the PPD of the 1960s attacked the Church for its involvement in politics, in the late 1990s it was defending ecclesiastical input. San Juan mayor Sila Calderón lashed out at the PNP for assailing the Catholic hierarchy.[99]

Religious leaders of various denominations found it difficult to support the government when the media reported *viequenses* had the highest cancer rates in Puerto Rico.[100] Evangelical minister Jorge Raschke stated that the health and lives of the people of Vieques could not be bought. He rebuked the Clinton-Rosselló accord as an "abuse of power" and an "immoral act."[101] José Lebrón, president of the Evangelical Foundation, declared: "For the Church, Vieques is essentially a problem of morality and conscience."[102] The Reverend Samuel Pagán, resident of the Evangelical Seminary, lauded the civil disobedience campaign as an act of "evangelical obedience."[103] When Rosselló called on Puerto Ricans to oppose Church involvement in the Vieques civil disobedience campaign, Methodist bishop Juan Vera, recalling Jesus' acts of disobedience, responded that the governor's comments showed an ignorance of the biblical tradition.[104] David Noriega remarked that Rosselló was the last person who should complain about church activism. After all, it was the governor himself who invited religious leaders to join his Vieques commissions in the first place.[105]

Despite these changes in federal attitude, the ruling PNP remained deeply concerned that persisting protests presented Puerto Rico to the United States in a nationalist light. Those fears were fueled by another peace rally attended by 150,000,[106] organized only half a year after a demonstration of roughly equal size had called for the political prisoners' release. Support for the civil disobedience campaign was widespread among most sectors, except for statehood supporters.[107] For them, cultural nationalism, while deeply entrenched in Puerto Rican society, was a clandestine sentiment one could acknowledge at home but certainly not in Washington.

English-language activist Jim Boulet pledged to use these protests as evidence of Puerto Rican nationalism in his campaign to thwart federal support for Puerto Rican statehood.[108] PNP leaders feared such displays could even propel federal lawmakers to promote independence.[109] To counter this image, statehood advocates spent considerable financial resources to organize pro-American rallies.[110] Rosselló's backers hoped these gestures might sway Congress; they were wrong. Congress ended the year 2000 without seriously tackling the status question. In the spring of 2000 the Rosselló administration found itself backing a proposal drafted by an outgoing president who was unable to secure congressional support even to discuss Puerto Rico's status.

On Vieques itself, activists were preparing for the first anniversary of David Sanes's death. Archbishop González commented that his demise "touched something very deep in the Puerto Rican soul."[111] Governor Rosselló claimed that the events of the past year profoundly affected U.S.–Puerto Rican relations, leading eventually to a choice between statehood and independence.[112] While some federal authorities were anxious to expel the protestors, Attorney General Reno was eager to avoid a repeat of the violent outcomes in the federal assaults at Ruby Ridge, Idaho, in 1992 and the Davidian compound in Waco, Texas, in 1993.[113] As a sign of federal resolve, the Pentagon sent the USS *Nashville* and USS *Bataan* to the region.[114] On May 4, 2000, more than three hundred federal authorities arrived in Vieques to arrest several hundred protestors. In addition to the arrests of several political figures, sixty clerics were taken into custody.[115] Their arrests triggered further protests throughout the main island.[116] Once released, the former detainees were received as heroes.[117] Six days after these arrests, the navy resumed its war games and its bombing of Vieques.[118]

Statehood supporters hoped the Vieques controversy had finally ended.[119] David Noriega claimed this was just the beginning.[120] The yearlong encampment on Vieques affected both how Puerto Rican islanders viewed the United States and how Americans looked upon Puerto Rico. A week after the navy resumed its Vieques operations, Standard and Poor's reported that "the population's strong sense of nationalism could become a source of instability and political risk in the future."[121] This society's cultural nationalism was put on full display for the world to see, which alarmed several powerful interests in the metropolis. What made this public expression of cultural identity so poignant to many was not only the energetic participation of separatist, civic, and many church-based organizations but also the very active involvement of ethnic Puerto Ricans living in the continental United States. These nationalists, from Washington's perspective, were living among us.

By June 2000 the aircraft carrier USS *George Washington* completed its training exercises in Vieques and proceeded to the Persian Gulf.[122] Its presence in Vieques marked four days of intense demonstrations culminating in over a hundred arrests.[123] The large numbers of arrests strained the federal judicial system and obliged the federal district court in Puerto Rico to seek the assistance of prosecutors from the Judge Advocate General and the district court in Miami.[124] While most Americans celebrated July 4 with elation, thousands protested outside the federal penitentiary in Guaynabo where the Vieques protestors were incarcerated.[125] In the words of one sympathizer, the federal prison in Guaynabo was transformed into the "Federal Bastille."[126] On the same date, thousands protested in the southern city of Ponce, and hundreds demonstrated in New York City.[127] Though recent experiences in Vieques were painful, Rev. Wilfredo Estrada, secretary general of Puerto Rico's Biblical Society, insisted that they "transformed the Puerto Rican soul" and served as a "process of national reconciliation."[128]

Elections 2000

American political figures presented several options regarding Vieques's status as a military training facility. Presidential candidate Al Gore called for an end to navy training on Vieques as soon as possible.[129] His Republican challenger, George W. Bush, pledged to respect the will of the people of Vieques.[130] Senator Lott suggested that the military should simply purchase the entire island of Vieques.[131] While discussing the possible transfer of some of the military-owned lands back to the *viequenses*, Senator Inhofe maintained no lands should be reassigned until the navy obtained something in return, such as the resumption of bombing with live ammunition.[132] As political leaders in the United States pondered the fate of Vieques, pundits in Puerto Rico were busy anticipating how events in Vieques might impact the upcoming fall 2000 elections in Puerto Rico.

Public opinion appeared to be moving in the military's favor. Whereas an August 1999 poll showed that 37 percent negatively viewed the military's role in Puerto Rico, a new survey revealed that only 30 percent felt the same way in June 2000. Overall, 44 percent saw the military's role in a positive light compared to 36 percent in 1999. This more optimistic view of the military was evident across the ideological spectrum, particularly among statehood supporters and those professing no partisan affiliation (see Table 4.1). Still, with the exception of statehood advocates, most Puerto Ricans supported a continuation of the civil disobedience campaign in Vieques.[133] Once more Puerto Ricans appeared to differentiate between the U.S. military on the whole and its operations in Vieques in particular. What impact would the resumption of military activity in Vieques have on the fall 2000 elections?

Table 4.1. Opinion on the U.S. Military Presence in Puerto Rico, June 2000 (percent)

Party	Status Preference	Positive	Negative
PNP	Statehood	64	16
PPD	Commonwealth	35	40
PIP	Independence	10	75
Nonaffiliated	(none)	37	30

Source: "Situación de Vieques," 5.

Throughout most of 1999 the PPD's gubernatorial candidate, Sila Calderón, maintained an advantage over her PNP contender, Carlos Pesquera.[134] Only a few weeks before the November 2000 elections, Pesquera had a four percentage point lead over Calderón.[135] The same survey revealed that PIP candidate Rubén Berríos, the former senator who camped out in the military's zone for over a year, was approaching double-digit support. As a pro-statehood political pundit observed, the PPD was adamant about saying only nice things about Berríos for fear of driving the party's more nationalistic members toward the Independence Party.[136] This segment of strategic voters—often referred to as *melones*—could frequently determine electoral outcomes.[137] The PPD's electoral strategy hinged on holding on to its base, including its more nationalist segment, and swaying undecided voters.

Analysts gave Calderón the edge over Pesquera in the debates.[138] They also noted a significant alteration in her line of attack. Calderón censured the PNP for lacking the will to resolve the Vieques crisis.[139] Federal actions ensured the prominence of the Vieques issue in the last leg of the 2000 campaign. President Clinton signed a $310 billion defense authorization bill, which included the transfer of navy-owned lands in western Vieques to civilians. The municipality of Vieques would receive 4,000 acres, the federal Department of the Interior would administer 3,100 acres, and the Puerto Rico Conservation Trust would oversee 800 acres.[140] Military training maneuvers would continue in eastern Vieques. Voters would have to wait until months after the elections to discover that these new civilian parcels accommodated seventeen toxic waste dumps.[141]

Throughout October the navy organized war games off the Isla Nena with thirty thousand American and NATO troops.[142] Thousands in New York City protested.[143] Challenging the navy in court was environmental attorney Robert Kennedy Jr., who was connected to the Vieques cause by New York labor leader Dennis Rivera.[144] If elected, Calderón promised to resume the search for a national consensus. After all, "Puerto Rico has acknowledged that it has a moral debt with the people of Vieques."[145] As a backdrop for her last major campaign rally, the stage behind the gubernatorial candidate was swathed in an immense banner proclaiming *Paz para Vieques* (Peace for Vieques).[146] Candidate Calderón was adamant about linking her campaign with the Vieques movement.

The PPD also inserted Vieques into its campaign by joining the PIP in challenging Puerto Rico's first proposed presidential election. In July 2000 Jaime Pieras, a federal judge in San Juan, ruled that the right to vote in a U.S. presidential election was based on citizenship rather than place of residence.¹⁴⁷ Federal Department of Justice officials immediately challenged the principle that residents of a territory, except those in the District of Columbia, were entitled to vote in the 2000 presidential contest between Al Gore and George W. Bush.¹⁴⁸

In September 2000 Governor Rosselló signed into law a bill authorizing a presidential ballot in the November elections. Both the PIP and PPD challenged the statute in court.¹⁴⁹ Senator Berríos stated that if it was not declared unlawful, he would encourage his followers to mark on these ballots *Paz para Vieques*.¹⁵⁰ The PPD followed suit.¹⁵¹ Many speculated on the possible victory of *Paz para Vieques* over both Bush and Gore until the First Circuit Court of Appeals overturned Judge Pieras's decision.¹⁵² Only days before the election, Puerto Rico's Supreme Court ruled that the statute authorizing a presidential election was an "electoral fallacy of unequal proportion," putting an end to what promised to be a audacious test of federal-territorial relations.¹⁵³

At the ballot box, Calderón won the governorship with 48.6 percent of the vote compared to 45.7 percent for Pesquera and 5.2 percent for Berríos. A more impressive transformation occurred in Vieques, where the PNP suffered its worst municipal defeat. The PPD's mayoral candidate Dámaso Serrano won 64.8 percent of the vote; the PNP's Juana Rivera Guishard received 31.6 percent; while the PIP's Dulce María Albandoz garnered only 4 percent of the vote.¹⁵⁴ The Pentagon's decision to hold war games off the coast of Vieques on the eve of the Puerto Rican elections offset the statehood party's message that it was capable of bringing peace to Vieques. Though the PIP invested a considerable amount of time and energy in its Vieques crusade, it became abundantly clear that more Puerto Rican voters opted to defeat the PNP rather than reward the PIP. The most effective way to accomplish this was by embracing the autonomist nationalism of the PPD, one of the two largest parties, rather than the separatist message of the PIP.

Postelection Consensus

The peace coalition campaigning for Vieques was able to maintain its unity following the 2000 elections. PIP leader Rubén Berríos called on all sectors to support Governor-elect Calderón's endeavor to end the bombing campaign.¹⁵⁵ Catholic Church spokespersons announced that the activist bishop of Caguas, Alvaro Corrada del Río, would be transferred to the dioceses of Tyler, Texas.¹⁵⁶ His successor, Rubén González Medina, announced his commitment to carry on the struggle.¹⁵⁷ In a symbolic act of reaffirmation, the Coalición Ecuménica pro Vieques (Pro-Vieques Ecumenical Coalition) announced that a replica of the ecumenical chapel built in the navy's restricted zone would be erected on a hill overlooking the capitol building in San Juan.[158]

Calderón insisted that the Clinton-Rosselló pact had to be renegotiated.[159] Vieques's new mayor insisted that any referendum on the navy's future operations include an option for an immediate end to all bombing.[160] Puerto Rico's first woman governor had a sense of the new Bush administration's unwillingness to compromise when Secretary of Defense–designate Donald Rumsfeld insisted that live-fire training on Vieques was vital to U.S. national security interests.[161] Admiral Kevin Green also insisted that the navy's presence was vital to check regional drug trafficking.[162] The new Bush administration, as was the case with its predecessor, seemed unwilling to sincerely study alternatives to bombing on Vieques, such as St. Kitts or islands off the coast of Colombia or Panama.[163]

While the peace coalition maintained a harmony of interests following the 2000 elections, the pro-statehood party found itself bitterly divided. Rosselló's secretary of state and head of the Vieques commission, Norma Burgos, was elected to the Senate. She represented the most culturally nationalistic wing of the PNP. Despite severe criticisms from within her party, Senator Burgos claimed that there was no contradiction between defending the rights of *viequenses* and her loyalty to the United States.[164] Key PNP leaders insisted that this elected official did not speak for the party.[165] Palpable manifestations of Puerto Rican nationalism, even its cultural variant, struck fear into the hearts of a political party aware that Congress was the only institution constitutionally authorized to fulfill its quest—permanent annexation. For statehood leaders, Puerto Rican ethnic pride was a sentiment best kept in the closet.

Norma Burgos's cooperation with Commonwealth and independence supporters fueled fears within her party that public displays of Puerto Rican nationalism were harming federal-territorial affairs. Following torrential rains early in 2001, Governor Calderón petitioned the White House to declare twenty-two municipalities federal disaster areas. PNP Representative Melinda Romero Donnelly suggested that President George W. Bush's decision to designate only six disaster areas proved how far relations with Washington had decayed.[166] Her father, Carlos Romero Barceló, echoed the concern that policy-makers in the United States perceived Puerto Ricans as "anti-American."[167] Analysts also pointed to stern reactions from Capitol Hill. Representative James Hansen of Utah, chair of the House Committee on Resources, insisted that Congress would not even address Puerto Rico's status question until the Vieques issue was resolved.[168] Moreover, Hansen threatened to use his influence to cut federal education funds to Puerto Rico to assure the military's continued operations in Vieques.[169]

A handful of Vieques residents were willing to go to extremes in order to demonstrate their uncompromising allegiance to the United States. In the first few months of 2001 Luis Sánchez, president of the promilitary organization Viequenses Pro Marina (Pro-Navy Vieques Islanders), proclaimed the start of a campaign to lobby Congress for *viequense* independence.[170] His goal was not to have Vieques secede from the United States; rather, his objective was to separate the Isla Nena from Puerto Rico and for it to become a separate U.S. territory. Separation, however, was rejected even from the staunchest statehood promoters on the main island.[171]

Attempts by statehood leaders to veil forthright public displays of Puerto Rican nationalism were continually thwarted by the parade of activists and political figures from the U.S. mainland professing their support for the plight of Vieques. New York senators Hillary Rodham Clinton and Charles Schumer, both Democrats, petitioned Secretary of Defense Rumsfeld to end the bombing immediately.[172] This time a Republican, New York governor George Pataki, also joined in the fray. In the midst of campaigning for reelection, Pataki consulted with Puerto Rican elected officials and community activists in New York.[173] While visiting the Isla Nena, Pataki called for an immediate end to the bombing and promised to take up the issue with President Bush.[174] Involvement in overseas issues, particularly those highly valued by local ethnic communities, is hardly a novelty in New York politics. Still, one is hard pressed to recall a time when elected officials from both major parties openly embraced a political issue so dear to the Puerto Rican community. Vieques became an integral part of New York politics and affirmed the critical input of mainland Puerto Ricans in the *viequense* equation.[175]

Pataki's visit came only days before the second anniversary of David Sanes's death.[176] To commemorate the occasion, the territorial legislature passed a bill fining "excess noise" on Puerto Rico's coasts and coastal waters.[177] Though generic on the surface, the law was drafted with the navy's raucous Vieques activities in mind. Peace activists also challenged the military's war games, on environmental grounds, in federal court.[178] Failing to stop the navy in court, the resumption of another round of navy war games sparked yet another wave of civil disobedience, culminating in the arrests of more than a hundred individuals.[179] Former senator Rubén Berríos was sentenced to four months in jail.[180] As he proclaimed, "Vieques is the cruelest expression of the political domination of the United States over Puerto Rico."[181]

Military officials tried to counter these protests by celebrating the transfer of eight thousand acres in western Vieques to civilian use. Admiral Green portrayed this conveyance as a positive step, blaming strains in civil-military relations on "professional agitators, news hunters, and anti-Americans."[182] Hardly any Puerto Ricans saw it that way. While gathering in the Vatican to celebrate the beatification of the first Puerto Rican, Carlos Manuel Rodríguez, hundreds of Puerto Ricans shouted *Paz para Vieques*.[183] Soon after Denise Quiñones was coronated as Miss Universe and Félix "Tito" Trinidad won the world middleweight boxing title, they announced their yearnings for peace in Vieques.[184] The U.S. military establishment failed to understand the depths of Puerto Rican commitment to this cause.

5

Politics in El Barrio

The death of David Sanes Rodríguez in 1999 served as a catalyst sparking a year-long civil disobedience campaign in Vieques and numerous demonstrations on the main island. Responding to public outrage, Governor Pedro Rosselló assembled representatives of various ideological persuasions, clerics, and community activists. For most of 1999 their recommendations were adopted as the official stance of the Puerto Rican people and their government. Sanes's death triggered an unleashing of cultural nationalism on a mass scale representing most sectors of Puerto Rican society.

The crisis in Vieques likewise invigorated ethnic Puerto Ricans in the United States. Mainland Puerto Rican leaders often stood on the front lines of legislative attacks on the antimilitary protestors and calls to free the political prisoners. The efforts of these leaders were matched with grassroots activism in various American urban centers, particularly New York City, the largest mainland Puerto Rican enclave. In the words of Jorge Farinacci, a main island activist with the Vieques and independence causes: "We Puerto Ricans who live on the big island have to recognize and appreciate the importance of the work being carried out by the different political, civic, and cultural sectors in the Puerto Rican community in New York. . . . Once again New York's *boricuas* have demonstrated that their commitment to Puerto Rico is at par or beyond that which has historically existed on the island. We are one people and neither colonialism nor distance can separate us."[1]

His appreciation is rather remarkable given the mainland community's reputation. Traditional scholarship on Puerto Rican mainland politics often began by referring to the community's electoral inactivity and general political apathy.[2] Of course, some of these same students of politics ignored the existence of other forms of political mobilization short of voting.[3] Contemporary scholarship challenges such assumptions of political complacency.[4] The events of 1999 are a case in point. Many failed to acknowledge the long tradition of political activism on the part of mainland Puerto Ricans. Marginalized by the established party machines, politics here often took the form of social activism: the struggle for workers' rights, civil rights, affordable housing, bilingual education, and so forth. Thus, the outpouring of support for the Vieques struggle in the continental United States was only the latest chapter in a long history of Puerto Rican political activism.

Activism and Migration

Puerto Ricans were lured to the United States before the Spanish-American War. By the late nineteenth century the United States had replaced Spain as Puerto Rico's largest trading partner.[5] Travel between Puerto Rico and the United States increased substantially after the change in sovereignty and was greatly facilitated following the enactment of the 1917 Jones Act.[6] Most of that early migration was unidirectional. For the past few decades, Puerto Ricans have come to expect a constant back and forth that is illustrated by referring to the mythical air bus—*la guagua aérea*—that links *puertorriqueños* in North America with their relations in the Caribbean. As Juan Flores put it, "Under the present conditions of transportation and communication, Puerto Rico is part of New York, and like it or not, New York is present in Puerto Rico."[7]

By the 1930s Puerto Ricans were the largest Hispanic group in New York City.[8] Given these demographic realities, Puerto Rican politics *were* New York Latino politics until the 1990s.[9] Mainland Puerto Rican politics has followed a distinctive path from the one usually associated with European immigrants.[10] Electoral barrio politics fell under the rubric of liberal reformism—the struggle to modify the system and create an opening for the social and economic demands of citizens. For years, many were frustrated by the urban system's aversion to openness. In response, activists often embraced the ideologies of the revolutionary Left, pursuing the politics of protest and agitation rather than the ballot box.

Before the Spanish-American War, Cuban and Puerto Rican independence activists established New York as their headquarters in exile.[11] New York City overtook New Orleans as the premier destination of Spanish Caribbean immigrants following the U.S. Civil War.[12] Nineteenth-century Latin New York was quite a different place than Latin New York a century later. Most of these immigrants were professionals, white-collar workers, or artisans. In contrast, most of twentieth-century migrants came with few skills and were poorly educated.[13] Puerto Rico's unemployment crisis early in the twentieth century was due, in large measure, to fundamental structural changes in the insular economy. These changes accelerated with the transfer of sovereignty from Spain to the United States.[14]

The Club Borinquen (Borinquen Club), the Liga Antillana (Antillean League), and the Liga de Artesanos (Artisans League) raised funds and served as information centers for the Cuban–Puerto Rican revolutionary movement in nineteenth-century New York City.[15] Political activism among these two Caribbean communities in New York subsided significantly following the Spanish-American War, with the noted exception of the labor activism of the International Cigar Makers Union, which was affiliated with the American Federation of Labor (AFL). Continuing a practice started in Cuban plants in the 1860s, many cigar-manufacturing facilities hired "readers." While the artisans rolled cigars, these individuals read from newspapers and works of literature.[16] Following the reading, cigar makers discussed current events, contending theories, or philosophical viewpoints. In a way, working in these cigar plants was akin to attending a nondegree-awarding center of higher education. For many decades, *tabaqueros* (tobacco workers) took on the role of the "political vanguard of a radicalized Puerto Rican working-class movement."[17] Radical ideologies, from anarchism to socialism to separatism, dominated the community's early leadership.[18] It would be difficult to justify categorizing this group as apolitical.

Early-twentieth-century political activism in the Puerto Rican community tended to eschew mainstream political parties. While influential in its day, even the Socialist Party at that time was xenophobic and declined to welcome Puerto Ricans.[19] When choosing between the two principal mainland parties, most Puerto Ricans overwhelmingly favored the Democrats.[20] In Brooklyn and Harlem, they organized local party branches and clubs.[21] Democratic Party appeals to immigrants and workers were strengthened by its urban machine that controlled the bulk of local patronage.[22] Though associated with corruption, urban machines were instrumental in incorporating immigrants into the political process. Immigrant votes were exchanged for government jobs or favors dispensed by local party bosses. Such practices may be ethically indefensible; still, they played a mayor role in socializing newcomers to the American electoral process. Those taking a "blame the victim" approach reprimanding Latinos for relatively low voter turnout rates ignore the less-than-law-abiding manner in which previous waves of immigrants were integrated into the system.

Puerto Rican leanings toward the Democratic Party were influenced by the connection many felt toward the island's long-time hegemonic party, the PPD, and to its founder, Luis Muñoz Marín, an ardent New Dealer who was associated with the mainland Democratic Party. This inclination was strongest among those who left the island in the 1940s and 1950s—the period marking the PPD's zenith. Many also linked the mainland Republican Party with its pro-statehood and pro–big business counterpart on the island.[23] Yet neither major party showed a keen interest in politically mobilizing the mainland Puerto Rican electorate.[24]

Cities may have established commissions to deal with Puerto Rican affairs and study neighborhood problems, but Democratic Party city machines generally ignored this community.[25] When city officials sought political input from Puerto Ricans, they preferred working with the Puerto Rican government's office in New York City rather than with community activists.[26] If the city Democratic machines were unfriendly, the Republican Party was not much better. For example, the first Puerto Rican elected official in New York City was Oscar García Rivera. Elected to the State Assembly in 1937 as a Republican, with the support of the American Labor Party, he represented a district in East Harlem. However, the Republican Party refused to renominate him because he "hung around too much with Communists and members of the American Labor Party."[27] Political party apathy toward Puerto Ricans was also encouraged by the decline of urban party machines, which coincided with the large waves of Puerto Rican migration in the mid-twentieth century.

As a general rule, immigrants must mobilize themselves first before parties are willing to bring them into the system; after all, the incorporation of new groups into the system usually foretells their demands for a share of resources.[28] That mobilization function was performed by the urban machines, and no large-scale organizations stepped in to fill that void. Puerto Ricans attempting to register to vote were often harassed by Board of Election officials. As Bernardo Vega noted in his famed memoirs, a few of New York's Puerto Ricans participated in Al Smith's 1918 mayoral campaign, but the community did not begin a concerted effort to mobilize its electoral base until the 1930s and 1940s—the years associated with the rise of Fiorello La Guardia and Vito Marcantonio.[29] These Italian Americans were among the first city politicians to actively court the Puerto Rican vote.[30] From his base in East Harlem, Marcantonio fought for his constituents, Puerto Rican and non-*boricua*, and advocated Puerto Rican independence.[31]

Early Puerto Rican political involvement stretched beyond electoral mobilization. New York's *tabaqueros* organized activities in solidarity with striking sugar cane workers on the island.³² Even in the 1920s New York Puerto Ricans debated the contentious status question of the island and political controversies engrossing Spain and Latin America.³³ When the links between the community's working-class intelligentsia—exemplified by the *tabaqueros*—and the larger socialist and labor movements of the time are understood, it is not surprising to find that many community activists of the period supported the Republican regime in Spain during the Spanish Civil War.³⁴

The Politics of Exclusion

Political interaction between *puertorriqueños* and Anglo-Americans in the United States was shaped by how the larger American society regarded Puerto Ricans. More often than not, the viewpoint expressed by mainstream society was decidedly negative. One of the most enduring American myths professed that all newcomers were obliged to assimilate into the mainstream—the proverbial "melting pot" thesis. Adoption of American cultural traits and norms was interpreted as a sign of patriotism. The reverse also held true. "The concept of Americanism as an act of *choice*— the decision to learn English, to apply for citizenship—and a choice of specific beliefs, acts and modes of behaviour implied the corresponding concept of 'un-Americanism.'"³⁵ Yet Puerto Ricans largely did not comply with this dictum. As Glazer and Moynihan noted: "Something new perhaps had been added to the New York scene—an ethnic group that will not assimilate to the same degree as others do but will resemble the strangers who lived in ancient Greek cities, or the ancient Greeks who set up colonies in cities around the Mediterranean."³⁶ Why were most Puerto Ricans so unwilling to fall into line?

Given future plans to return to the island, many Puerto Rican migrants in the great waves of the 1940s and 1950s saw little value in culturally merging with their immediate surroundings. Their cultural identities were already embedded in another place. "They had an imaginary line, a memory and a culture that made their 'assimilation' almost impossible. But that memory also allowed them to adapt themselves—selectively and conflictually—to the new circumstances in a society, in general, that scorned them."³⁷ Even as the children of Puerto Rican migrants came to share many of the cultural attributes associated with their new home, they were treated as outsiders.

At the time, most Puerto Ricans were unaware that their presence, along with that of other multiracial groups, contested the classic American racial paradigm dividing society into neatly bifurcated categories of white and black.[38] Society at large, and white society in particular, responded by racializing Puerto Ricans.[39] "If anything taught the Puerto Ricans—including white Puerto Ricans—what life is like in the United States, it was the awareness of discrimination."[40] Bernardo Vega reported in his memoirs that an armed robbery committed by a Puerto Rican in April 1924 help stigmatize the community with the stain of criminality. The members of this ethnic society were also associated with disease due to a damaging comment made by Eleanor Roosevelt in 1934.[41] Thanks to the tumultuous events of the early 1950s—the attempted assassination of President Truman at Blair House by nationalists, the armed attack of the U.S. House of Representatives, and the nationalist Gesta de Jayuya uprising led by Pedro Albizu Campos—Puerto Ricans were also associated with political violence.[42]

Negatives images of Puerto Ricans are nothing new in American society. In the midst of discussing the navy's future, Senator James Inhofe called Puerto Ricans short-sighted and "ungrateful."[43] There are few communities in the United States that are asked to prove their gratitude by allowing their communities to be used for target practice. His comments recalled columnist Don Feder's reference to Puerto Rico as a "Caribbean Dogpatch."[44] Despite promises of freedom and equality, Latino communities frequently lacked political clout and economic opportunities.[45]

Assimilation apologists, such as Linda Chávez, downplay the role of entrenched sociocultural hierarchies.[46] They ignore or underestimate the depths of the socioeconomic pecking order in the United States that consigned white Protestants at the apogee of American society.[47] Accompanying this ethno-racial pecking order was a linguistic hierarchy—one that favored Anglophones over non-English speakers.[48] There remains a de facto religious ranking favoring Christians over non-Christians, though the intra-Christian hierarchy has largely subsided.[49] Even when Puerto Ricans learned English, they tended to pick up the dialects of their immediate surroundings. This language variant was associated with the poor, the less educated, and inner-city blacks.[50] Blackness, or association with African Americans, was a permanent mark of exclusion. Therefore, "immigrants from Europe came to be American by striving not to be black."[51] Ethnic whites, on the other hand, were destined to assimilate.

> Immigrants were disparaged for their cultural peculiarities, and the implied message was, "You will become like us whether you want to or not." When it came to racial minorities, however, the unspoken

dictum was 'No matter how much like us you are, you will remain apart.' Thus, at the same time that the nation pursued a policy aimed at the rapid assimilation of recent arrivals from Europe, it segregated the racial minorities who, by virtue of their much longer history in American society, had already come to share much of the dominant culture.[52]

Not surprisingly, some lighter-skinned Puerto Ricans attempted to pass for Spaniards.[53] In contrast to racial minorities, Americans of northern European ancestry had only to change their family names to veil their socially stigmatized past.[54] For most Puerto Ricans, racially mixed to varying degrees, this whitening process was not an option.

In response to these social pressures, Puerto Ricans on the island and on the U.S. mainland embraced the Spanish language as a marker of cultural identity and symbol of solidarity with Latin Americans and U.S.-based Latinos.[55] For many English-dominant Puerto Ricans, the Spanish language endures as a representation of cultural distinctiveness vis-à-vis white, Anglophone Americans. This attachment to Spanish may be described as "defensive lingualism."[56] Language identities and loyalties do not depend on fluency.[57] Lack of fluency in Spanish has left English-dominant Puerto Ricans vulnerable to discrimination from insular Puerto Ricans who view their mainland coethnics as culturally impure.[58] Yet insular Puerto Ricans have no immunity to North American cultural influences. The plentiful adoption of English words in colloquial insular Spanish reveals that island-mainland linguistic differences are a matter of degree and not of kind.[59]

Ethnic discrimination had a profound impact on Puerto Rican politics on the U.S. mainland. Local political party organizations had a vested interest in maintaining Puerto Ricans, as with other Latinos, electorally marginalized.[60] In the third quarter of the twentieth century the Democratic Party was transformed in many cities into the party of white ethnics.[61] Party leaders feared that white voters could be alienated by an influx of Puerto Ricans; white officeholders were anxious about their possible displacement by an ethnic Puerto Rican leadership. Participation in the electoral process was often organized by activists whose power base was centered in their communities rather than in the party apparatus. Such an independent support base posed a threat to the traditional party leadership.[62]

Throughout much of the twentieth century New York City officials turned to the Commonwealth government's office not only for Puerto

Rican spokespersons but also for input into problems faced by the city's Puerto Rican community.[63] During the 1968 riots after the assassination of Martin Luther King Jr., Mayor John Lindsay consulted with officials at the Commonwealth's office rather than local leaders such as Bronx borough president Herman Badillo.[64] This case is not isolated. Foreign governments have used their diplomatic offices to politically mobilize their ethnic communities in the United States.[65] The island government's offices in other cities such as Chicago and Hartford also performed a similar intermediary function between local government and their respective Puerto Rican communities.[66] Commonwealth government input added to the sense that the community's presence in the city was temporary.[67] "Homeland governments are not reliable champions or defenders of the interests of their diaspora communities."[68] Once Badillo was elected to Congress, he became a spokesperson not only for New York Puerto Ricans but also for *puertorriqueños* on the island.[69] The tables began to turn.

A New Generation

Some sought change from within the system and opted to work with government-supported nonprofit organizations. Others rejected the system entirely, seeking alternative spaces in the form of community-based organizations. This two-pronged strategy of fighting for rights within the political system and advocating revolutionary change to overhaul the system was a hallmark of mainland Puerto Rican politics in the 1960s and early 1970s and paralleled the African American experience.[70] "Just as labor organizes to resist class domination, racial/ethnic minorities undertake *ethnically based strategies,* hoping to establish an autonomous foothold in a racially divided society. Disadvantaged groups seek to transform racial and cultural differences from a barrier into a resource, recasting racial identity as a bonding mechanism and a basis for self-esteem and group pride."[71] Many mainland Puerto Rican political organizations in this period prided themselves on their rejection of capitalism and openly embraced the struggle for Puerto Rico's independence. Joining the independence movement was a means of affirming cultural authenticity as *puertorriqueños*.[72] "Although members of diaspora communities no longer inhabit their national homelands, these homelands still play an important role in shaping their sense of collective identity."[73]

Through government-funded organizations, a new generation of Puerto Rican leaders acquired their first political experience in the

1960s.[74] A new cohort of educated mainland Puerto Ricans were transformed into "poverty-crats" thanks to the President Lyndon Johnson's War on Poverty. They developed some of the organizational skills that could subsequently be transferred to the realm of electoral politics.[75] Though *boricuas* no longer represent the majority of Latinos in New York City, Puerto Rican elected officials are now integral parts of "the system." In the past several decades, immigration from the Dominican Republic, Mexico, and other Latin American countries has significantly diminished the numeric dominance of *puertorriqueños* in the city.[76] While immigrants from other parts of Latin America now constitute most of the city's Latino residents, Puerto Ricans—U.S. citizens since 1917—comprise the vast majority of New York's Latino electorate.[77]

The island of Puerto Rico may be the ethnic *patria* and the birthplace of their ancestors, but for a new generation New York was home. Socialization here was sculpted by the experiences of daily living in American barrios. Their most intimate contact with U.S. society was through their neighbors—often African American. Among the struggles deeply influencing young Puerto Ricans of this generation were the Vietnam War, the civil rights movement, and the Black Power movement.[78]

From its origins as a Chicago street gang, the Young Lords Party was founded in 1969 as an inner-city political movement inspired by the Black Panther Party.[79] Albizuan nationalism blended with black nationalism and Marxism.[80] Concentrated primarily in large metropolitan areas in the Northeast and Midwest, the leadership of the Young Lords Party was unaware of the concurrent Chicano movement, whose political struggle was profoundly influenced by César Chávez's agro-labor movement in the Southwest.[81] The radical Puerto Rican organizations that eventually established themselves in the Southwest were primarily offshoots of preexisting northeastern associations such as the mainland branch of the PSP.[82] Black Panthers served as the model for the Young Lords Party, but the broader Black Power movement also had a profound impact on the articulation of mainland Puerto Rican identity and the appropriation of nationalist symbols.[83] Black organizations such as the Student Nonviolent Coordinating Committee (SNCC) cooperated with the campaign to free the Puerto Rican political prisoners arrested in the 1950s.[84] Puerto Ricans and African Americans also collaborated on the campaign to demilitarize Vieques.[85]

Winning elections was not the Young Lords Party's main objective. Instead, it focused on implementing change at the community level through socialist principles.[86] "In particular, the Young Lords are illustrative of intergenerational distance between migrants and second-generation Puerto Ricans and transformed articulations of Puerto Ricanness in the sociopolitical context of the United States."[87] As community servants, the Lords established food and clothing programs.[88] As social progressives, they promoted women's rights and challenged racism, even within Puerto Rican groups.[89] Their commitment to street-level social activism maintained one foot in the U.S. experience, but through their support for Puerto Rican independence, the Young Lords kept one foot on the island.[90]

Colonialism on the island was connected to the neocolonialism or internal colonialism of mainland Puerto Ricans.[91] These concepts were yet another example of the intellectual heritage of African American nationalists who drew parallels between the exploitation and suffering of colonial peoples in the developing world with the plight of blacks in American society.[92] Along with other Puerto Rican organizations, the Young Lords campaigned for the U.S. Navy's withdrawal from Vieques.[93] Vieques was symptomatic of the Puerto Rican colonial condition. Dedicated to improving the lot of their neighbors, the Lords earned local respect. At the same time, their revolutionary rhetoric brought on the scorn of law enforcement agencies.[94] A similar fate was met by a radical from an earlier era—Pedro Albizu Campos.

Albizu Campos represented an icon and a role model for Puerto Rican radicals of the 1960s and 1970s. The Albizuan spirit calling on Puerto Ricans to take pride in their cultural identity traversed any particular locality.[95] "For the emergent generation of Puerto Rican radicals the legacy of Pedro Albizu Campos was to be appropriated and invested with a number of meanings. As a symbol of unwavering militant opposition to U.S. colonialism, Albizu Campos could be viewed as Puerto Ricans' Malcolm X."[96] Barrio residents saw in Albizu Campos an individual who, like many, was black, was raised in poverty, lived in the United States (while studying at Harvard in the 1910s), and was willing to stand up and challenge injustices inflicted upon his people.[97] Albizu Campos was, in the eyes of the Young Lords, an undisputed champion of the Puerto Rican nation.[98] In this manner, Albizu Campos was transformed to fulfill a nationalist mission in American inner-city communities.[99] Albizu Campos as national hero would serve as the ethno-mythical link joining *puertorriqueños* in the diaspora with Puerto Ricans on the island.[100] Though most contemporary independence sympathizers on the island rejected Albizu Campos's revolutionary methods, they acknowledged him, nonetheless, as one of the greatest *independentistas*.

The Young Lords Party was not the only activist organization. Generally speaking, the Lords appealed to mainland-raised Puerto Ricans; the preferred option for many island-raised Puerto Ricans living in the U.S. was the Movimiento Pro Independencia (MPI) (Pro-Independence Movement).[101] The MPI later renamed itself the Partido Socialista Puertorriqueño (PSP). The transition from MPI to PSP coincided with the organization's decision to embrace English-dominant and mainland-born Puerto Ricans.[102] Still, the MPI/PSP was also associated with middle-class Puerto Ricans from the island.[103] Besides the Lords and the MPI, other mainland-based Puerto Rican political organizations included El Comité-MINP (Puerto Rican National Left Movement), the Puerto Rican Student Union, and the Movement for National Liberation.[104] Puerto Rican student organizations worked with black student groups in the United States and other student groups on the island, particularly the Federación Universitaria Pro Independencia (FUPI) (Federation of Pro-Independence University Students) at the University of Puerto Rico.[105]

These organizations were committed to the Puerto Rican struggle. While they sounded radical, and indeed many adhered to Marxist and socialist principles, they were not armed groups. There were, however, two well-known organizations that sought Puerto Rico's independence through revolutionary means, the Fuerzas Armadas de Liberación Nacional and Macheteros. Though part of the political fringe, their existence was a sign that despite—or perhaps because of—a century of racism, ethnic discrimination and the persecution of independence supporters, the ideal of a sovereign Puerto Rican homeland remained. "Given that people need a sense of identity, and a sense of strong and legitimate authority to turn to in times of crises, suppression or denial of nationalist claims is likely to lead only to more intense nationalism and the emergence of more extreme groups."[106] Under conditions of colonialism on the island and the relegation of Puerto Ricans on the mainland to the status of second-class citizens, revolutionary organizations flourish.

Barrio Vieques

Throughout the Vieques crisis, the Puerto Rican community in the United States was an active participant. In response to the crisis, members of the mainland community sponsored events to raise awareness about the issue, staged numerous demonstrations, and used their political clout to pressure their elected officials to change Pentagon policy. Indeed, the three Puerto Rican members of the House of Representatives took a leading role in the struggle to demilitarize Vieques and galvanize their local communities. Only three weeks after David Sanes's death Representative Nydia Velázquez of New York and Representative Luis Gutiérrez of Illinois were protesting the Vieques bombing in front of the White House.[107]

There are numerous communities in the United States with deep emotional ties to distant lands. Yet what fueled the zeal of Vieques protestors on the mainland was the ability to analogize from Vieques to the inner-city barrio. Peaceful protests in Vieques were reminiscent of the civil rights era three decades before. Fears of an armed takeover of the protestors' encampments by federal marshals evoked images of police brutality in urban America. Federal assurances to improve the economic lot of *viequenses*—contingent, of course, on their willingness to allow the resumption of military training and bombing practice—sounded all too familiar to inner-city *puertorriqueños* who had heard government pledges to improve their neighborhoods one too many times. This time resignation gave way to collective action and to an emboldened leadership willing to directly challenge federal policy toward this Puerto Rican municipality.

In August 1999 a delegation of Puerto Rican leaders traveled to the White House insisting that the navy leave Vieques. Vieques leader and activist Ismael Guadalupe presented an "ultimatum" from his community. He was joined by New York City Council members Adolfo Carrión, Margarita López, and José Rivera; New York State Assembly member Roberto Ramírez; and New York state senator Efraín González.[108] Ramírez was one of several Puerto Ricans leaders who warned office seekers that the Vieques controversy would affect how New York Latinos would vote in the 2000 elections.[109] Many of these same people backed the release of the political prisoners.

To social progressives in the community, and not just *independentistas*, the prisoners were heroes in the larger Puerto Rican movement and victims of political oppression. Their conditional release was in the eyes of many activists yet another example of injustice.[110] In New York, Father Luis Barrios, an Episcopal priest and local activist, proclaimed that "these Puerto Ricans are prophets of love with a burning desire to sacrifice those who have kept their homeland colonized on God's altar."[111] Rallies supporting their release on Las Américas Expressway in San Juan were matched by demonstrations down New York's Third Avenue.[112] New York City Council members Margarita López and José Rivera withheld their support for Hillary Rodham Clinton and Al Gore until the two candidates expressed their views on the political prisoners.[113] While visiting

Vieques, members of the New York City Council underscored that they represented over a million Puerto Ricans.[114] The release of the prisoners was an issue of "social justice" that *puertorriqueños* in New York could not ignore.[115]

Mainland political leaders demonstrated their commitment to Puerto Rico and to Vieques. The reverse was not always true. Carlos Pesquera, the PNP's 2000 gubernatorial candidate, opposed allowing Puerto Ricans in the United States to vote in a future plebiscite on the island's status.[116] For years, stateside Puerto Ricans lobbied Congress to give them a say in the island's eventual status.[117] To the casual observer, it may seem peculiar that a party advocating the Commonwealth's incorporation into the Union wanted to hush the voices of Puerto Ricans who were already living in the States. What appeared incongruous at first glance was actually a strategic decision based on a prudent understanding of the political preferences of the mainland Puerto Rican community. Most political activists on the mainland favored either independence or autonomy.

Whereas pro-independence organizations—such as the PIP, MPI/PSP, the Nationalist Party, the Young Lords, and the Puerto Rican Student Union (PRSU)—tried to organize the mainland community politically, the same could not be said for statehood organizations. The attitude of many mainland Puerto Ricans is: "We already know what statehood is; we have lived it."[118] Vieques becomes a metaphor for the larger domain of U.S.–Puerto Rican relations.[119]

> Contrary to the litany of the politicians on duty, over here as well as over there, that insist upon classifying the conflict in Vieques as an insurmountable challenge, many Puerto Ricans living in the United States have managed to transform the fight against the U.S. Navy into a renewed impetus for struggle and vindication. It is a momentum that clamors not only for the rights of Puerto Ricans in Vieques but also for the rights of other human beings in our environs that are also victims of abuse.[120]

Previously apolitical celebrities, such as Ricky Martin, publicly proclaimed, "Vieques I am with you."[121] Actress Rosie Pérez was arrested in front of the United Nations building for civil disobedience in solidarity with the plight of Vieques.[122] As a vibrant symbol of injustice, Vieques galvanized observers to become political activists and even risk arrest for civil disobedience.[123]

Parades and Symbolism on a Mass Scale

Many of the demonstrations protesting U.S. policy toward Vieques were small and spearheaded by a core group of activists. Mainland organizations supporting this cause, such as the Vieques Solidarity Group, had been active in the United States for a number of years, but their popular support was limited.[124] A once peripheral issue now took center stage. Organizers of the 2000 Puerto Rican Day Parade used their event to showcase ethnic pride and provide a large number of previously politically inactive Puerto Ricans the opportunity to express their views on Vieques publicly.[125] Similar assemblies, such as Philadelphia's Puerto Rican Day Parade, were used to call attention to a host of issues such as drugs, unemployment, discrimination, and black-Latino solidarity.[126] Such gatherings are evidence of a group's "political self-awareness."[127] Politics and ethnic marches go hand in hand. In the 1930s thousands of New York *boricuas* marched to protest another horrible episode on the island—the Ponce Massacre.[128]

Politics was never far from the parade, and in some years pro-independence organizations used this opportunity to protest U.S. colonialism on the island and the island's statehood movement.[129] The 1999 Puerto Rican Day parade was dedicated to two pro-statehood leaders—former governor Luis A. Ferré and the late José Celso Barbosa.[130] In 2000 the parade was dedicated to the struggle in Vieques and to the memory of the nationalist leader Pedro Albizu Campos. Governor Rosselló declined to attend the parade, attributing his refusal to do so to the Albizu Campos dedication.[131] Albizu Campos symbolized a brand of *puertorriqueñidad* that refused to submit. Particularly among more militant cultural nationalists, Albizu Campos was the "father of Puerto Rican national consciousness."[132] "In Puerto Rico, the image of Albizu has been freed from oblivion and rejection thanks to the work of many groups. Very slowly since the 70s the most illustrious Puerto Rican of this century has been approaching his rightful place. But the immigration Puerto Ricans already walked down that path fully. There Albizu already has his star in the firmament of the honored children of the motherland."[133] It was a celebration awash in Puerto Rican flags.[134] This was precisely the vision of Puerto Ricanness the Rosselló administration did not want the American public to witness.

Such a display of ethnic self-esteem, while acceptable in New York, was often problematic in Puerto Rico. In New York City, birthplace of the Puerto Rican flag, the one-starred flag is seen primarily as a badge of ethnic identity—just as the green-white-gold tricolor is associated with

Irish Americans. Nonetheless, in Puerto Rico the flag has never escaped its genesis as a symbol of a projected independent Puerto Rican homeland. Scholars debate who exactly created the Puerto Rican flag.[135] What is not disputed is that in 1895 Puerto Rican nationalists, collaborating with Cuban revolutionaries in their struggle to end Spanish colonial rule, reversed the colors on the Cuban flag, thus creating the Puerto Rican flag. Hence, from its genesis this banner was inextricably linked with the island's independence movement.[136]

On the island of Puerto Rico, the flag is always displayed on Commonwealth and municipal government buildings and in offices alongside the American flag.[137] In effect, the Puerto Rican flag, forever linked with the island's independence movement, is such a potent symbol that it must be diluted when displayed in public by situating it alongside an American flag. Its power in the parade, particularly when juxtaposed with images of Albizu Campos, gave this demonstration an added edge. Albizu Campos, Vieques, and the flag were clearly important representations of Puerto Rican history; yet they were no less political acts of defiance.[138] As David Guss noted, "festivals, for all their joy and color, are also battlegrounds where identities are fought over and communities are made."[139]

As interesting as the disparate reactions of mainland politicians and Governor Rosselló was the manner in which the 2000 parade was covered in various media. News agencies from Puerto Rico and Spanish-language media in New York highlighted the cultural and political significance of the event. They commented on the celebration of *puertorriqueñidad* and the potent symbolism of floats traveling down Fifth Avenue honoring Vieques and Pedro Albizu Campos. In contrast, American mainstream media ignored much of the parade's political message, focusing instead on its commercial aspects and on an assault on a group of women in Central Park that was supposedly linked to the parade. The clear message sent by these images in the mainstream U.S. media was "that Puerto Ricans cannot contain themselves when gathered in large groups."[140] Three-quarters of a century after another notorious incident documented by Bernardo Vega, the larger society was still eager to associate Puerto Ricans with criminal activity.[141] In the pursuit of ratings and profit, the mainstream media appear oblivious to their role in the continued criminalization and racialization of an entire community.

6

Transnational Identities

The highly politicized nature of Puerto Rican society is underscored by reactions to the crisis in Vieques. Unlike the comparatively subdued atmosphere frequently encountered in U.S. elections, voting in Puerto Rico is a boisterous affair characterized by thunderous caravans, buildings defaced with partisan slogans and advertisements, and an overly generous share of heated public discourse. The island's voter turnout rate outpaces any state in the Union, but Puerto Rican politics are not just about electing individual candidates or the quest for a patronage position. Voting in Puerto Rico is also a referendum on identity. Each of the island's three principal parties stakes out a different path toward a final resolution to the interminable status debate. Each avenue—statehood, greater autonomy, or complete sovereignty—obliges voters to define themselves in terms of their *puertorriqueñidad* and their sense of loyalty to the United States.

Peace activism on the Vieques front labored for years with a small but committed coterie of local organizations and independence sympathizers. Following David Sanes's death, protests over the fate of the Isla Nena ballooned into a mass movement. Numerous political, civic, and religious leaders used the Vieques crisis to galvanize public awareness and collective action to a degree previously unseen in Puerto Rico. Solidarity on this scale alarmed federal policy-makers accustomed to dealing with a society deeply divided over political affairs. Clerics, locals, and a host of political activists not only camped out—in effect becoming human shields—but also risked arrest again and again. Those who could not travel to the Isla Nena partook in the struggle through rallies and demonstrations on the main island. As a result of the events of April 1999, David Sanes Rodríguez entered the pantheon of Puerto Rican martyrs. Nationalism, albeit its cultural variant, flourished to an unprecedented degree. Then again, Puerto Rican cultural nationalism has always been stronger than its most legendary variant—secessionism.[1]

Just as interesting as the reactions in Puerto Rico was the response of the stateside Puerto Rican community. For years the literature on mainland Puerto Rican political participation focused on this group's exceedingly low voter turnout rates. Contrary to such assumptions, the *boricua* communities of North America joined in the fray. Mainland Puerto Rican participation in island politics was nothing new. *Independentistas* and labor activists organized in New York City for decades. This metropolis was also the focal point of a great deal of political activism in the tumultuous 1960s and early 1970s championing community rights and advocating Puerto Rico's independence. Support for independence among mainland Puerto Rican organizations is rather fascinating, perhaps even ironic, given that full sovereignty for Puerto Rico would not alter the political status of those residing on the continent. *Puertorriqueños* may live in distinct jurisdictions, but they are united by a shared marginalization in American society as colonials or neocolonials.[2] With a common citizenship and freedom of travel, the island-diaspora connection remains dynamic, as Puerto Ricans move back and forth on a regular basis. For hundreds of thousands of Puerto Ricans, notions of "over here" and "back there" take on a distinctively temporary flavor.

Like other diasporic communities—whether Jews or Palestinians living abroad, the Tibetans in India, Sikhs in Canada, or even Cubans settled in Southern Florida—the "cause" associated with the ancestral homeland endures in exile. "Although members of diaspora communities no longer inhabit their national homelands, these homelands still play an important role in shaping their sense of collective identity. People of the diaspora continue to be members of the nations whose homelands they have left behind."[3] Unlike its counterpart in the ethnic homeland, politics in diasporic communities are often temporally frozen at the time of departure. Observers of American ethnic politics have long observed an anti-British sentiment among Irish Americans far surpassing that found in Éire. In song and story, Celtic progeny on the western side of the Atlantic repeat disheartening stories about British rule and Ireland's suffering at the time of the Great Famine a century and a half ago. Irish American political consciousness rarely integrates the new economic and political relationships in the Anglo-Irish isles forged following World War II. The old struggles endure in the collective memories of a community physically disconnected from changing circumstances "back home."

A New Ethnicity, a New Temple

From the perspective of the U.S. Navy and its supporters, Vieques may have been the site of an unfortunate incident, but its value to the country's national defense outweighed other considerations. Indeed, congressional Republican leaders insisted that the death of one civilian, the frayed nerves of shell-shocked *viequenses*, the potential economic loss from military ownership of three-quarters of the island, and the health risks associated with the military's bombing did not outweigh American national security interests. According to the Pentagon, while there was no longer an imminent Soviet threat or a bona fide Communist menace, Vieques had a key role to play in a new international conflict—the "War on Drugs." This was also the spot where naval personnel practiced bombing runs before being deployed to the Balkans. Defense Department officials insisted Vieques was irreplaceable.

During the Cold War, it was easier to convince Puerto Ricans, particularly those favoring closer ties with the United States, that national security took precedence over other matters. Regional instability seemed close by: civil wars in Central America, a revolution-exporting regime in Cuba, and a Caribbean basin filled with semi- or nondemocratic regimes. By the 1990s that argument was more difficult to sell. Cuba no longer received financial backing from Moscow, and even the Soviet Union itself disintegrated as a sovereign state. The number of popularly elected regimes in the Caribbean increased. Costa Rican President Oscar Arias was awarded a Nobel Peace Prize for an accord that ended several civil wars and foreign-financed insurgencies. Poverty, social inequality, and drug trafficking still abounded, but the Caribbean was no longer the front line of a major global conflict.

If the U.S. Navy could end its shelling of Kaho'olawe, Hawaii, it should be able to do the same in Vieques. Puerto Ricans, regardless of residence or ideological persuasion, increasingly saw the conflict in Vieques as one of social justice and human rights. Many were convinced this crisis derived from Puerto Rico's colonial status. Out of the seventy-eight municipalities in Puerto Rico, this was where U.S. colonialism disclosed itself in its most naked form. From Barrio Puntas in the eastern town of Rincón to "El Barrio" in the borough of Manhattan, many maintained that the bombing would have ceased long ago were it not for the fact that the land being barraged was inhabited by Puerto Ricans. *Boricuas* in the Caribbean and North America transformed into a basilica of *puertorriqueñidad* the very spot where their people were treated most unfairly and inhumanely.

The recent struggle for Vieques has opened a new chapter in the perennial debate over where to pinpoint the epicenter of Puerto Rican identity. Mythmakers seek to objectify key cultural traits in order to showcase the group's uniqueness.[4] Among those traits are territorial boundaries imbued with particular cultural significance. For Israelis and Palestinians, Jerusalem serves as residential city and a spiritual focal point—particularly in the Old City.[5] Cultural epicenters are not dependent on habitation. Serbian attachment to Kosovo derives not from the Serb minority in the province but its status as the birthplace of Serbian culture.[6] The government in Beijing takes as an article of faith the territorial absorption of Hong Kong, Macao, and eventually Taiwan.[7] By delineating borders, states and groups attempt to define themselves.

Beyond the realm of social justice and human rights, the struggle over Vieques's fate is also representative of ethnic symbolism and notions of territoriality. Ethnic identities profess group membership in extended families. Such sentiments are not inherently political but are likely to become so with the appearance and subsequent development of profound problems or crises in the group's relationship with the state.[8] At the point where ethnic groups make territorial demands, they have crossed over to become "nations."[9]

> Like ethnic ideologies, nationalism stresses the cultural similarity of its adherents and, by implication, it draws boundaries vis-à-vis others, who thereby become outsiders. The distinguishing mark of nationalism is by definition its relationship to the state. A nationalist holds that political boundaries should be coterminous with cultural boundaries, whereas many ethnic groups do not demand command over a state. When the political leaders of an ethnic movement make demands to this effect, the ethnic movement therefore by definition becomes a nationalist movement.[10]

As Steinberg underscored, ethnic sentiments become foundations for conflict when cultural differences affect access to rights, privileges, and a livelihood. "If there is an iron law of ethnicity, it is that when ethnic groups are found in a hierarchy of power, wealth, and status, then conflict is inescapable."[11] Throughout the peace activists' occupation of navy-owned lands, federal authorities made it abundantly clear that they would resist changes in Vieques's status. Their interests superceded those of the *viequense* community, and they had the brute force to impose their will.

When discussing this topic, observers frequently err by assuming that nationalism is equivalent to separatism. By definition, the nationalist project is a territorial one. However, many nationalists, perhaps most, seek autonomy from the state, not independence.[12] Calls for autonomy vary tremendously, as do central state responses to regional demands for greater degrees of home rule. For more than a century autonomism has been the primary political goal of Puerto Ricans. This proclivity toward autonomism far surpasses the numbers who vote for the PPD or endorse the current Commonwealth status. At the heart of the contemporary statehood movement's *estadidad jíbara* (Creole statehood) thesis is the conviction that cultural autonomy can coexist within the framework of American federalism.[13] In Puerto Rico, "*todos somos autonomistas*" (we are all autonomists)—though to varying degrees.[14] The vast majority of Puerto Ricans are also cultural nationalists.[15] Puerto Ricans, whether in the Caribbean or in North America, face differing or even competing allegiances to the Puerto Rican "nation" and the United States. Schizophrenic or not, two loyalties pull at the heart of the average *puertorriqueño*. The struggle over Vieques is representative of that prevalent, yet variable, autonomist or cultural nationalism.

Most Vieques protestors and their sympathizers were engaged in a struggle for autonomy, not a plot to foment *independentista* fervor. Their goal was to give *viequenses* input into their lives, which have been deeply affected by decades of bombing and an economic stagnation perpetuated by the military's monopoly over land ownership in this municipality. Still, the determination to defend community rights, particularly in the case of ethnic enclaves under American jurisdiction, has often been interpreted in U.S. political circles as defiance and subversion. At the height of the civil rights movement in the 1960s, various leaders, regarded as subversives by government authorities, were kept under the constant surveillance of the FBI.[16] "The presence of latent nationalism on the Puerto Rican political scene represents a disturbing element whose ultimate significance, while it cannot be precisely evaluated, cannot be ignored."[17] Puerto Rican nationalism in any form has been a worry to U.S. policy-makers.

Throughout this process, Vieques was inducted into the Puerto Rican nationalist shrine. Ramón Emeterio Betances led an unsuccessful uprising against the Spanish Crown—the Grito de Lares—in 1868. Lares was consecrated by Pedro Albizu Campos as the epicenter of separatist nationalism in the 1930s.[18] "Lares became part of the national foundation myth."[19] Every September 23, thousands descend on the Plaza de la Revolución to remember that rebellion, recommit themselves to the cause, and remind the world that the island's independence movement lives.[20]

Independence supporters alone did not sanctify Vieques. The island's political parties played second fiddle to a host of civil and church-based organizations in this struggle.[21] Such a diverse base of support made a federal "deal" with protestors a much more difficult task. As civil rights activists in the United States learned long ago, a heterogeneous base coupled with an array of nonviolent action fortify movements.[22] Decentralization is one of the prime characteristics of contemporary social movements.[23] The PIP erected its beachfront encampment alongside the tents of community activists, labor union members, students, intellectuals, and clerics.

In a way, the Isla Nena took on the broader role as the locus of Puerto Rican cultural or autonomist nationalism. Vieques was objectified as the nationalist common denominator. By analogy, if Lares's Plaza de la Revolución is Puerto Rico's Alamo, then Vieques's Monte David could be considered to be Puerto Rico's National Civil Rights Museum—the memorial to the American civil rights movement in Memphis, Tennessee, built on the site of the Lorraine Motel where Martin Luther King Jr. was assassinated in 1968.

Intellectuals have long debated precisely where to locate the epicenter of Puerto Rican cultural life—that physical space that Laponce referred to as a group's "vital centre."[24] Geography also set the stage for selecting the paradigmatic *boricua*. Early in the twentieth century, Antonio Pedreira referred to the island's *jíbaro*, the highland peasant, as the "central root of our culture."[25] Selecting the *jíbaro* to play this vital role in Puerto Rican ethnogenesis would have a profound impact on the course of insular-metropolitan relations long after Spain's sovereignty. "Eventually, broad acceptance of the jíbaro by all classes came to represent not only a legitimation of a sense of Puerto Rican-ness, which all Puerto Ricans discursively shared, but also a form for contestation of the legitimacy of the North American colonial project and the corresponding colonial identity it assigned to Puerto Ricans."[26] By elevating the *jíbaro* to the apex of *puertorriqueñidad*, Creole writers in the nineteenth and early twentieth century declared themselves Puerto Rico's anointed ruling class.[27] Nineteenth-century criollos discursively redefined Puerto Ricans as a new *staatvolk*—society's newly christened dominant group.[28] Peninsular Spaniards, in the process, were reclassified as "others."

This thesis would be challenged later in the twentieth century by Jose González, who asserted that the island's *jíbaros* represented a new floor in the Puerto Rican multistoried sociocultural edifice—one that was built atop Puerto Rican blacks and racially mixed coastal communities.[29] If González tried to move the focal point of Puerto Rican identity from the highlands to the shores, Juan Flores sought to transfer it from the Caribbean to a metaphysical space linking the island with the U.S. mainland. After all, almost half of all Puerto Ricans now live on the North American continent. Today's diasporic communities compel us to redefine our previous notions of identity and cultural authenticity.[30] The Vieques crisis has created a noncorporeal space where the political struggles of Puerto Ricans in the Caribbean and North America converge. "Under the present conditions of transportation and communication, Puerto Rico is part of New York, and like it or not, New York is present in Puerto Rico."[31] On the mainland, *puertorriqueñidad* evolves in that space where *boricua* and African American gather, share lives, and influence one another.[32]

Of course, this discussion did not prevent activists in the mainland community from debating their own territorial parameters. Debates raged over interpreting the diasporic community as part of a "divided nation" or an oppressed "national minority" in the United States.[33] The Young Lords and El Comité-MINP, for example, opted for the oppressed minority approach, while the MPI/PSP insisted upon viewing Puerto Ricans as a divided nation.[34] Certainly the constant migration between the island and the continent prevented any one notion of territoriality from becoming hegemonic within the mainland community. Nationalism in the mainland community, beyond the search for Puerto Rican self-determination, has served a vital role as a vehicle for social reform.[35] Gordon Lewis has commented:

> The divided Puerto Rican nation is a nation divided against itself. That can be seen clearly in the prototypical difference between the island nationalist and the mainland nationalist. The first is warm, tolerant, indecisive, almost happy-go-lucky. The second is harsh, tough, and determined. The first talks theoretically of revolution. The second acts as a revolutionary, because he has been forced to do so by the humiliating discriminations of the ghetto. Many of the first type still believe in independence by the ballot box. It would be difficult to find many of the second type who so believe.[36]

Ethnic leaders on both sides of the *charco* (the puddle) may be concerned over the long-term consequences of island-mainland differences in definitions of Puerto Rican identity. Yet insular Puerto Ricans themselves live in a society where elites and the masses have long classified *puertorriqueñidad* in different ways.[37] Certainly a mainland-based identity would celebrate not only the African roots of Puerto Rican heritage but also the pervasive influence of African American culture on the *boricua* experience. In any case, mainland activists and organizations were willing to demonstrate that their visualization of *puertorriqueñidad* would not be dictated by leaders or intellectuals on the island.[38] They were also revealing their unwillingness—some might argue inability—to imagine themselves as Americans.

Flores's argument purports that identity may not be established in any one physical place. After all, at any given time hundreds or thousands of Puerto Ricans are riding the legendary *guagua aérea* linking San Juan with Boston, Chicago, Orlando, and New York. The Puerto Rican "nation" transcends the juridical boundaries of the Commonwealth and includes over three million *boricuas* on the North American continent.[39] Along the same lines, Ramón Grosfoguel suggests that as a result of Vieques, a formerly insular-centric identity has been transformed into an archipelagan ethnicity uniting Puerto Ricans on the main island, St. Croix, the U.S. mainland, and even Hawaii.[40] Indeed, "[w]hereas continental peoples view oceans as empty areas of limitation and separation, island peoples see them as central and interconnecting."[41] On the other hand, we may be witnessing a new *puertorriqueñidad* unbound by geographic restrictions. "The solidarity that the Puerto Rican community in the United States has exhibited towards Vieques exhibits the possibility of a true Puerto Rican nation that transcends borders."[42] Agustín Lao contends that this nation was a "translocal historical category whose boundaries shift between the archipelago of Puerto Rico and its U.S. diaspora."[43] Jorge Duany asserts that "massive migration—both to and from the Island—has undermined conventional definitions of the nation based exclusively on territorial, linguistic, or juridical criteria—and offers fresh possibilities for a non-territorial view of identity."[44] Perhaps we have moved beyond looking for Judaism's Wailing Wall, Islam's Al-Ka'bah (or Kábah), or Sikhism's Golden Temple. At this point we have a choice of accepting the thesis that Puerto Ricanness is unicentric, multicentric, or noncentric.

The foregoing debate highlights that while numerous scholars and activists esteem Puerto Rican cultural identity, each person views it from a different angle. Conceivably, a more interesting question than where Puerto Rican identity lies is why its locus is still debated. Ideally, ethnic mythmakers seek to raise their ideals to the level of a culturally hegemonic concept—one that is not questioned in society and is accepted as a commonsense notion.[45] Ethnogenesis is an artificial process, and the cultural traits ethnic leaders objectify coincide with their strategic interests. It is only logical that an emerging new elite—whether criollos in the nineteenth century or a new Nuyorican intelligentsia in the twentieth century—

would seek to redefine Puerto Ricanness to suit its interest.[46] Though Puerto Rican identity was articulated by a group of elites, it was accepted by the island's masses—although they would subsequently articulate it in different ways. Ethnic ideologies, as with other collective and mass-based ventures, are complex principles whose enunciation and dissemination rely on a high social subset of people, such as intellectuals.[47]

Ethnogenesis, in the case of peripheral elites such as Puerto Rico's criollos, is often triggered by a sense of persistent resentment toward the policies and attitudes of society's dominant group, as was the case with nineteenth-century Spanish *peninsulares* or Americans in the twentieth century.[48] The fact that ethnic mythmakers dare to question the locus of *puertorriqueñidad* indicates that the old criollo elites succeeded in entrenching the idea of a distinctive Puerto Rican nation but not all of the objective cultural traits associated with that culture, including a spiritual center.

If those descended from the nineteenth-century hacienda-owning families found it in their strategic interest to forge a new Puerto Rican identity centered on the island's highland *jíbaro*, it is only logical that a new elite or collection of elites, a twentieth-century city-dwelling intelligentsia, would seek to shift that identity elsewhere. Along the same lines, it makes perfect sense that new generations of U.S.-born-and-raised Puerto Ricans would want to shift the *boricua* cultural heartland closer to them. After all, "[e]thnicity is a creative and improvisational process, fluid and ever-changing."[49] This debate also attests to the fact that there is no single elite in Puerto Rican society capable of hegemonizing any one interpretation of where to center the nation.

At no time should it be assumed that the new emerging identity is any less nationalistic or any less territorial. Centuries ago Aristotle contended that "man is by nature a political animal."[50] Ivo Duchacek added that "in politics man still remains basically a territorial animal."[51] Michael Hechter insisted that "*territoriality* is one objective criterion that does seem to be a necessary characteristic of the nation. The presence of a real or putative homeland is properly regarded as a defining feature of the nation."[52] William Miles observed that "though theories of nationalism often downplay this reality, cognitive identification is often more with territory than with inhabitants."[53] The precise physical parameters of the nation may be disputed, but the national myth always needs a finite temporal space to serve as the sociocultural homeland. Though divided from their spiritual center for almost two millennia, Jews throughout the world continued to reinforce the link to a faraway land by reiterating every Passover, "Next year in Jerusalem." Scattered throughout the Arabian peninsula, North Africa, and some western cities, Palestinians embrace the same dream.

Nationalists of all stripes insist that cultural boundaries coincide with clear geographic borders. Within their niche, regardless of territorial extent, nationalists insist on the right to determine their own destiny. If popular perceptions of those geographic frontiers become culturally hegemonic, rival interpretations of border permanency could lead to intra- as well as interstate conflict. The loss of Algeria, for example, toppled the French Fourth Republic, and southern Ireland's break from the United Kingdom nearly brought the country to civil war.[54] Once congealed, hegemonic ideals constrain the activities of future political elites, limiting their maneuverability, even in the realm of peacemaking.[55]

In their quest for local autonomy, Puerto Ricans in the United States have fought to establish their own space. Urban ethnic enclaves become, in effect, an extension of the ultramarine ethnic homeland. "If, however, the homeland is located in a state or states dominated by other nations, then the hub of the transnational national community may be displaced or decentered and come to be located in the diaspora itself."[56] We see that struggle in the immense metal Puerto Rican flag arching over Chicago's Division Street, the fight to create Villa Victoria in Boston's South End, the effort to establish Puerto Rican "homelands" in New York City's Lower East Side and East Harlem, and even in the quest to create and preserve Casitas in the South Bronx.[57] The focus of even the most militant activists was the struggle in the nearby homeland rather than the one in the Caribbean.[58] "Like the Young Lords and unlike older generations, the FALN members had no visions of 'returning to the Island'; for them, 'home' was Chicago's barrio."[59] In this light, Vieques became an extraterritorial setting where both mainland and main island Puerto Ricans could embrace a more assertive variety of cultural nationalism. For *puertorriqueños* outside of Vieques, the Isla Nena became the new scene of a clash between Americans and Puerto Ricans over social justice, cultural rights, and political autonomy.

Identity and Collective Action

Throughout the year-long occupation of navy lands, local residents provided an invaluable lifeline, bringing in food, water, clothing, and news to the protestors living in Puerto Rico's newest residential development—Monte David. Local activism was matched with large-scale activism on the main island and in mainland communities. Organizers staged protests in front of the White House, at military installations, and down major thoroughfares such as Las Américas Expressway in San Juan and Manhattan's Fifth Avenue. Puerto Ricans are a very political people, but rarely has one issue triggered such a widespread display of collective action.

With a strong sense of ethnic pride and a feeling of anger toward what most in the Puerto Rican community saw as an act of social injustice, veteran protesters were joined on the front lines by thousands of individuals, in different capacities, who usually did not participate in such overt forms of political activism. Individual sacrifices for collective goals remain a long-observed trait in social movements. People's participation in such movements, including the Vieques crusade, questions the universal applicability of certain renowned social science theories that insist all individuals are motivated by strictly defined self-interest.[60]

The relatively small group of individuals willing to camp out on Vieques or risk imprisonment confirms that the most ardent activists are relatively few in number and members of what could be described as an ultra-activist subset. However, not all of those who lived on Vieques or were detained for civil disobedience on the mainland were hardcore activists. Group identities and social ties are responsible for generating large-scale protests.[61] The key to understanding collective action is an individual's identification with the group.[62] Incentives earmarked for participants are insufficient for generating collective action unless they are connected with a broader ideological appeal.[63] When it comes to collective movements, especially ethnic ones, social and emotional sentiments lead an individual's interest to mesh with those of the group and community.[64]

Our desires to be accepted by our communities as good citizens or moral persons may be so strong that we forgo any economic or material sanctions resulting from our actions.[65] "Simply put, we convey to each other signals of praise or blame, approval or disapproval, recognition or rejection, honour or contempt, socially organised to sustain the collective good, and our susceptibility of these signals is what encourages collective action."[66] The degree to which individuals partake in collective projects depends on the sense of group loyalty or solidarity. Camaraderie may be necessary, but it is not per se a sufficient condition. A sense of obligation is necessary to trigger large-scale collective action, and such a sentiment is easily fostered in a state of crisis.

In Vieques and for Vieques, individuals responded to the preexisting and resilient cultural identity found in most Puerto Ricans. For generations, Puerto Ricans, whether in the Caribbean or in North America, were deterred from seeking inclusion in American mainstream society and its political system. On the island, Puerto Ricans were colonials, while on the mainland they were relegated to the status of neocolonials. Additionally, Puerto Ricans were marginalized in the metropolitan economy. Thus, economics reinforced the institutionalized social and political hierarchy that left *boricuas* as long-term, if not permanent, second-class citizens. Federal responses—both civilian and military—to the ecological devastation on Vieques, the economic distress of this community, and ultimately to the death of David Sanes Rodríguez reinforced in a rather brusque manner the outrage over nonequality. His demise alerted Puerto Ricans, regardless of their place of residence, that their people were under assault. Colonialism, racism, and socioeconomic marginalization insinuated that the military exercises leading to Sanes's death would not have been conducted so close to civilian population centers if the local inhabitants were white North American continentals.

Protesting military policy in Vieques became a vehicle for openly expressing pride in *puertorriqueñidad* and anger over the perceived injustices inflicted on one particular ethnic group. The crisis in Vieques focused that resentment on one particular spot. In the process, it became the newly anointed locus of Puerto Rican national consciousness. Protests and rallies served a dual function of pursuing a collective goal but also emotionally or spiritually empowering the individual. After more than a century of U.S. rule, a strong sense of Puerto Rican identity persisted and under certain conditions even flourished. Defense planners either failed to see the sociocultural and political implications of their activities in Vieques or were indifferent to them. As is often the case at the juncture of politics, culture, and identity, contenders grasp the same conflict in diametrically opposed ways.

7

A New Era

On the surface, the crisis in Vieques appeared to be a conflict between the military and a neighboring civilian community. Such disputes are not unheard of either in the United States or elsewhere. Any case can be described in terms of its unique properties, and Vieques is no exception. However, civil-military relations in Vieques deteriorated to an unprecedented degree in recent Puerto Rican–U.S. relations. Vieques became a metaphor for the larger encounter between Puerto Ricans—both colonials and neocolonials—and the United States.

Unknowingly, the U.S. armed forces became a major player in the evolution of Puerto Rican identity. *Puertorriqueñidad* antedated the arrival of U.S. troops during the Spanish-American War. Among its political manifestations was separatism, though this remained a minority view. Its most common manifestation came in the form of autonomism. Federal policies in the 1900s aimed at culturally assimilating the Puerto Rican people paradoxically had the opposite effect: they fortified preexisting notions of Puerto Rican uniqueness. The death of David Sanes Rodríguez in the spring of 1999 and the federal government's seeming indifference to the dangers military maneuvers posed to the *viequenses* widened the chasm separating Americans and Puerto Ricans.

These events were interpreted in light of a decades-long relationship in which the armed forces obtained what they wanted, starting with the acquisition of three-quarters of Vieques. Even after bombing practices shifted from Culebra to Vieques, the health concerns of the local community were still largely dismissed. Only a few years after the Pentagon finally signed the 1983 Fortín Accord, it became evident to community residents that the military lost what little interest it had in carrying out the letter or the spirit of the agreement. In this light, the death of David Sanes Rodríguez was simply the latest calamity in *viequense*-Pentagon, and Puerto Rican–American, relations.

Military officials pointed out, and rightly so, that their institution was not a social services agency. Its function is to defend the state's interests—to guard or promote them through force of arms if needed. Vieques was assessed from a "national security" perspective. Of course, the military's numerous installations throughout the United States have a long history of contributing to the economic vitality of their immediate surroundings and, in so doing, accruing community favor. In Vieques, the military's presence actually undermined the local economy by denying locals their traditional livelihoods and denying them a new one. What the military establishment and its supporters assessed in terms of defense interests, Puerto Ricans viewed as a struggle for civil and human rights.

The social and political movement in Vieques opened up new spaces with which to reinvigorate an already established Puerto Rican identity, both in the United States and on the island. The idea of Puerto Ricans as a distinct nationality is stronger now than in the past, regardless of the electoral fortunes of any independence party. That national identity vis-à-vis Americans is interpreted differently based on place of residence. Insular Puerto Ricans often objectify Americans as nondescript North American continentals. In contrast, mainland Puerto Ricans visualize Americans in light of their experiences. That "other" is more racialized (as white) and more firmly entrenched in a particular class (middle class or higher).

To Puerto Ricans on the island, Vieques served as a reminder of classic colonialism. Federal authorities could impose their will over the needs and aspirations of a community under their tutelage. To those on the mainland, Vieques was an example of "internal colonialism," reminiscent of their struggles in inner-city barrios. The present served as a reminder that the past, or aspects of it, endured. Violations of the spirit of the 1983 Fortín Accord became tools in the construction and reconstruction of ethnogenesis. Failure to promote economic development, while wreaking havoc with the emotional and physical well-being of *viequenses*, served as "evidence"—in the words of mythmakers—that the negative attitudes of American administrators in the early twentieth century were alive, though in another form.

Racism and ethnic discrimination have been hallmarks of Puerto Rican collective experiences. After several generations in North America, mainland *boricuas* have learned a great deal from the historic trajectories of African Americans. Indeed, the black civil rights movement was a great inspiration for its Puerto Rican counterpart. Black nationalist organizations, such as the Black Panthers, served as models for the Young Lords.

Malcolm X, an icon of pride and resistance, had a counterpart in inner-city Puerto Rican communities—Pedro Albizu Campos. African Americans also presented a guide for participation in mainstream politics, primarily through the Democratic Party. In numerous ways, mainland Puerto Ricans are much less apprehensive about openly expressing their ethnic pride and cultural nationalism than are their insular coethnics. Future attempts by Congress to resolve Puerto Rico's status quagmire will undoubtedly have to contend with the three million stateside *boricuas* who will insist on having a voice in the final outcome.

In addition to influencing the fate of the Commonwealth of Puerto Rico and its juridico-political relationship with the United States, *puertorriqueños* on the mainland have also shaped the parameters of *boricua* cultural identity. Ethnic mythmakers on the mainland are less apprehensive about highlighting the African elements of Puerto Rican culture and the traits associated with more socially and economically marginalized classes than are many of their insular counterparts. But Puerto Ricans have also been instrumental in reinforcing the bonds between cultural identity and territoriality. Mainland community organizations, in their grassroots struggles for equality and justice, have redefined street corners, blocks, and neighborhoods as parcels of a new diasporic homeland.

The North American barrio was transformed into an extrapatrial extension of Puerto Rico. The territorial objectification of the barrio as a part of the larger Puerto Rican nation facilitated the espousal of Vieques, the new front line in the nation's civil rights and cultural struggles, as the epicenter of Puerto Rican cultural nationalism. Territoriality is as important to Puerto Rican ethnicity as it is to any other nationalist movement. For decades, the separatist wing of Puerto Rican nationalism rejoiced in its celebration of the Grito de Lares every September 23. As a result of David Sanes Rodríguez's martyrdom, the more prevalent Puerto Rican cultural nationalism now had its own shrine on the beaches of Vieques and its own anniversary—April 19.

If military officials were able to ascertain Vieques's strategic implications, why were they, along with federal civilian policy-makers, unable to see the broader social implications of the navy's activities? Some activists might contend that the armed forces are simply indifferent to the plight of *viequenses* in particular and Puerto Ricans in general. They point to the military's institutional interest in invading Puerto Rico during the Spanish-American War and the less-than-benign governance of the island's appointed governors in the first half of the twentieth century. Many of these executives themselves had strong connections to the armed forces.

Protestors might also point to the military's indifference over the plight of the people of Culebra in the third quarter of the twentieth century. These allegations speak to the military as an institution and not to any particular individual. Still, they cast an ominous shadow over the interactions of individual military personnel and Puerto Rican civilians. But as the old adage articulates, *no hay peor ciego que aquel que no quiere ver* (the worst blind man is he who does not want to see).

Each state, society, or community is held together by a series of myths based on a selective interpretation of its history. If they achieve a culturally hegemonic status, such myths cross a threshold whereupon no mainstream community member, including its leaders, will challenge the "commonsense" nature of the norm or principle. Within Puerto Rican communities, regardless of location, the Vieques crisis has been entrenched in the popular mind as a struggle for human rights and social justice. With extremely few exceptions, *puertorriqueños* reject the assertion that Vieques's use for target practice is justifiable in the name of national security.

Of course, the same pattern applies to American society and, by extension, to its armed forces. As do all societies, the United States has its own myths. Scholars question whether these myths have penetrated every level of U.S. society. In particular, nonwhite communities seem to have rejected these myths and to have created alternative interpretations of current and past events. But for the majority of those in the United States—the constellation of Americans of European ancestry—a profound myth impacting the Vieques crisis is the assumption that the U.S. government, as a democratic polity, always adheres to principles of fairness and social justice.

Key writings—such as the Declaration of Independence, the Constitution's Bill of Rights and the Civil War Amendments, the *Federalist Papers*, and even Tocqueville's narrative of nineteenth-century American society—lend credence to the tradition that the United States is an inherently democratic society. We are exhorted that democracies are, by nature, objectively good and virtuous. If a polity is democratic, then the defense of such a regime is not only justifiable but a duty every citizen should uphold. Therefore, if the U.S. Navy needs Vieques to prepare for the nation's defense, the military's actions are warranted and patriotic. The flip side of this belief is that those opposed to the U.S. military are unpatriotic, anti-American, and quite possibly subversive.

Throughout the crisis, the mainstream American media and numerous federal policy-makers insisted that those opposed to the navy's presence were radicals with possible ties not only to the independence movement (ignoring the myriad nonseparatist organizations committed to the Vieques cause) but quite possibly to terrorist organizations. In an attempt to link the Vieques and political prisoners' clemency issues, the federal government labored diligently to reinforce this connection in the minds of the American public. Under such circumstances, the possibilities of a mutually acceptable compromise were slim. Governor Rosselló's attempt to curry favor with the Clinton White House may have been well received in Washington, but it was vehemently opposed by the Puerto Rican people as expressed in rallies, protests, and the results of the 2000 Commonwealth elections. So far, the new Bush administration has yet to show any more compassion to its Puerto Rican territorials than did its predecessor. This perceived indifference may help to explain why more than 68 percent of *viequenses* voted for an immediate halt to the navy's bombing campaign in a July 29, 2001, referendum.

As previously underscored, mythmaking is based on a subjective and selective interpretation of the past. Mythmakers often omit references to the evolution of democracy in the United States. Many of the "Founding Fathers" of the Republic saw no contradiction between their claims of democracy and their personal dependency on the institution of slavery, the marginalization and subsequent extermination of indigenous peoples, and the electoral exclusion of the poor and women. From their perspective, their regime, led by a bourgeoisie and petite bourgeoisie, was a far more progressive political system than were the more restrictive monarchies and constitutional monarchies-aristocracies in Europe.

What about the present? Clearly the United States falls under the category of a liberal democratic regime despite occasional difficulties and crises such as the legendary 2000 presidential elections. Of course, the democratic label refers to how a political system governs internally. It says little about how one conducts external affairs. As the Supreme Court made clear in the infamous "Insular Cases" at the dawn of the twentieth century, the overseas territories were possessions of the United States and not integral parts of it. The right to select one's representatives and government officials, a hallmark of all democratic regimes, was severely restricted in Puerto Rico by the federal government for the first half of the twentieth century. That period also coincided with a concentrated effort by Washington to assimilate the island's populace culturally. On the mainland, Puerto Rican communities were often disenfranchised, de facto, by a system interested in keeping Puerto Ricans electorally inert. In many mainland jurisdictions, literacy requirements—the de facto disenfranchisement of non-English speakers—prevented many Latinos from exercising their rights as citizens until the 1970s. In a manner of speaking, Puerto Ricans became domestic foreigners.

Challenges to the age-old myths of democracy and social justice in the third quarter of the twentieth century served as a major shock to the established political order. One wonders whether the system has fully recovered. The civil rights movements, anti–Vietnam War rallies, women's rights demonstrations, Stonewall riots, and other crusades all threatened the underlying creed that American society was perennially good and just. Proponents of the status quo ante faced these domestic sources of opposition, all the while challenging the Soviet Union and Marxist ideals for influence around the globe. One of the old order's responses to the counterculture was the conservative backlash of the 1980s, which insisted that there was nothing fundamentally wrong with U.S. society and that those advocating change exhibited dubious loyalties. *Viequenses* learned the depths of these convictions. Those opposed to the military were painted as anti-American, secessionist, and sympathetic to Communist doctrines. After all, many of the Vieques activists also supported the release of the Puerto Rican political prisoners. Sanctioned more severely than others found guilty of comparable crimes because of their connection to the island's independence movement, the prisoners became yet another set of pawns in the larger Vieques game. Military apologists refused to entertain the possibility that the navy's Vieques activities could be wrong in any way.

By releasing the prisoners President Clinton, the first chief executive impeached in more than a century, knew that what little political capital he held with lawmakers regarding Puerto Rico was spent on the prisoners' issue. After that point, there was nothing left with which to tackle the Vieques crisis. Time and the diligent research of historians may confirm this suspicion, but it appears that Clinton's decision to grant clemency to the prisoners was his attempt to wash his hands of Vieques in such a way that the blame would fall on congressional Republicans and the resolute will of the military establishment. His plan was to bequeath the Vieques dispute to his vice president, Al Gore. In the end, he handed the controversy to the former governor of Texas, George W. Bush. With a strident commitment to refortify the country's military—particularly in the aftermath of the September 11, 2001, attacks on the World Trade Center and the Pentagon—there appears to be little chance that President Bush will weigh the aspirations of the Puerto Rican community above the wishes of the defense establishment.

With little political muscle to pull the navy out of Vieques, all Clinton could offer the Puerto Rican government was his commitment to tackle the island's interminable status dilemma. To Pedro Rosselló—a governor profoundly disappointed at his failure to win insular backing for statehood in two plebiscites or from the U.S. Congress in the course of eight years in office—this offer from the Clinton White House had to sound like sweet tidings. Yet what appealed to Rosselló did not entice Vieques activists in the least, nor did it cajole the Puerto Rican people.

What does this crisis say about the future of Puerto Rican–U.S. relations? The current Commonwealth status provides Washington with the fig leaf to claim that Puerto Ricans are empowered to govern themselves while endowing federal authorities with the power to impose their will regardless of popular opinion. But something momentous appears to be looming in Puerto Rico at the dawn of the twenty-first century. Puerto Ricans appear to be less apprehensive about expressing their cultural identity or asserting their cultural nationalism. Threats from Washington, both subtle and gross, no longer have the retarding influence they once had.

At this stage, we are not witnessing the emergence of a neoseparatist movement but instead a more assertive cultural nationalism akin to the nationalism exhibited by African Americans. While Puerto Rican nationalism defies assimilation, it remains willing to negotiate a peaceful coexistence. Much of the credit for this unreserved ethnic identity lies in the diaspora and not solely in the experiences of Puerto Rican islanders. This assertiveness in no way implies that the federal government, and in particular the military establishment, is any more sensitive to the impact of its activities in Vieques or other Puerto Rican communities. With a community determined to defend its rights and heritage, only Washington can determine whether this will inaugurate a new chapter of cooperation or one of intense conflict.

Notes

Chapter 1. Settlement and Fortifications

1. Rodríguez Beruff, *Política militar*, 146–47.
2. Langhorne, *Vieques*, 1.
3. According to a noted Vieques scholar, contrary to a popular myth, there is no evidence that there existed an indigenous leader, or *cacique*, called Bieque. See Pastor Ruiz, *Vieques antiguo*, 98. The English referred to Vieques as Crab Island. As Tió noted, some old Spanish maps referred to Vieques as *Buruquena*. *Buruquenas* are freshwater crabs. See Tió in Bonnet Benítez, *Vieques*, xv.
4. Pastor Ruiz, *Vieques antiguo*, 28, 30.
5. Langhorne, *Vieques*, 11.
6. Bonnet Benítez, *Vieques*, 26–27.
7. Pastor Ruiz, *Vieques antiguo*, 31.
8. Langhorne, *Vieques*, 11.
9. Santana, "Puerto Rico," 71.
10. Pastor Ruiz, *Vieques antiguo*, 40; Meléndez López, *La batalla*, 12.
11. Pastor Ruiz, *Vieques antiguo*, 40. St. Thomas, part of the Danish West Indies for most of the 1800s, was occupied by the British for a brief interlude early in the century. Ireland, *Boundaries*, 354–55.
12. Hamilton, Madison, and Jay, *Federalist Papers*, 87.
13. Trías Monge, *Historia constitucional*, 1:135.
14. Figueroa, *Breve historia*, 174.
15. Tocqueville, *Democracy in America*, 409–10.
16. Meléndez López, *La batalla*, 12–13.
17. Bonnet Benítez, *Vieques*, 38. Some speculate that the name Leguillou derived from the name Le Guillén. Pastor Ruiz, *Vieques antiguo*, 32.
18. Delgado Cintrón, *Culebra*, 15.
19. Bonnet Benítez, *Vieques*, 92.
20. Langhorne, *Vieques*, 33–34.
21. Bonnet Benítez, *Vieques*, 44–45.
22. Pastor Ruiz, *Vieques antiguo*, 31–32. Puerto Rico's governor, Miguel López de Baños, submitted a report on Vieques and its eight hundred residents in 1839. The majority were "free people of color" and slaves. One-third of the inhabitants were non-Spanish subjects—mostly French with a few English and Danish residents. Bonnet Benítez, *Vieques*, 108.

23. Pastor Ruiz, *Vieques antiguo,* 31–32. The construction of the fort and main settlement in Vieques coincided with the ascent of Queen Isabel II. In her honor, the town's official name is "Isabel Segunda." Ibid., 51.

24. Bonnet Benítez, *Vieques,* 67.

25. See Figueroa, *Breve historia,* 392–407. González Vales, "The Challenge," 117.

26. González Vales, "The Challenge," 110–12.

27. Ferrer, *Insurgent Cuba.*

28. Puerto Rican ethnogenesis, some argue, began in the nineteenth century. Maldonado-Denis "Prospects," 36; Pedredira, *Insularismo,* 118; Picó, *Historia general,* 115. Others contend that this was an embryonic national identity that did not ripen until the early twentieth century. González, *Puerto Rico.*

29. Quintero Rivera, *Conflictos de clase,* 24.

30. Stavans, *Hispanic Condition,* 21.

31. Chatterjee, *Nation,* 36–37; Fanon, *Wretched,* 108–9.

32. Barreto, *Language.*

33. See Anderson, *Imagined Communities;* Gellner, *Nations and Nationalism;* Hechter, *Internal Colonialism.*

34. Gorenburg, "Not with One."

35. Connor, *Ethnonationalism,* 77–78, 196.

36. Barth, Introduction, 33; Rogowski, "Causes and Varieties," 94.

37. Anderson, *Imagined Communities,* 58; Jiménez de Wagenheim, *Puerto Rico's Revolt,* 39.

38. Quintero Rivera, *Conflictos de clase,* 30.

39. Eriksen, *Ethnicity,* 6; Handler, *Nationalism,* 13–15.

40. Barth, Introduction, 38; Roosens, *Creating Ethnicity,* 12.

41. Weinstein, *Civic Tongue,* 12.

42. Laitin, *Hegemony and Culture,* 106; Toland, "Introduction," 3; Chatterjee, *Nation,* 73.

43. Barreto, *Language;* Ferrao, "Nacionalismo."

44. Guerra, *Popular Expression,* 14–15.

45. Ibid.; Janer, "Colonial Nationalism"; Scarano, "*Jíbaro* Masquerade."

46. Godreau-Santiago, "Missing the Mix." Some argue that this nineteenth-century ethnic myth treated the island's African components as if they were illnesses. Trigo, "Anemia."

47. For example, fishermen in Lajas, Puerto Rico, frequently made references to "tradition" in their rhetorical arsenal when combating government proposals to restrict their access to the waters in La Parguera. Valdés-Pizzini, "Fishermen Associations," 169.

48. Cabán, *Constructing,* 120; Maldonado-Denis, *Puerto Rico,* 56; Picó, *Historia general,* 221.

49. Sprout and Sprout, *Toward,* 24.

50. Cabán, *Constructing,* 20–22.

51. Grusky, "U.S. Navy," 107.
52. Rodríguez Beruff, *Política militar,* 148, 27.
53. Mahan, *Letters and Papers,* 1: 482.
54. Pratt, *History,* 395. The preferred location for a canal was Nicaragua. Debates over the canal's location ended with Panama's secession from Colombia in 1903. Pratt, *History,* 400–409.
55. Meléndez López, *La batalla,* 16; Pastor Ruiz, *Vieques antiguo,* 80–81.
56. Bonnet Benítez, *Vieques,* 102.
57. Pratt, *History,* 395.
58. Rodríguez Beruff, *Política militar,* 28.
59. Estades Font, *La presencia militar,* 13.
60. Petrullo, *Puerto Rican Paradox,* 29.
61. Estades Font, *La presencia militar,* 80; Rodríguez Beruff, *Política militar,* 28.
62. Cuba's separatist movement in the 1890s motivated Spain into conceding greater autonomy to Cuba and Puerto Rico. Ferrer, *Insurgent Cuba,* 171; Gould, *La ley Foraker,* 18–19; Ramos de Santiago, *El gobierno,* 38–39.
63. Ramírez Lavandero, *Documents,* 37, 36.
64. Trías Monge, *Puerto Rico,* 13.
65. Torres Rivera, *Militarismo,* 32.
66. Cabán, *Constructing,* 38–39. Trías Monge, a former chief justice of Puerto Rico's Supreme Court, has argued that this treaty has been interpreted in an "illegitimate way." It has been construed to allow the federal government to maintain Puerto Rico as a de facto colony in perpetuity. American absolute dominion over Puerto Rico, deriving from the Treaty of Paris, lies at the justification of the U.S. Navy's presence in Puerto Rico. Trías Monge, "La Marina," 116.
67. Lipset, *Continental Divide,* 26.
68. Kaufmann, "American Exceptionalism," 443–44; Kaufmann, "Ethnic or Civic," 134.
69. Fredrickson, *Comparative Imagination,* 63.
70. Maldonado-Denis, *Emigration Dialectic,* 75.
71. Cabán, *Constructing,* 81.
72. Danforth, *Macedonian Conflict,* 21.
73. Trías Monge, *Puerto Rico,* 107.
74. Maldonado-Denis, *Puerto Rico,* 65–66.
75. Mahan, *Letters and Papers,* 3: 498, 596.
76. Said, *Orientalism,* 207, 204.
77. Carroll, *Report,* 59.
78. Barreto, *Language,* 51–60.
79. Hobsbawm, "Mass-Producing Tradition," 279.
80. Negrón de Montilla, *Americanization;* Osuna, *History.*
81. Roosevelt, *Public Papers,* 1937 vol., 161.
82. Roosevelt, *Public Papers,* vol. 3, 391–92.

83. Birch, *Nationalism*, 10.

84. Connor, *Ethnonationalism*, 21.

85. Verrill, *Porto Rico*, 18–19.

86. *Downes vs. Bidwell*, 182 U.S. 244, 287 (1901). The Supreme Court in *Downes*, one of the "Insular Cases," distinguished between "incorporated" and "unincorporated" territories. The incorporated territories—such as the District of Columbia, Arizona, and New Mexico—were possessions and integral parts of the country. In contrast, the unincorporated territories—such as the Philippines and Puerto Rico—were simply possessions, and the constitutional rights enjoyed by mainlanders did not automatically apply to their residents. Leibowitz, *Defining Status*, 26.

87. *Congressional Record*, vol. 33, 3612.

88. White, *Puerto Rico*, 185.

89. Ramírez Lavandero, *Documents*, 64–65.

90. Go, "Chains of Empire," 336; Cabán, *Constructing*, 152.

91. Said, *Orientalism*, 37.

92. White, *Puerto Rico*, 171–73.

93. The first election for governor was held in 1948. Ramírez Lavandero, *Documents*, 103–6.

94. Puerto Ricans could refuse U.S. citizenship, but those doing so could not vote; the franchise was limited to U.S. citizens. Fernós Isern, *Estado Libre Asociado*, 32. The coincidence of imposing citizenship on the eve of World War I fueled speculation that another motivation was the desire to conscript Puerto Ricans. Others argued citizenship was imposed in order to preclude independence. Maldonado-Denis, *Puerto Rico*, 106. Still others countered that while citizenship was imposed paternalistically—"worthy" Puerto Ricans versus "ungrateful" Filipinos—it was not done for military reasons. Cabranes, "Citizenship," 492.

95. Delgado Cintrón, *Culebra*, 15–16; Meléndez López, *La batalla*, 17–18.

96. Meléndez López, *La batalla*, 19.

97. Verrill, *Porto Rico*, 18–19.

98. Meléndez López, *La batalla*, 17–19.

99. Delgado Cintrón, *Culebra*, 16–17.

100. García and Quintero Rivera, *Desafío*, 60–61.

101. Meléndez López, *La batalla*, 19.

102. Ribes Tovar, *Albizu Campos*, 137.

103. Rivera, *Puerto Rico*.

104. Cabán, *Constructing*, 229.

105. Ironically, he volunteered in the U.S. Army during World War I. Ribes Tovar, *Albizu Campos*, 40–43.

106. Mahajani, *Philippine Nationalism*, 161, 324.

107. Tugwell, *Stricken Land*, 83–84.

108. Ribes Tovar, *Albizu Campos*, 159.

109. Bothwell González, *Puerto Rico*, 2: 507.

110. Ferrao, *Pedro Albizu Campos,* 156–61. The jury in his first trial—comprising seven Puerto Ricans and five Americans—deadlocked on the charges. A second jury—this time made up of ten Americans and two Puerto Ricans—found him guilty. Ibid., 163.

111. Petrullo, *Puerto Rican Paradox,* 160–61.

112. Quintero Rivera, "La ideología populista," 134.

113. Tugwell, *Stricken Land,* 83.

114. Bothwell González, *Orígenes y desarrollo,* 185.

115. Berríos Martínez, *La independencia,* 185; Mari Bras, *El independentismo,* 81.

116. Frambes-Buxeda, "Albizu," 88.

117. Ramos-Zayas, "La patria," 6.

118. Carroll, *Report,* 57.

Chapter 2. Target Practice

1. *Building,* 1: 3.

2. Dooley, "Wartime San Juan," 921. German U-boats posed a continual threat to shipping on the Atlantic, leading to severe food shortages in Puerto Rico. Ibid., 935.

3. *Building,* 1: 4, 27.

4. The accord gave the United States a ninety-nine-year lease and the right to build bases in eight colonies: Antigua, the Bahamas, Bermuda, British Guyana, Jamaica, Newfoundland, St. Lucia, and Trinidad. *Ibid.,* 2: 3.

5. Craven and Cate, *Army,* 123.

6. *Building,* 2: 5; Craven and Cate, *Army,* 161.

7. *Building,* 2: 6, 8; Langley, "Roosevelt Roads," 272.

8. Meléndez López, *La batalla,* 28.

9. Rodríguez Beruff, *Política militar,* 157.

10. Meléndez López, *La batalla,* 33.

11. Veaz, "Las expropiaciones," 198.

12. Grusky, "U.S. Navy," 107.

13. U.S. House, 1981, *Naval Training Activities,* 3.

14. Huntington, *Political Order,* 386.

15. Fernández, R., *Los Macheteros,* 61.

16. Grusky, "U.S. Navy," 108.

17. U.S. Navy, *Continued Use,* 2-204.

18. Grusky, "U.S. Navy," 108; McCaffrey, "Culture," 72, 73.

19. Albizu Campos, *La conciencia,* 50.

20. Tugwell, *Stricken Land,* 68n.

21. *Building,* 2: 8, 9.

22. U.S. House, 1980, *Naval Training Activities,* 27.

23. Roosevelt Roads covers 32,161 acres, of which 25,552 are in Vieques. García Muñiz, "U.S. Military," 85.

24. U.S. Navy, *Continued Use*, 2-196.
25. In order to downplay the impact of the navy's activities in Vieques, military cartographers designate a 980-acre "impact area" within the AFWTF; however, the navy uses all of eastern Vieques for training purposes. McCaffrey, "Culture," 36–37.
26. U.S. Navy, *Continued Use*, 1-11, 2-208.
27. Langley, "Roosevelt Roads," 274.
28. Ibid., 273.
29. U.S. Navy, *Continued Use*, 1-12.
30. Torres Rivera, "Puerto Rico," 47.
31. Grusky, "U.S. Navy," 119.
32. McCaffrey, "Culture," 71–72.
33. Bothwell González, *Puerto Rico*, 1–1: 622–23.
34. Bayrón Toro, *Elecciones y partidos*, 192–209.
35. Meléndez López, *La batalla*, 76.
36. Meléndez, *Movimiento anexionista*, 99. Centering its platform on labor issues, the Partido Socialista (Socialist Party) of the 1930s and 1940s saw no incongruity with supporting statehood. In contrast, the Partido Socialista Puertorriqueño, founded in the 1970s, was unmistakably Marxist and pro-independence.
37. Weisskoff, *Factories*, 121.
38. Lewis, *Notes*, 38.
39. Ramírez Lavandero, *Documents*, 103–6.
40. Mills, *Power Elite*, 171–223.
41. Meléndez López, *La batalla*, 81–82, 85–86.
42. Samoiloff, *Calamity*, 7.
43. Rabin Siegal, *Compendio*, 9; Samoiloff, *Calamity*, 11.
44. Samoiloff, *Calamity*, 20.
45. Rabin Siegal, *Compendio*, 9.
46. Ibid., 9.
47. Samoiloff, *Calamity*, 4.
48. Millar, *Current*, 357.
49. Samoiloff, *Calamity*, 1.
50. Meléndez, "Colonialism," 42.
51. Acosta, "El grito," 163; McCaffrey, "Culture," 86–87.
52. Grusky, "U.S. Navy," 110.
53. McCaffrey, "Culture," 85–86, 87, 111.
54. Rabin Siegal, *Compendio*, 6.
55. Movimiento Ecuménico Nacional de Puerto Rico, *Vieques*, 47–48.
56. Ortiz Ramos, *Con Rubén*, 38–39.
57. Gottlieb, *Nation*, 23.
58. Wells, *La modernización*, 352–53.
59. Delgado Cintrón, *Culebra*, 18, 19.

60. Maldonado-Denis, *Puerto Rico,* 178. While the relationship between education and support for the PIP is positive, it is not statistically significant. Barreto and Eagles, "Modelos ecológicos," 153, 157.

61. Rüdig, "Peace and Ecology," 29.

62. Delgado Cintrón, *Culebra,* 21, 293.

63. Ibid., 22.

64. U.S. House, 1980 *Naval Training Activities,* 52.

65. Ibid., 5; Noriega Rodríguez, "Seguridad nacional," 128.

66. Carr, *Puerto Rico,* 313.

67. Murillo, "The Value"; Rodríguez Beruff, "Guerra"; Torres Rivera, "Puerto Rico."

68. McCaffrey, "Culture," 146.

69. Valdés-Pizzini, "Fishermen Associations," 165, 170.

70. McCaffrey, "Culture," 147; Valdés-Pizzini, "Fishermen Associations," 167.

71. McCaffrey, "Culture," 11.

72. Valdés-Pizzini, "Fishermen Associations," 171.

73. McCaffrey, "Culture," 156, 329.

74. Grusky, "U.S. Navy," 112.

75. Fernández, R., *Los Macheteros,* 59–60.

76. Grusky, "U.S. Navy," 112.

77. U.S. House, 1980 *Naval Training Activities,* 190–91, 191–92.

78. Ibid., 101.

79. McCaffrey, "Culture," 173.

80. U.S. House, 1981 *Naval Training Activities,* 14.

81. Grusky, "Navy," 215.

82. Samoiloff, *Calamity,* 32.

83. Romero-Barceló and Goodrich, "Memorandum of Understanding," 1. A copy of this document was provided by the Office of the Resident Commissioner in San Juan.

84. Meléndez, *Movimiento anexionista,* 224.

85. Grusky, "U.S. Navy," 112.

86. Grusky, "Navy," 228.

87. Grusky, "U.S. Navy," 113.

88. Grusky, "Navy," 218.

89. Ibid., 220.

90. Grusky, "U.S. Navy," 110, 115–16.

91. McCaffrey, "Culture," 93.

92. Ibid., 91–99.

93. Baker, "Clinton's Defense," 132.

94. National Defense Research Institute, *Sexual Orientation,* 24–25.

95. Rabin Siegal, *Compendio,* 12.

96. McCaffrey, "Culture," 231.

97. Lewis, *Notes,* 30.
98. U.S. House, *Vieques Lands,* 2–4.
99. Carlos Romero-Barceló, a founding member of the PNP, was elected mayor of San Juan in 1968 and 1972. In 1976 he was elected governor and reelected in 1980. He lost a bid to win a third term in 1984. In 1992 and 1996 Romero-Barceló was elected resident commissioner. He lost a reelection bid in 2000.
100. U.S. House, *Vieques Lands,* 49, 10.
101. Ibid., 19, 20–21.
102. Barreto, *Politics,* 132.
103. It has also been suggested that the Pentagon helped derail the 1989–91 congressional status debates. Rodríguez Beruff, "La cuestión."
104. García Muñiz, "U.S. Military," 94–95.

Chapter 3. The Canonization of David Sanes

1. Morales, "El Grito de Lares," 9.
2. Duchesne et al., "Algunas tesis," 38.
3. Rosselló also supported two constitutional amendments that, by law, were presented to the electorate via referendum. Reminiscent of President Franklin D. Roosevelt's clash with the U.S. Supreme Court in the 1930s, Governor Rosselló proposed adding seats to the island's Supreme Court. That referendum was defeated, as was a companion amendment limiting the right to bail.
4. Cordero, "En marcha," 26.
5. Cotto, "Necesario," 7.
6. Cotto, "Refutan a Romero," 6.
7. Noriega Rodríguez, *El Instituto,* 201–3.
8. Estades Santaliz, "Sorprendido," 4.
9. Luciano, "Lazo político," 6.
10. Estrada Resto, "Augura Noriega," 5.
11. "Rosselló mantiene," 22.
12. Estrada Resto, "Protestan," 22.
13. Rodríguez Cotto, "Premio," 5.
14. Morín, "Indigenous Hawaiians," 14.
15. Trask, *From a Native,* 92.
16. Arbona, "Kanaloa es Vieques," 12.
17. Merrill, "Kaho'olawe Lives," 235.
18. Bush, *Public Papers,* 1440.
19. Essoyan, "Hawaiians Win," A19.
20. Bush, *Public Papers,* 1470.
21. "Hawaii," 20.
22. "State," D2.
23. "Military," B20.
24. Colombani, "En alerta," 28; Rabin Siegal, "El FBI," 8.
25. Rivera Marreo, "Anticipan cesantías," 37.

26. Ferraiuoli Suárez, "Acusa Vieques," 42.
27. Rabin Siegal, "La batalla," 8.
28. Ferraiuoli Suárez, "Trae $100 millones," 18.
29. Penchi, "En progreso," 34; Rabin Siegal, "La batalla," 8.
30. Ferraiuoli Suárez, "Testifica," 7.
31. "Buscan frenar," 52.
32. Ferraiuoli Suárez, "Nube negra," 8.
33. García San Inocencio, "La hora," 55.
34. Colombani, "Bomba cobra," 6.
35. Ruiz Marrero, "Condenan tragedia," 3.
36. Martínez, "Freno," 5.
37. Torres Gotay and Mulero, "Pide perdón," 8.
38. Rodríguez Orellana, "Puerto Rico."
39. Irizarry Mora, "Agenda," 108.
40. Rivera and Mulero, "Se reúne hoy," 29.
41. Torres Gotay and Mulero, "Unidos," 4.
42. Ghigliotty, "Voto legislativo," 32.
43. Mulero, "Temen más," 30.
44. Ferraiuoli Suárez, "Manuela a favor," 6.
45. Rivera Marrero, "Fecha," 15.
46. Estrada Resto, "Entre dos aguas," 6.
47. Berríos Martínez, "Puerto Rico's Decolonization," 110.
48. Ortiz Ramos, *Con Rubén*, 4.
49. Rochon, "West European," 108.
50. Rodríguez Beruff, "Vieques," 48.
51. Lleras Silva, "Defensa nacional . . . II," 7.
52. Lleras Silva, "Defensa nacional," 7.
53. Estrada Resto, "Entre dos aguas," 6.
54. Mulero, "La Marina," 29; Mulero, "Decide la Marina," 5.
55. Delgado, "Cita de status," 27; Mulero, "Llamado al consenso," 26.
56. Mulero, "Reciban apoyo," 26.
57. Mulero, "Exigen," 30.
58. Gopin, "Religion," 5.
59. Movimiento Ecuménico Nacional de Puerto Rico, *Vieques,* 33, 35.
60. Agosto Cintrón, *Religión y cambio,* 40, 32–33.
61. Picó, *Al filo del poder,* 20.
62. Agosto Cintrón, *Religión y cambio,* 84.
63. Torres, *Between Melting Pot,* 71–72.
64. Díaz-Stevens, "Aspects," 169.
65. Agosto Cintrón, *Religión y cambio,* 142.
66. Greenberg, "Church," 379.
67. Rivera Marrero, "Acto de fe," 6.
68. "Arzobispo de San Juan," 2.

69. Valdivia, "Llegó el Obispo," 4.
70. "Mensaje," 1.
71. Muriente Pérez, "Monseñor González," 10.
72. "Mensaje," 1. The expression "plantain stain" refers to something enduring or permanent.
73. Ibid., 2.
74. "Arzobispo de San Juan," 2.
75. González Nieves, *Ecological*, 62.
76. Cotto, "Clara la identidad," 5.
77. González, "Adónde se van," 12.
78. Rivera, *Puerto Rico;* Trías Monge, *Puerto Rico,* 183.
79. Barreto, "Constructing Identities."
80. Estrada Resto, "Maniobra," 8.
81. Mari Narváez, "Rubén Berríos," 3.
82. Colón Martínez, "Doña Norma," 11.
83. Rivera, Manuel, "Advertencia," 33.
84. Rivera Renta, "Posible expulsión," 22.
85. Varela, "Rivera hijo," 16.
86. "Intocable," 38.
87. Dávila, "Perdón senatorial," 30.
88. Mulero, "Fuera," 4.
89. Mulero, "Destaca CRB," 34.
90. Mulero, "No perdona," 4.
91. "El choque," 6.
92. Torres Gotay, "Listos," 5.
93. Santana, M., "Esperan por Clinton," 4.
94. Estrada Resto, "Sólo dos," 4.
95. Estrada Resto, "Cautela," 30; Estrada Resto, "En la 'lista,'" 24.
96. Colombani and Torres Gotay, "Vinculan," 8.
97. Mulero, "Asenso asombros," 5.
98. Ghigliotty, "En pie," 5.
99. "Atribuyen a Hillary," 14.
100. Mulero and Estrada Resto, "Responde Clinton," 5.
101. Colón, "Desconfían del comité," 5.
102. Mulero, "Dan forma," 5.
103. Estrada Resto, "Decepción," 5.
104. Estrada Resto, "Defiende el panel," 5.
105. Torres Gotay, "A repelar," 4.
106. "Indigna el 'robo,'" 4.
107. Mulero, "Mea culpa," 5.
108. U.S. Navy, *Continued Use*, 3–12.
109. Mulero, "Pesquisan," 4.
110. Depleted uranium, more dense than lead, is sandwiched between a shell's

outer and inner steel plates. As it pierces its target it "self sharpens"; small particles flake off, ignite, and then explode. Sheheane, "Depleted Uranium," 32.

111. Mulero, "Se lava," 4.
112. Sheheane, "Depleted Uranium," 33.
113. Torres Gotay, "La Marina," 4.
114. Mulero, "Despega el 'chantaje,'" 4.
115. U.S. House, 1980 *Naval Training Activities,* 89.
116. Torres Gotay, "Ceiba con Vieques," 6.
117. Estrada Resto, "¡Basta ya!," 4.
118. Mulero, "Roto el diálogo," 15.
119. Mulero, "'Tergiversada,'" 5; Mulero, "Ningún lugar," 4.
120. Barreto, *Politics,* 47–48.
121. Romero-Barceló, *Statehood,* 95.
122. Duchesne et al., "La estadidad"; Grosfoguel, "Divorce."
123. Carrión, "El imaginario," 96.
124. Ghigliotty, "David Sanes," 4.
125. Parés Arroyo, "Exonerada la víctima," 5.
126. McCaffrey, "Culture," 244.
127. Pérez, "Otorgan contrato," 68.
128. "Llevarían a la ONU," 5.
129. Mulero, "Revés," 4.
130. Rivera Marrero, "Entusiasmo," 26.
131. Torres Gotay, "No baja," 4.
132. Colón, "Tildan de tiranía," 5.
133. Rivera Marrero, "Respalda Manuela," 5.
134. Ghigliotty, "Asomo," 35; Ghigliotty, "Clamor más allá," 5.
135. Torres Gotay, "Unidos," 4.
136. "Lo bueno," 6.
137. Meléndez, "El estudio," 71.
138. Anderson, *Party Politics,* 12.
139. Barreto and Eagles, "Modelos ecológicos."
140. "Vieques une," 5.
141. "Lo bueno," 6.
142. Ramos Avalos, "Vieques," 146.
143. Estades Santaliz, "La lucha," 29.

Chapter 4. Clemency and Consensus

1. Martell, "In the Belly," 190; "Los 15," 20.
2. González and Bazinet, "Clemency," 10.
3. Motley, *U.S. Strategy,* 18.
4. Fernández, *Los Macheteros.*
5. McCoy, "FALN Prisoners," 15.
6. Hernández Colón, "Presos políticos," 133.

7. Serrano, "Sin condiciones," 6.
8. McCoy, "FALN Prisoners," 15.
9. Ramos-Zayas, "La patria," 275–76.
10. Torres Gotay, "Conmociona," 6.
11. Torres Gotay,"Sobrepasa la marcha," 18.
12. Mulero, "'Sí,'" 22.
13. Mulero, "Petición," 28.
14. Estades Santaliz, "Gore apoya," 4.
15. Mulero, "Firma Clinton," 32.
16. Mulero, "En libertad," 28.
17. Ghigliotty, "Rosselló aplaude," 28.
18. *Congressional Record,* vol. 145, no. 116, H8008.
19. Estades Santaliz, "Los necesitamos," 32.
20. Mulero, "Clinton confiesa," 30.
21. Mulero, "Firman," 12.
22. Montano, "Multitudinario," 62.
23. Mulero, "Una 'bomba,'" 28.
24. Pyle, "Hillary reitera," 25.
25. Mulero, "Callejón," 18.
26. Rivera, "Critican," 15.
27. Mulero, "Dennis Rivera," 14.
28. Abrams, "Dos congresistas," 22.
29. Allen, "Rudy," 4.
30. Mulero, "No suelta," 24.
31. "Policía," 66.
32. McQuillan, "Terror Act," 27.
33. Mulero, "El dilema," 4.
34. *Congressional Record,* vol. 145, no. 116 S10687, S10688, H8005, H8007, H8008.
35. House Concurrent Resolution 180 passed 311 to 41. Ten did not vote, and oddly 72 answered "present." Ibid., H8019–20.
36. *Congressional Record,* vol. 145, no. 117, S10720. The Senate also voted to censure the president, 95 to 2. *Congressional Record,* vol. 145, no. 119, S10818.
37. *Congressional Record,* vol. 145, no. 119, S10817.
38. Ibid., S10817.
39. Mulero, "Amenaza Lott," 8.
40. Mulero, "Censura Trent Lott," 5.
41. Mulero, "Firme el Gobierno," 6.
42. Mulero, "Polémico el voto," 4.
43. Estrada Resto, "Nada de bombardeo," 5.
44. Estrada Resto, "La Fortaleza," 6.
45. García, "Presencia espiritual," 6.
46. Mulero, "Propuestas," 5; Mulero, "Desobediencia," 10.

47. Fernández, "Presos," 99.
48. Rodríguez Cotto, "Peña Clos truena," 39.
49. Estrada Resto, "'Dañino' el debate," 16; Rodríguez Cotto, "Estrategia," 25.
50. Ramos Avalos, "Puerto Rico," 131.
51. Estrada Resto, "Sí de Rosselló," 34.
52. Ghigliotty, "Vieques domina," 26.
53. Ghigliotty, "Los ex presos," 26–27; Ghigliotty, "Apoyan a Vieques," 22.
54. Rodríguez Cotto, "Organizan," 35; Estrada Resto, "Toman," 30.
55. Rodríguez Cotto, "Divide al PNP," 5.
56. Mulero, "Serrano," 16.
57. Mulero, "Alto apoyo," 26.
58. Rozell and Wilcox, *Interest Groups,* 85.
59. Eisenhower, *Public Papers,* 1038.
60. Parés Arroyo, "Consulta al pueblo," 26.
61. U.S. House, *Report on the Inspection,* 1–2.
62. "La situación," 4.
63. Torres Gotay, "Pasan un susto," 14.
64. Estrada Resto, "No al plan," 5; Mulero, "Censura el rol," 5.
65. Mulero, "Se queda," 4.
66. Mulero, "Gutiérrez," 5.
67. Mulero, "Admite," 30.
68. Bosque Pérez, "Carpetas," 54.
69. Mulero, "FBI entregará," 34.
70. Serrano, "Se abre," 16.
71. Colombani, "Agentes del FBI," 36.
72. Estrada Resto, "A pagar," 4.
73. Villarreal, "Toledo señala," 64.
74. Rivera Marrero, "Propone donar," 5.
75. Villanueva, "El consenso," 111.
76. Colombani, "A descorrer," 32; Rivera Marrero, "Inquietud partidista," 34.
77. Tió, "Vieques," 133.
78. Berríos Martínez, "Vieques," 141.
79. Delgado, "Culpa Clinton," 5.
80. Mulero, "El status," 42.
81. García, "Rompe el consenso," 4.
82. Estrada Resto, "Detalla Rosselló," 8.
83. Estrada Resto, "Sólo en Vieques," 4; Estrada Resto, "Gobernador rechaza," 6.
84. Torres Gotay, "El PIP," 8.
85. Ghigliotty, "Vieques," 22; Roldán Soto, "Llama aguajeros," 5.
86. Duchesne et al., "La estadidad," 30.

87. Mulero, "Desmienten sacrificio," 27.
88. Mulero, "Clinton reta," 30.
89. Mulero, "Sin garras," 8.
90. Mulero, "Aplauso federal," 5.
91. Mulero, "Contento," 5.
92. "Referendum en Vieques," 4–5.
93. Ibid.
94. *Escrutinio Elecciones*, 149.
95. "Referendum en Vieques," 4–5.
96. Alonso, *Muñoz Marín*, 63–65.
97. Fernández, "Jugando con fuego," 95.
98. "Pide un regaño," 10.
99. "Calderón deplora," 30.
100. Valdivia, "No cede," 8; Valdivia, "Confirmado," 73.
101. Torres Gotay, "Un abuso," 6.
102. Lebrón Velázquez, "La marcha," 129.
103. Pagán, "Las iglesias," 138.
104. García and Roldán, "Líderes cristianos," 6.
105. Noriega Rodríguez, "Desobediencia," 135.
106. Roldán Soto, "Ejército de paz," 5.
107. "Escaso apoyo," 6.
108. Mulero, "Utilizan a Vieques," 34.
109. Mulero, "Pesquera advierte," 5.
110. The PNP spent $100,000 on advertising and $80,000 for other event-related expenses. Rodríguez Cotto, "Satisfecho," 23.
111. Valdivia, "Destaca el Arzobispo," 5.
112. Torres, "Expresión," 8.
113. Mulero, "Canta victoria," 19.
114. Torres Gotay, "Reforzado," 4.
115. Colombani, "Alegan maltrato," 27; Rodríguez Cotto, "Líderes religiosos," 18.
116. Caquías Cruz, "Manifestación," 12; Maldonado Arrigoitía, "El paro," 10; Nieves Ramírez, "Cierran filas," 14; Santana, "Hasta hoy," 8; Valdivia, "Protesta y palos," 6.
117. Colombani, "Reciben como héroes," 30.
118. Torres, "Vuelve a tirar," 6.
119. Fernández, "Dejen a Vieques," 133.
120. Noriega Rodríguez, "El día después," 153.
121. Casellas and Trinidad, "Advierte," 64.
122. Roldán Soto, "'Termina' el bombardeo," 4.
123. Roldán Soto, "Revalúa el PIP," 4.
124. Colombani, "Abogados," 20.
125. Roldán Soto, "Masivo apoyo," 6.

126. Santori, "La bastilla," 103.
127. Santana, "Marchan," 8; Vinicio, "'Viento en popa,'" 3.
128. Estrada, "Vieques," 138.
129. Mulero, "Cambia Gore," 4.
130. Mulero, "Apoyo al plan," 76.
131. Mulero, "Urge Lott," 10.
132. Mulero, "Inhofe insiste," 8.
133. "Situación de Vieques," 5, 6.
134. "Brecha," 4.
135. "Aventaja Pesquera," 26.
136. Fernández, "Fracaso," 117.
137. Barreto, *Politics,* 86.
138. Luciano, "Calderón," 31.
139. Rivera Marrero, "'Sin voluntad,'" 5.
140. Delgado, "Visto bueno," 4.
141. Torres Gotay, "17 vertederos," 6.
142. Mulero, "Ejercicios," 4.
143. Vinicio, "Vieques decisivo," 3.
144. Torres, "Vieques," 5.
145. Calderón, "Renacer viequense," 115.
146. Rivera Marrero, "Calderón pide," 4.
147. Colombani, "Sí judicial," 68.
148. Colombani, "No federal," 72.
149. Rivera Marrero, "PPD se unirá," 26; Torres, "Ya es ley," 22.
150. Estrada Resto, "Reitera el PIP," 30.
151. Rivera Marrero, "El PPD," 30.
152. Delgado, "Boston anula," 30.
153. Colombani, "'Falacia electoral,'" 4.
154. Roldán Soto, "Reitera su promesa," 13.
155. Torres Gotay, "Pide Berríos," 6.
156. Valdivia, "Nombran a Corrada," 12.
157. Valdivia, "Compromiso con Vieques," 24.
158. Rosario, "Al Capitolio," 14.
159. Sosa Pascual, "Reafirma la Marina," 16.
160. "Nuevo alcalde," 24.
161. Rivera Marrero, "Rumsfeld no sorprende," 5.
162. Green, "Nuestra gran responsabilidad," 112.
163. "Saint Kitts," 28; Mulero, "Suena Colombia," 30; Mulero, "Le ofrecen," 5.
164. Rodríguez Sánchez, "Admite la senadora," 31.
165. Rodríguez, "Misla y McClintock," 31.
166. Ghigliotty, "Gesta reparar," 42.
167. García, "Preocupa a CRB," 42.

168. Mulero, "Vieques antes," 47.
169. Mulero, "Piden a Hansen," 14.
170. Rivera, "Pide gobierno propio," 28.
171. Rodríguez Sánchez, "Parga le aclara," 32.
172. Mulero, "Senadores," 20.
173. "Pataki," 2; Acosta, J., "Pataki anuncia," 2.
174. Rivera Marrero, "Convencido Pataki," 5.
175. González, "En acción," 12.
176. This anniversary was particularly severe on the Sanes Rodríguez family. On that day, April 19, 2001, David Sanes's mother passed away. Torres Gotay, "Golpea," 4.
177. Rodríguez, "Radican ley," 4.
178. Mulero, "Vía libre," 4.
179. Torres Gotay, "Consiguen deterer," 4.
180. Covas Quevedo, "Sentencian a Berríos," 17.
181. Berríos Martínez, "Solamente ante Dios," 126.
182. Green, "Algo más," 107.
183. Valdivia, "Mensaje papal," 16.
184. Castro, "El poder," 41; Colón, "'Siempre lo soñé,'" 2.

Chapter 5. Politics in El Barrio

1. Farinacci, "Nueva York," 10.
2. Glazer and Moynihan, *Beyond the Melting Pot,* 100.
3. Hardy-Fanta, *Latina Politics.*
4. Jennings, "Introduction," 7.
5. Cabán, *Constructing,* 69.
6. Sánchez Korrol, *From Colonia,* 28–31.
7. Flores, *Divided Borders,* 103.
8. Haslip-Viera, "Evolution," 7.
9. Jones-Correa, *Between Two Nations,* 114.
10. Guzmán, "Puerto Rican Barrio," 144.
11. Haslip-Viera, "Evolution," 5; Sánchez Korrol, *From Colonia,* 167–68.
12. Vega, *Memoirs,* 46–47.
13. Haslip-Viera, "Evolution," 4, 13.
14. Jennings, *Puerto Rican Politics,* 29; Sánchez Korrol, *From Colonia,* 18–25.
15. Sánchez Korrol, *From Colonia,* 168; Vega, *Memoirs,* 66.
16. Vega, *Memoirs,* 83, 21–22.
17. Falcón, "History," 23.
18. Rodríguez-Morazzani, "Political Cultures," 30.
19. Vega, *Memoirs,* 97.
20. Falcón, "History," 22.
21. Sánchez Korrol, *From Colonia,* 173.

22. Jennings, *Puerto Rican Politics,* 125–26.
23. Ibid., 125–26, 140–41.
24. Vega, *Memoirs,* 111.
25. Sánchez, "Puerto Rican Politics," 271.
26. Jennings, *Puerto Rican Politics,* 38.
27. Falcón, "History," 32.
28. Jones-Correa, *Between Two Nations,* 65.
29. Vega, *Memoirs,* 111, 107–11, 182.
30. Sánchez Korrol, *From Colonia,* 184.
31. Falcón, "History," 34.
32. Vega, *Memoirs,* 116.
33. Ibid., 127; Falcón, "History," 30.
34. Vega, *Memoirs,* 194.
35. Hobsbawm, "Mass Producing Tradition," 280.
36. Glazer and Moynihan, *Beyond the Melting Pot,* 100.
37. Díaz-Quiñones, *La memoria rota,* 49.
38. Omi and Winant, *Racial Formation;* Rodríguez, C., "Racial Themes."
39. Racialization, an initial response by native-born white Americans to all immigrants, is common where the target group lacks control over their labor. The economic marginalization of African Americans and Latinos perpetuated their status as permanent "others." Urciuoli, *Exposing Prejudice,* 17–23.
40. Vega, *Memoirs,* 181.
41. Ibid., 136, 176.
42. Cruz, *Identity and Power,* 44.
43. Rivas, "Boricuas son miopes," 7.
44. Feder, "No Statehood," 27.
45. Barrios, "Realidades latinas," 16.
46. Chávez, *Out of the Barrio.*
47. Oboler, *Ethnic Labels,* 26; Urciuoli, *Exposing Prejudice,* 16.
48. Barreto, *Language.*
49. Anti-Catholic sentiment was very strong in nineteenth-century American society. Moynihan, *Pandaemonium,* 31. An overlooked legacy of Senator Joseph McCarthy and his ideological witch-hunts in the 1950s was a shift in the popular locus of the "Antichrist" from the Vatican to the Kremlin, thus opening the door for white Catholics to enter the American mainstream. O'Brien, *God Land,* 36.
50. Urciuoli, *Exposing Prejudice,* 66.
51. Glick Schiller, "Who Are," 17.
52. Steinberg, *Ethnic Myth,* 42.
53. Vega, *Memoirs,* 97.
54. Waters, *Ethnic Options.*
55. Barreto, *Language,* 87–93; Sánchez Korrol, *From Colonia,* 76.
56. Landau, "Diaspora," 78.

57. Miles, *Bridging Mental Boundaries*, 120.
58. Acevedo, "Look," 63; Ginorio, "Puerto Rican Ethnicity," 201; Ramos-Zayas, "La patria," 157.
59. Maldonado-Denis, *Emigration Dialectic*, 96.
60. Jones-Correa, *Between Two Nations*, 79.
61. Baver, "Puerto Rican Politics," 44; Jennings, *Puerto Rican Politics*, 133.
62. Jennings, *Puerto Rican Politics*, 76, 87, 93.
63. Baver, "Puerto Rican Politics," 45.
64. Jennings, *Puerto Rican Politics*, 78.
65. González, *Mexican Consuls;* Smith, "Mexicans," 70.
66. Ramos-Zayas, "La patria," 54; Cruz, *Identity and Power*, 69.
67. Jennings, *Puerto Rican Politics*, 77.
68. Esman, "Diasporas," 347.
69. Baver, "Puerto Rican Politics," 49.
70. Ibid., 49.
71. Torres, *Between Melting Pot*, 11.
72. Ramos-Zayas, "La patria," 214–15. Indeed, on the island, statehood and Commonwealth parties feel a greater need to openly discuss cultural issues than does the PIP, given the popular perception that *independentistas* are inherently "more Puerto Rican." Frambes-Buxeda, "El papel," 178n.
73. Danforth, *Macedonian Conflict*, 80.
74. Jones-Correa, *Between Two Nations*, 114.
75. Jennings, *Puerto Rican Politics*, 197, 241.
76. Flores, "Pan-Latino," 110.
77. Falcón, "Puerto Ricans," 187; Jones-Correa, *Between Two Nations*, 116.
78. Torres, "Introduction," 3.
79. Young Lords, *Resolutions*, 3.
80. Lewis, *Notes*, 268–69.
81. Guzmán, "La Vida Pura," 156; Gutiérrez, *Walls and Mirrors*, 183.
82. Rodríguez, "Boricuas."
83. Morales, "Palante," 211.
84. Carson, *In Struggle*, 278.
85. Early, "African-American," 324.
86. Lucas, "Puerto Rican Politics," 106.
87. Ramos-Zayas, "La patria," 60.
88. Young Lords, *Resolutions*, 5.
89. Morales, "Palante," 217–19.
90. Young Lords, *Resolutions*, 6.
91. Whalen, "Bridging Homeland," 113; Ramos-Zayas, "La patria," 68.
92. Ture and Hamilton, *Black Power*, 16–23; Malcolm X, *Malcolm X Speaks*, 46–47, 50–51.
93. Whalen, "Bridging Homeland," 122.
94. Lucas, "Puerto Rican Politics," 107.

95. Gutiérrez Olmedo, "Necesitamos reconciliación," 32.
96. Rodríguez-Morazzani, "Political Cultures," 38.
97. Ramos-Zayas, "La patria," 266.
98. Young Lords, *Resolutions*, 9.
99. Ramos-Zayas, "La patria," 268–69.
100. A similar case is found in Mongolian nationalism. Adulation of the thirteenth-century figure Temüjin (Chinggis Khan) in contemporary nationalist discourse binds Mongols in China (Inner Mongolia), Russia (Buryatia and Tuva), and Mongolia in a new pan-ethnic identity. Bulag, *Nationalism*, 70.
101. Rivera, "Our Movement," 195–96.
102. Velázquez, "Coming Full Circle," 51.
103. Rodríguez-Morazzani, "Political Cultures," 41–42.
104. Torres, "Introduction," 5.
105. Serrano, "Rifle," 126–27.
106. Goldstone, "Soviet Union," 117–18.
107. "Marcha," 7.
108. Vázquez, "Denuncian," 6.
109. Mulero, "Clama a Clinton," 6; Pineda, "Pesa Vieques," 35.
110. Vega, "Liberación incondicional," 3.
111. Barrios, "Los profetas," 14.
112. Aquino, "Manifestantes," 3.
113. Vega, "Cuál es," 2.
114. Vázquez, "Funcionarios electos," 5.
115. Rivas, "Consejales de NY," 9.
116. Vázquez, "No apoyo," 2.
117. Barreto, *Politics*, 141.
118. Torres, "Introduction," 17.
119. Rivera, "Tras Vieques," 14.
120. Monteverde-Torres and Frontera, "Puertorriqueños," 18.
121. Rodríguez Cotto, "Ricky," 80.
122. "Arrestada Rosie," 6.
123. Aquino, "Prosiguen arrestos," 3.
124. Torres, "Introduction," 11. For a list of other mainland organizations, see Arce, "La solidaridad," 16.
125. It was originally founded as a "Hispanic" parade in the 1950s. By the early 1960s two distinct parades emerged—one Puerto Rican and one pan-Hispanic, the Defile de la Raza. Estades, "Symbolic Unity," 101.
126. Schneider, "Defining Boundaries," 39.
127. Jennings, *Puerto Rican Politics*, 25.
128. Sánchez Korrol, *From Colonia*, 197; Vega, *Memoirs*, 192.
129. "Luis A. Ferré," 8; Valentín, "José Celso," 12.
130. Estades, "Symbolic Unity," 103.
131. Andreu, "Líderes políticos," 19.

132. Barrio, "El desfile," 12.
133. González, "La nación," 12.
134. Arce, "Mil y un," 22–23.
135. Rosario Natal, "El debate," 44.
136. In his quest to appease the hard-core nationalists in his party, Luis Muñoz Marín appropriated several symbols clearly connected with the island's independence movement, including the one-starred flag and the nationalist anthem—"La Borinqueña." Dávila, *Sponsored Identities,* 32.
137. Morris, *Puerto Rico,* 159.
138. "Vieques and Albizu," 6.
139. Guss, *Festive State,* 172.
140. Murillo, "Puerto Rico."
141. Vega, *Memoirs,* 136.

Chapter 6. Transnational Identities

1. Carrión, "National Question," 71–72.
2. Marquez and Jennings, "Representation," 545.
3. Danforth, *Macedonian Conflict,* 80.
4. Handler, *Nationalism,* 13–15.
5. Lustick, *Unsettled States,* 387–88.
6. Udovički, "Nationalism," 298.
7. Kryukov, "Self-determination." Since 1949 Taiwanese have developed a mixed or hybrid identity embracing a sense of local Taiwan and pan-Chinese loyalties. Wong and Sun, "Dissolution."
8. Connor, *Ethnonationalism,* 80; Daniel, "Identidad cultural," 46.
9. Anderson, *Imagined Communities;* Gellner, *Nations and Nationalism;* Smith, *Ethnic Revival.*
10. Eriksen, *Ethnicity,* 6.
11. Steinberg, *Ethnic Myth,* 170.
12. Connor, *Ethnonationalism,* 83.
13. Meléndez, *Movimiento anexionista,* 152.
14. Rivera, *Puerto Rico.*
15. Trías Monge, *Puerto Rico,* 183.
16. Carson, *In Struggle,* 262.
17. Anderson, *Party Politics,* 45.
18. Alvarez-Curbelo, "El discurso populista," 27.
19. Carrión, "Puerto Rican Nationalism," 135.
20. Popular festivals in Puerto Rico have been heavily commercialized in recent years. Dávila, *Sponsored Identities.* Still, most of the items sold at the Grito de Lares festivities convey an unmistakably nationalist message extolling the island's cultural identity and glorifying Albizu's legend.
21. Pantojas García, "La noción," 24.
22. Morris, "Birmingham Confrontation," 623.

23. Breyman, "Were the 1980s," 314.
24. Laponce, *Languages*, 139.
25. Pedreira, *Insularismo*, 132.
26. Guerra, *Popular Expression*, 15.
27. Ibid., 5–9, 267; Janer, "Colonial Nationalism," 33.
28. Connor, *Ethnonationalism*, 196.
29. González, *Puerto Rico*.
30. Díaz-Quiñones, *La memoria rota*, 49.
31. Flores, *Divided Borders*, 103.
32. Ibid.; Flores, *From Bomba*.
33. Velázquez, "Another West Side," 89.
34. Torres, "Introduction," 15.
35. Ramos-Zayas, "La patria," 30–34.
36. Lewis, *Notes*, 265.
37. Dávila, *Sponsored Identities*; Guerra, *Popular Expression*; Janer, "Colonial Nationalism."
38. Hernández, "Identity and Culture," 129–30.
39. Alicea Ortega, "Puerto Rico," 22.
40. Grosfoguel, "David Sanes," 112.
41. Miles, *Bridging Mental Boundaries*, 11.
42. Arce, "La solidaridad," 16.
43. Lao, "Islands," 171.
44. Duany, "Nation on the Move," 7.
45. Laitin, *Hegemony and Culture*, 19; Mallon, *Peasant and Nation*, 12.
46. Barreto, "Constructing Identities."
47. Rudé, *Ideology*, 4.
48. Greenfeld, *Nationalism*, 14–17; Anderson, *Imagined Communities*, 58; Lafaye, *Quetzalcóatl*, 8.
49. Stephen, "Creation and Re-creation," 18.
50. Aristotle, *Politics*, 3.
51. Duchacek, "Antagonistic Cooperation," 3.
52. Hechter, *Containing Nationalism*, 14.
53. Miles, *Bridging Mental Boundaries*, 8.
54. Lustick, *Unsettled States*.
55. Myths based on colonial accounts facilitated efforts by contemporary Costa Rican political elites to quell conflict and, on the contrary, thwarted efforts by Nicaraguan leaders to do likewise. Cruz, "Identity and Persuasion."
56. Danforth, *Macedonian Conflict*, 82.
57. Ramos-Zayas, "La patria," 332; Hardy-Fanta, *Latina Politics*, 103; Aponte-Parés, "Lessons," 48–50; Flores, *From Bomba*, 71–76. The word "casitas" literally means "little houses." Built in many Puerto Rican communities throughout the United States, these structures recall the wooden houses that used to be built in Puerto Rico before the 1950s. They serve as a reminder of Puerto

Rico's agrarian past and a territorial marker proclaiming the neighborhood's status as a Puerto Rican enclave.

58. The struggle to maintain a particular space has even led to intra-Latino conflicts between Puerto Ricans and other Latinos in New York and Chicago. Dávila, "Latinizing Culture"; Ramos-Zayas, "La patria," 89–91.

59. Ramos-Zayas, "La patria," 281.

60. Olson, *Logic*.

61. Chong, *Collective Action*, 35.

62. Dawes, van de Kragt, and Orbell, "Cooperation," 99; Kelly and Kelly, "Who Gets Involved," 77.

63. Lichbach, "What Makes Rational Peasants," 416.

64. Hardin, *One for All*, 5.

65. Chong, *Collective Action*, 9.

66. Barnes, "Status Groups," 263.

Bibliography

Abrams, Jim. 1999. "Dos congresistas atacan el indulto." *El Nuevo Día*, San Juan (August 20): 22.
Acevedo, Gladys. 2000. "A Look at How Mainland Puerto Ricans Believe Themselves to Be Perceived by Their Insular Counterparts and Its Impact on Their Ethnic Self-Identity and Group Belongingness." Ph.D. diss., City University of New York.
Acosta, Ivonne. 1999. "El grito de Vieques." Editorial. *El Nuevo Día*, San Juan (April 29): 163.
Acosta, José. 2001. "Pataki anuncia viaje a Vieques." *El diario/La prensa*, New York (April 2): 2.
Agosto Cintrón, Nélida. 1996. *Religión y cambio social en Puerto Rico, 1898–1940* (Religion and social change in Puerto Rico). Río Piedras, P.R.: Ediciones Huracán.
"Alarma por casos de cáncer." 1999. *El Nuevo Día*, San Juan (May 15): 4.
Albizu Campos, Pedro. 1977 [1972]. *La conciencia nacional puertorriqueña* (The Puerto Rican national consciousness). 3rd ed. México, D.F.: Siglo Veintiuno Editores.
Alicea Ortega, Luz M. 2000. "Puerto Rico y Nueva York: Dos hogares boricueños." *Diálogo* (May): 22.
Allen, Michael O. 1999. "Rudy: Show Me the Files—Puerto Rican Pardons." *Daily News*, New York (August 15): 4.
Alonso, María M. 1998. *Muñoz Marín vs. the Bishops: An Approach to Church and State*. Hato Rey, P.R.: Publicaciones Puertorriqueñas.
Alvarez-Curbelo, Silvia. 1993. "El discurso populista de Luis Muñoz Marín: Condiciones de posibilidad y mitos fundacionales en el período 1932–1936." In *Del nacionalismo al populismo: Cultura y política en Puerto Rico* (From nationalism to populism: Culture and politics in Puerto Rico), ed. Silvia Alvarez-Curbelo and María E. Rodríguez Castro. Río Piedras, P.R.: Ediciones Huracán.
Anderson, Benedict. 1983. *Imagined Communities: Reflections on the Origin and Spread of Nationalism*. London: Verso Editions.
Anderson, Robert W. 1965. *Party Politics in Puerto Rico*. Stanford, Calif.: Stanford University Press.
———. 1983. "Political Parties and the Politics of Status." *Caribbean Studies* 21, nos. 1–2: 1–43.

Andreu, Leila A. 2000. "Líderes políticos repudian controversia de desfile." *El diario/La prensa*, New York (March 24): 19.

Aponte-Parés, Luis. 1999. "Lessons from el Barrio—The East Harlem Real Great Society/Urban Planning Studio: A Puerto Rican Chapter in the Fight for Urban Self-Determination." In *Latino Social Movements: Historical and Theoretical Perspectives*, ed. Rodolfo D. Torres and George Katsiaficas. New York: Routledge.

Aquino, Fernando. 1999. "Manifestantes en NY se unen al llamado." *El diario/La prensa*, New York (August 30): 3.

———. 2000. "Prosiguen arrestos voluntarios por Vieques." *El diario/La prensa*, New York (January 7): 3.

Arbona, Ramón. 1999. "Kanaloa es Vieques triunfante." *Claridad*, Santurce, P.R. (May 21–27): 12.

Arce, Maritere. 2000. "Mil y un sititios para la bandera." *El diario/La prensa*, New York (June 11): 12.

———. 2000. "La solidaridad con Vieques trasciende las fronteras." Special Supplement. *El diario/La prensa*, New York (June 11): 16, 18.

Aristotle. 1988. *The Politics*, ed. Stephen Everson. Cambridge: Cambridge University Press.

"Arrestada Rosie Pérez ante la ONU." 2000. *El Nuevo Día*, San Juan (January 7): 6.

"Arzobispo de San Juan." 1999. *El Visitante: Semanario católico de Puerto Rico*, San Juan (April 3): 2.

"Atribuyen a Hillary pesquisa Vieques." 1999. *El Nuevo Día*, San Juan (June 26): 14.

"Aventaja Pesquera." 2000. *El Nuevo Día*, San Juan (October 17): 26–27.

Baker, John C. 1996. "Clinton Defense Policy-Making: Players, Process, and Policies." In *Clinton and Post-Cold War Defense*, ed. Stephen J. Cimbala. Westport, Conn.: Praeger.

Barnes, Barry. 1992. "Status Groups and Collective Action." *Sociology* 26, no. 2: 259–70.

Barreto, Amílcar A. 1998. *Language, Elites, and the State: Nationalism in Puerto Rico and Quebec*. Westport, Conn.: Praeger.

———. 2001. *The Politics of Language in Puerto Rico*. Gainesville: University Press of Florida.

———. 2001. "Constructing Identities: Ethnic Boundaries and Elite Preferences in Puerto Rico." *Nationalism and Ethnic Politics* 7, no. 1: 21–40.

Barreto, Amílcar A., and D. Munroe Eagles. 2000. "Modelos ecológicos de apoyo partidista en Puerto Rico, 1980–1992." *Revista de Ciencias Sociales* 9: 135–65.

Barrios, Luis. 1999. "Los profetas revolucionarios del amor." Editorial. *El diario/La prensa*, New York (August 20): 14.

———. 1999. "Realidades latinas para el 2000." Editorial. *El diario/La prensa*, New York (December 26): 16.

———. 2000. "El desfile de la conciencia nacionalista puertorriqueña." Editorial. *El diario/La prensa*, New York (June 11): 12.

Barth, Fredrik. 1969. Introduction to *Ethnic Groups and Boundaries: The Social Organization of Culture Difference*, ed. Fredrik Barth. Boston: Little, Brown.

Baver, Sherrie. 1984. "Puerto Rican Politics in New York City: The Post-World War II Period." In *Puerto Rican Politics in Urban America*, ed. James Jennings and Monte Rivera. Westport, Conn.: Greenwood Press.

Bayrón Toro, Fernando. 1989. *Elecciones y partidos políticos de Puerto Rico* (Elections and political parties of Puerto Rico). 4th ed. Mayagüez, P.R.: Editorial Isla.

Benítez, Celeste. 1998. *El día en que Puerto Rico habló: El plebiscito de 1993* (The day that Puerto Rico spoke: The 1993 plebiscite). Río Piedras, P.R.: Editorial Cultural.

Berríos Martínez, Rubén. 1983. *La independencia de Puerto Rico: Lucha y razón* (The independence of Puerto Rico: Struggle and cause). México, D.F.: Editorial Línea.

———. 1997. "Puerto Rico's Decolonization." *Foreign Affairs* 76, no. 6: 100–114.

———. 1999. "Vieques: Metáfora y preludio." Editorial. *El Nuevo Día*, San Juan (November 3): 141.

———. 2001. "Solamente ante Dios." Editorial. *El Nuevo Día*, San Juan (May 17): 126.

Birch, Anthony. 1989. *Nationalism and National Integration*. London: Unwin Hyman.

Bonnet Benítez, Juan A. 1976. *Vieques en la historia de Puerto Rico* (Vieques in the history of Puerto Rico). San Juan: F. Ortiz Nieves.

Bosque Pérez, Ramón. 1997. "Carpetas y persecución política en Puerto Rico: La dimensión federal." In *Las Carpetas: Persecución política y derechos civiles en Puerto Rico* (The files: Political persecution and civil rights in Puerto Rico), ed. Ramón Bosque Pérez and José J. Colón Morera. Río Piedras, P.R.: Centro para la Investigación y Promoción de los Derechos Civiles.

Bothwell González, Reece B. 1979. *Puerto Rico: Cien años de lucha política* (Puerto Rico: A hundred years of political struggle). Vol. 1–1, *Programas y manifiestos, 1869–1952*. Río Piedras, P.R.: Editorial Universitaria.

———. 1979. *Puerto Rico: Cien años de lucha política* (Puerto Rico: A hundred years of political struggle). Vol. 2, *Documentos varios, 1869–1936*. Río Piedras, P.R.: Editorial Universitaria.

———. 1988. *Orígenes y desarrollo de los partidos políticos en Puerto Rico, 1869–1980* (Origins and development of political parties in Puerto Rico). Río Piedras, P.R.: Editorial Edil.

"Brecha de 6 puntos entre Sila y Pesquera." 2000. *El Nuevo Día*, San Juan (June 7): 4–5.

Breyman, Steve. 1997. "Were the 1980s' Anti-Nuclear Weapons Movements New Social Movements?" *Peace and Change* 22, no. 3: 303–29.

Building the Navy's Bases in World War II (History of the Bureau of Yards and Docks and the Civil Engineer Corps, 1940–1946). 1947. Vol. 1. Washington, D.C.: Government Printing Office.

———. 1947. Vol. 2. Washington, D.C.: Government Printing Office.

Bulag, Uradyn E. 1998. *Nationalism and Hybridity in Mongolia*. Oxford: Clarendon Press.

"Buscan frenar las maniobras en Vieques." 1999. *El Nuevo Día*, San Juan (February 10): 52.

Bush, George. 1991. *Public Papers of the Presidents of the United States (George Bush, 1990)*. Vol. 2, *July 1 to December 31, 1990*. Washington, D.C.: Government Printing Office.

Cabán, Pedro A. 1999. *Constructing a Colonial People: Puerto Rico and the United States, 1898–1932*. Boulder, Colo.: Westview.

Cabranes, José A. 1978. "Citizenship and the American Empire: Notes on the Legislative History of the United States Citizenship of Puerto Ricans." *University of Pennsylvania Law Review* 127: 391–492.

Calderón, Sila M. 2000. "Renacer viequense." Editorial. *El Nuevo Día*, San Juan (October 23): 115.

"Calderón deplora los ataques al Arzobispo." 2000. *El Nuevo Día*, San Juan (March 11): 30.

Caquías Cruz, Sandra. 2000. "Manifestación y amenaza en el Fuerte Allen." *El Nuevo Día*, San Juan (May 5): 12.

Carr, Raymond. 1984. *Puerto Rico: A Colonial Experiment*. New York: Vintage Books.

Carrión, Juan M. 1993. "The National Question in Puerto Rico." In *Colonial Dilemma: Critical Perspectives on Contemporary Puerto Rico*, ed. Edwin Meléndez and Edgardo Meléndez. Boston: South End Press.

———. 1995. "Puerto Rican Nationalism and the Struggle for Independence." In *The National Question: Nationalism, Ethnic Conflict, and Self-Determination in the 20th Century*, ed. Berch Berberoglu. Philadelphia: Temple University Press.

———. 1999. "El imaginario nacional norteamericano y el nacionalismo puertorriqueño." *Revista de Ciencias Sociales* 7: 66–101.

Carroll, Henry K. 1975 [1899]. *Report on the Island of Porto Rico: Its Population, Civil Government, Commerce, Industries, Productions, Roads, Tariff, and Currency*. New York: Arno Press.

Carson, Clayborne. 1981. In *Struggle: SNCC and the Black Awakening of the 1960s*. Cambridge: Harvard University Press.

Casellas, Carmen T., and Pablo J. Trinidad. 2000. "Advierte S&P sobre el nacionalismo en la isla." *El Nuevo Día*, San Juan (May 17): 64.

Castro, Elliott. 2001. "El poder de Tito Trinidad." *Claridad*, Santurce, P.R. (May 18–24): 41.

Chatterjee, Partha. 1993. *The Nation and Its Fragments: Colonial and Postcolonial Histories*. Princeton, N.J.: Princeton University Press.

Chávez, Linda. 1991. *Out of the Barrio: Toward a New Politics of Hispanic Assimilation*. New York: Basic Books.

Chong, Dennis. 1991. *Collective Action and the Civil Rights Movement*. Chicago: University of Chicago Press.

"El choque por la gobernación." 1999. *El Nuevo Día*, San Juan (May 27): 4–6.

Clachar, Arlene. 1997. "Ethnolinguistic Identity and Spanish Proficiency in a Paradoxical Situation: The Case of Puerto Rican Return Migrants." *Journal of Multilingual and Multicultural Development* 18, no. 2: 107–24.

Colombani, Juanita. 1999. "En alerta los pescadores de Vieques." *El Nuevo Día*, San Juan (January 28): 28.

———. 1999. "Bomba cobra una vida civil en Vieques." *El Nuevo Día*, San Juan (April 20): 6.

———. 2000. "A descorrer el velo político." *El Nuevo Día*, San Juan (January 10): 32.

———. 2000. "Alegan maltrato los congresistas." *El Nuevo Día*, San Juan (May 5): 27.

———. 2000. "Reciben como héroes a los arrestados." *El Nuevo Día*, San Juan (May 5): 30.

———. 2000. "Sí judicial al voto presidencial isleño." *El Nuevo Día*, San Juan (July 21): 68.

———. 2000. "Abogados de la Marina juzgarán a desobedientes." *El Nuevo Día*, San Juan (July 27): 20.

———. 2000. "No federal al voto presidencial." *El Nuevo Día*, San Juan (August 9): 72.

———. 2000. "Agentes del FBI se 'disfrazan' de pipiolos en Lares." *El Nuevo Día*, San Juan (September 26): 36.

———. 2000. "'Falacia electoral' el voto federal para el Supremo." *El Nuevo Día*, San Juan (November 3): 4–5.

Colombani, Juanita, and Benjamín Torres Gotay. 1999. "Vinculan la decisión al caso sobre Instituto del Sida." *El Nuevo Día*, San Juan (June 2): 8.

Colón, David. 1999. "Tildan de tiranía la actitud de la flota militar." *El Nuevo Día*, San Juan (July 16): 5.

Colón, Wilma. 1999. "Desconfían del comité de Clinton." *El Nuevo Día*, San Juan (June 12): 5.

———. 2001. "Siempre lo soñé." Miss Universe Supplement. *El Nuevo Día*, San Juan (May 12): 2.

Colón Martínez, Noel. 1999. "Doña Norma está aprendiendo . . ." *Claridad*, Santurce, P.R. (May 28–June 3): 11.

Colón Morera, José J. 1993. "Economic Constraints and Political Choices: U.S. Congressional Deliberations on the Status of Puerto Rico, 1989–1991." Ph.D. diss., Boston University.

Congressional Record. 1900. (April 2) Vol. 33. Washington, D.C..

———. 1999. Vol. 145, no. 116 (September 9). Washington, D.C.

———. 1999. Vol. 145, no. 117 (September 10). Washington, D.C.

———. 1999, Vol. 145, no. 119 (September 14). Washington, D.C.

Connor, Walker. 1994. *Ethnonationalism: The Quest for Understanding*. Princeton, N.J.: Princeton University Press.

Cordero, Gerardo. 1998. "En marcha el diálogo del PIP." *El Nuevo Día*, San Juan (December 21): 26.

———. 1999. "Trazan su raya respecto a los presos políticos." *El Nuevo Día*, San Juan (July 5): 16.

Cotto, Cándida. 1999. "Necesario incrementar campaña pro presos políticos." *Claridad*, Santurce, P.R. (January 29–February 4): 7.

———. 1999. "Refutan a Romero sobre patriotas presos." *Claridad*, Santurce, P.R. (April 16–22): 6.

———. 1999. "Clara la identidad nacional del arzobispo." *Claridad*, Santurce, P.R. (May 14–20): 5.

Covas Quevedo, Waldo D. 2001. "Sentencian a Berríos a cuatro meses de cárcel." *El Nuevo Día*, San Juan (May 17): 17.

Craven, Wesley F., and James L. Cate, eds. 1983 [1948]. *The Army Air Forces in World War II*. Vol. 1, *Plans and Early Operations, January 1939 to August 1942*. Washington, D.C.: Office of Air Force History.

Cruz, Consuelo. 2000. "Identity and Persuasion: How Nations Remember Their Pasts and Make Their Futures." *World Politics* 52, no. 3: 275–312.

Cruz, José E. 1996. "Los puertorriqueños y la política en los Estados Unidos: Una evaluación preliminar." *Revista de Ciencias Sociales* 1: 86–111.

———. 1998. *Identity and Power: Puerto Rican Politics and the Challenge to Ethnicity*. Philadelphia: Temple University Press.

Danforth, Loring M. 1995. *The Macedonian Conflict: Ethnic Nationalism in a Transnational World*. Princeton, N.J.: Princeton University Press.

Daniel, Justin. 1999. "Identidad cultural e identidad política en Martinica y en Puerto Rico: Mitos y realidades." *Revista de Ciencias Sociales* 7: 33–65.

Dávila, Arlene M. 1997. *Sponsored Identities: Cultural Politics in Puerto Rico*. Philadelphia: Temple University Press.

———. 1999. "Latinizing Culture: Art, Museums, and the Politics of U.S. Multicultural Encompassment." *Cultural Anthropology* 14, no. 2: 180–202.

Dávila, Jesús. 1999. "Anda el penepé tras un candidato para Vieques." *El Nuevo Día*, San Juan (March 2): 26.

———. 1999. "Exige CRB acción de los estadistas." *El Nuevo Día*, San Juan (May 1): 25.
———. 1999. "Otra voz contra la marina." *El Nuevo Día*, San Juan (May 29): 4.
———. 1999. "Perdón senatorial a Berríos." *El Nuevo Día*, San Juan (June 2): 30.
Dawes, Robyn M., Alphons van de Kragt, and John M. Orbell. 1990. "Cooperation for the Benefit of Us—Not Me, or My Conscience." In *Beyond Self-Interest*, ed. Jane J. Mansbridge. Chicago: University of Chicago Press.
Delgado, José A. 1999. "Cita de status en el Senado." *El Nuevo Día*, San Juan (May 3): 27.
———. 1999. "Sin opción la Marina." *El Nuevo Día*, San Juan (June 15): 4.
———. 2000. "Culpa Clinton al status político." *El Nuevo Día*, San Juan (February 17): 5.
———. 2000. "Boston anula la decisión de Pieras." *El Nuevo Día*, San Juan (October 14): 30.
———. 2000. "Visto bueno del Presidente." *El Nuevo Día*, San Juan (October 31): 4.
Delgado Cintrón, Carmelo. 1989. *Culebra y la Marina de Estados Unidos* (Culebra and the United States Navy). Río Piedras, P.R.: Editorial Edil.
"Desfile podría tornarse en acto de protesta." 2000. *El diario/La prensa*, New York (May 2): 13.
Díaz-Quiñones, Arcadio. 1993. *La memoria rota: Ensayos sobre cultura y política* (The broken memory: Essays on culture and politics). Río Piedras, P.R.: Ediciones Huracán.
Díaz-Stevens, Ana M. 1996. "Aspects of Puerto Rican Religious Experience: A Sociohistoric Overview." In *Latinos in New York: Communities in Transition*, ed. Gabriel Haslip-Viera and Sherrie L. Baver. Notre Dame, Ind.: University of Notre Dame Press.
Dooley, Edwin L. 1999. "Wartime San Juan, Puerto Rico: The Forgotten American Home Front, 1941–1945." *Journal of Military History* 63, no. 4: 921–38.
Downs, Anthony. 1957. *An Economic Theory of Democracy*. New York: Harper Collins.
Duany, Jorge. 2000. "Nation on the Move: The Construction of Cultural Identities in Puerto Rico and the Diaspora." *American Ethnologist* 29, no. 1: 5–30.
Duchacek, Ivo D. 1977. "Antagonistic Cooperation: Territorial and Ethnic Communities." *Publius* 7, no. 4: 3–29.
Duchesne, Juan, Chloé Georas, Ramón Grosfoguel, Agustín Lao, Frances Negrón, Pedro A. Rivera, and Aurea M. Sotomayor. 1997. "La estadidad desde una perspectiva democrática radical." *Diálogo* (February): 30–31.
Duchesne, Juan, Chloé Georas, Ramón Grosfoguel, Agustín Lao, and Pedro A. Rivera. 1999. "Algunas tesis democráticas ante el plebiscito de 1998." *Diálogo* (March): 38–39.
Early, James. 1998. "An African American-Puerto Rican Connection—An Auto-Bio-Memory Sketch of Political Development and Activism." In *The Puerto*

Rican Movement: Voices from the Diaspora, ed. Andrés Torres and José Velázquez. Philadelphia: Temple University Press.

Eisenhower, Dwight D. 1961. *Public Papers of the Presidents of the United States (Dwight D. Eisenhower, 1960–61)*. Washington, D.C.: Government Printing Office.

Eriksen, Thomas H. 1993. *Ethnicity and Nationalism: Anthropological Perspectives*. London: Pluto Press.

"Escaso apoyo a que la Marina siga en Vieques." 2000. *El Nuevo Día*, San Juan (March 7): 5–6.

Escrutinio Elecciones Generales 1996 (Resultados por municipio). (General election tally 1996 [Results by municipality]). 1996. San Juan: Comisión Estatal de Elecciones.

Esman, Milton J. 1986. "Diasporas and International Relations." In *Modern Diasporas in International Politics*, ed. Gabriel Sheffer. New York: St. Martin's Press.

Essoyan, Susan. 1990. "Hawaiians Win Halt to Island Bombing." *Los Angeles Times* (October 23): A19.

Estades, Rosa. 1996. "Symbolic Unity: The Puerto Rican Day Parade." In *Historical Perspectives on Puerto Rican Survival in the United States*, ed. Clara E. Rodríguez and Virginia Sánchez Korrol. Princeton, N.J.: Markus Wiener.

Estades Font, María E. 1988. *La presencia militar de Estados Unidos en Puerto Rico, 1898–1918: Intereses estratégicos y dominación colonial* (The United States military presence in Puerto Rico, 1898–1918: Strategic interests and colonial domination). Río Piedras, P.R.: Ediciones Huracán.

Estades Santaliz, Amelia. 1999. "Sorprendido por el giro del escándalo del sida." *El Nuevo Día*, San Juan (February 27): 4.

———. 1999. "La lucha de Vieques persiste a todo vapor." *El Nuevo Día*, San Juan (August 11): 29.

———. 1999. "Repudio a las condiciones del indulto." *El Nuevo Día*, San Juan (August 12): 33.

———. 1999. "Los nesecitamos luchando en la calle." *El Nuevo Día*, San Juan (August 13): 32.

———. 1999. "Gore apoya que se vaya la Marina." *El Nuevo Día*, San Juan (August 20): 4.

Estrada, Wilfredo. 2000. "Vieques y la sanidad del alma borincana." Editorial. *El Nuevo Día*, San Juan (August 9): 138.

Estrada Resto, Nilka. 1999. "Protestan Vieques y Culebra contra puertos." *El Nuevo Día*, San Juan (January 9): 22.

———. 1999. "Augura Noriega que habrá más acusados." *El Nuevo Día*, San Juan (March 11): 5.

———. 1999. "Cautela ante invitación de Rosselló." *El Nuevo Día*, San Juan (April 30): 30.

———. 1999. "Entre dos aguas Rosselló ante las protestas." *El Nuevo Día*, San Juan (May 1): 6.
———. 1999. "Maniobra sin garantía." *El Nuevo Día*, San Juan (May 13): 8.
———. 1999. "Sólo dos términos." *El Nuevo Día*, San Juan (June 2): 4.
———. 1999. "En la 'lista corta' de los favoritos de Gore." *El Nuevo Día*, San Juan (June 2): 24.
———. 1999. "Decepción con el panel creado por Clinton." *El Nuevo Día*, San Juan (June 15): 5.
———. 1999. "Defiende el panel de allá." *El Nuevo Día*, San Juan (June 16): 5.
———. 1999. "¡Basta ya! Unánime a la Marina." *El Nuevo Día*, San Juan (July 1): 4.
———. 1999. "'Dañino' el debate sobre la clemencia." *El Nuevo Día*, San Juan (September 18): 16–17.
———. 1999. "Nada de bombardeo, insiste Rosselló." *El Nuevo Día*, San Juan (September 23): 5.
———. 1999. "'Sí' de Rosselló a un proyecto de independencia." *El Nuevo Díá*, San Juan (September 23): 34.
———. 1999. "Toman con pinzas en el PNP la idea de la marcha." *El Nuevo Día*, San Juan (September 24): 30.
———. 1999. "La Fortaleza censura el reinicio de los bombardeos." *El Nuevo Día*, San Juan (October 19): 6.
———. 1999. "No al plan de Clinton." *El Nuevo Día*, San Juan (December 4): 5.
———. 1999. "A pagar por las persecuciones." *El Nuevo Día*, San Juan (December 15): 4.
———. 2000. "Detalla Rosselló la directriz presidencial." *El Nuevo Día*, San Juan (February 2): 8.
———. 2000. "Sólo en Vieques el referendum." *El Nuevo Día*, San Juan (February 4): 4.
———. 2000. "Gobernador rechaza una consulta con opción de cero bombardeo." *El Nuevo Día*, San Juan (February 10): 6.
———. 2000. "Reitera el PIP escribir 'Paz para Vieques' en la papeleta." *El Nuevo Día*, San Juan (September 14): 30.
Falcón, Angelo. 1984. "A History of Puerto Rican Politics in New York City: 1860s to 1945." In *Puerto Rican Politics in Urban America*, ed. James Jennings and Monte Rivera. Westport, Conn.: Greenwood Press.
———. 1996. "Puerto Ricans in Postliberal New York: The 1992 Presidential Election." In *Ethnic Ironies: Latino Politics in the 1992 Elections*, ed. Rodolfo O. de la Garza and Louis DeSipio. Boulder, Colo.: Westview.
Fallon, Joseph E. 1991. "Federal Policy and U.S. Territories: The Political Restructuring of the United States of America." *Pacific Affairs* 64, no. 1: 23–41.
Fanon, Frantz. 1963. *The Wretched of the Earth*. Translated by Constance Farrington. New York: Grove Press.

Farinacci, Jorge. 2001. "Nueva York: Se intensifica la solidaridad." Editorial. *Claridad*, Santurce, P.R. (May 18–24): 10.

Feder, Don. 1998. "No Statehood for Caribbean Dogpatch." Editorial. *Boston Herald* (November 30): 27.

Fernández, Ismael. 1999. "Presos, Vieques y la estadidad." Editorial. *El Nuevo Día*, San Juan (September 13): 99.

———. 2000. "Jugando con fuego." Editorial. *El Nuevo Día*, San Juan (February 14): 95.

———. 2000. "Dejen a Vieques en paz." Editorial. *El Nuevo Día*, San Juan (May 9): 133.

———. 2000. "Fracaso de la melonada." Editorial. *El Nuevo Día*, San Juan (October 17): 117.

Fernández, Ronald. 1987. *Los Macheteros: The Wells Fargo Robbery and the Struggle for Puerto Rican Independence*. New York: Prentice Hall.

Fernós Isern, Antonio. 1988. *Estado Libre Asociado de Puerto Rico: Antecedentes, creación y desarrollo hasta la época presente* (Commonwealth of Puerto Rico: Background, creation and development until the present period). 2nd ed. Río Piedras, P.R.: Editorial de la Universidad de Puerto Rico.

Ferraiuoli Suárez, Bibiana. 1999. "Testifica sobre su cáncer la Isla Nena." *El Nuevo Día*, San Juan (February 20): 7.

———. 1999. "Nube negra en Vieques." *El Nuevo Día*, San Juan (February 20): 8.

———. 1999. "Trae $100 millones en beneficios el Ejército Sur." *El Nuevo Día*, San Juan (February 26): 18.

———. 1999. "Acusa Vieques a la Marina por su sufrimiento." *El Nuevo Día*, San Juan (March 4): 42.

———. 1999. "Manuela a favor de la salida." *El Nuevo Día*, San Juan (April 21): 6.

Ferrao, Luis A. 1990. *Pedro Albizu Campos y el nacionalismo puertorriqueño* (Pedro Albizu Campos and Puerto Rican nationalism). Río Piedras, P.R.: Editorial Cultural.

———. 1993. "Nacionalismo, hispanismo y élite intelectual en el Puerto Rico de la década de 1930." In *Del nacionalismo al populismo: Cultura y política en Puerto Rico* (From nationalism to populism: Culture and politics in Puerto Rico), ed. Silvia Alvarez-Curbelo and María E. Rodríguez Castro. Río Piedras, P.R.: Ediciones Huracán.

Ferrer, Ada. 1999. *Insurgent Cuba: Race, Nation, and Revolution, 1868–1898*. Chapel Hill: University of North Carolina Press.

Figueroa, Loida. 1979. *Breve historia de Puerto Rico: Desde sus comienzos hasta 1892* (Brief history of Puerto Rico: From its beginnings until 1892). 6th rev. ed. Vol. 1. Río Piedras, P.R.: Editorial Edil.

Flores, Juan. 1993. *Divided Borders: Essays on Puerto Rican Identity*. Houston: Arte Público Press.

———. 1999. "Pan-Latino/Trans-Latino." In *Identities on the Move: Transnational Processes in North America and the Caribbean Basin*, ed. Liliana R. Goldin. Albany, N.Y.: Institute for Mesoamerican Studies, University at Albany.

———. 2000. *From Bomba to Hip Hop: Puerto Rican Culture and Latino Identity*. New York: Columbia University Press.

Frambes-Buxeda, Aline. 1980. "El papel de los grupos políticos y características de la cultural política." *Homines* 4, no. 2: 173–81.

———. 1993. "Albizu, un boricua en su laberinto." In *Huracán del Caribe: Vida y obra del insigne puertorriqueño, Don Pedro Albizu Campos* (Hurricane in the Caribbean: Life and work of the eminent Puerto Rican, Pedro Albizu Campos), ed. Aline Frambes-Buxeda. San Juan: Editorial Libros Homines, Universidad Interamericana de Puerto Rico.

Fredrickson, George M. 2000. *The Comparative Imagination: On the History of Racism, Nationalism, and Social Movements*. Berkeley: University of California Press.

García, Gervasio L., and Angel G. Quintero Rivera. 1982. *Desafío y solidadidad: Breve historia del movimiento obrero puertorriqueño* (Defiance and solidarity: Brief history of the Puerto Rican workers movement). Río Piedras, P.R.: Ediciones Huracán.

García, Pepo. 1999. "En la recta final el etudio de la comisión." *El Nuevo Día*, San Juan (June 22): 6.

———. 1999. "Afrenta contra el pueblo viequense." *El Nuevo Día*, San Juan (September 24): 6.

———. 1999. "Presencia espiritual del Arzobispo." *El Nuevo Día*, San Juan (September 25): 6.

———. 2000. "Rompe el consenso la oferta aceptada." *El Nuevo Día*, San Juan (February 1): 4.

———. 2001. "Preocupa a CRB lo que se palpa en los EE.UU." *El Nuevo Día*, San Juan (May 9): 42.

García, Pepo, and Camile Roldán. 2000. "Líderes cristianos reaccionan." *El Nuevo Día*, San Juan (February 10): 6.

García Muñiz, Humberto. 1991. "U.S. Military Installations in Puerto Rico: An Essay on Their Role and Purpose." *Caribbean Studies* 23, nos. 3–4: 79–97.

García San Inocencio, Víctor. 1999. "La hora de Vieques." Editorial. *El Nuevo Día*, San Juan (January 19): 55.

Gellner, Ernest. 1983. *Nations and Nationalism*. Ithaca, N.Y.: Cornell University Press.

Ghigliotty, Julio. 1999. "Voto legislativo contra la Marina." *El Nuevo Día*, San Juan (April 21): 32.

———. 1999. "Protesta el PIP en Sabana Seca." *El Nuevo Día*, San Juan (April 30): 16.

———. 1999. "En pie la agenda de la Marina." *El Nuevo Día*, San Juan (June 22): 5.

———. 1999. "Asomo el proverbial divisionismo en la marcha." *El Nuevo Día*, San Juan (July 1): 35.
———. 1999. "Clamor más allá de líneas partidistas." *El Nuevo Día*, San Juan (July 5): 5.
———. 1999. "David Sanes murió por 'error humano.'" *El Nuevo Día*, San Juan (August 3): 4.
———. 1999. "Rosselló aplaude de nuevo." *El Nuevo Día*, San Juan (August 13): 28.
———. 1999. "Los ex presos se aguzan y optan por no asistir." *El Nuevo Día*, San Juan (September 24): 26–27.
———. 1999. "Vieques domina el Grito de Lares." *El Nuevo Día*, San Juan (September 24): 26.
———. 1999. "Apoyan a Vieques guardando la distancia." *El Nuevo Día*, San Juan (November 29): 22.
———. 2000. "Vieques como protagonista." *El Nuevo Día*, San Juan (February 1): 22.
———. 2001. "Gesta reparar las malas relaciones con los EE.UU." *El Nuevo Día*, San Juan (May 18): 42.
Ginorio, Angela B. 1987. "Puerto Rican Ethnicity and Conflict." In *Ethnic Conflict: International Perspectives*, ed. Jerry Boucher, Dan Landis, and Karen Arnold Clark. Beverly Hills, Calif.: Sage Publications.
Glazer, Nathan, and Daniel P. Moynihan. 1970. *Beyond the Melting Pot: The Negroes, Puerto Ricans, Jews, Italians and Irish of New York City*. 2nd ed. Cambridge: MIT Press.
Glick Schiller, Nina. 1999. "Who Are These Guys? A Transnational Reading of the U.S. Immigrant Experience." In *Identities on the Move: Transnational Processes in North America and the Caribbean Basin*, ed. Liliana R. Goldin. Albany, N.Y.: Institute for Mesoamerican Studies, University at Albany.
Go, Julian. 2000. "Chains of Empire, Projects of State: Political Education and U.S. Colonial Rule in Puerto Rico and the Philippines." *Comparative Study of Society and History* 42, no. 2: 333–62.
Godreau-Santiago, Isar P. 1999. "Missing the Mix: San Antón and the Racial Dynamics of 'Nationalism' in Puerto Rico." Ph.D. diss., University of California, Santa Cruz.
Goldstone, Jack A. 1998. "The Soviet Union: Revolution and Transformation." In *Elites, Crises, and the Origin of Regimes*, ed. Mattei Dogan and John Higley. Lanham, Md.: Rowman and Littlefield.
González, Gilbert G. 1999. *Mexican Consuls and Labor Organizing: Imperial Politics in the American Southwest*. Austin: University of Texas Press.
González, José L. 1993. *Puerto Rico: The Four-Storeyed Country and Other Essays*. Translated by Gerald Guinness. Princeton, N.J.: Princeton University Press.
González, Juan, and Kenneth R. Bazinet. 1999. "Clemency for Puerto Ricans." *Daily News*, New York (August 12): 10.
González, Manuel de J. 1999. "Adónde se van es asunto de ellos." *Claridad*, Santurce, P.R. (May 14–20): 12.

———. 2000. "La nación por la Quinta Avenida." *Claridad*, Santurce, P.R. (June 16–20): 12.

———. 2001. "En acción la inteligencia de la Marina." *Claridad*, Santurce, P.R. (April 13–19): 12.

González Nieves, Roberto O. 1984. "Ecological, Ethnic and Cultural Factors of Church Practice in an Urban Roman Catholic Church." Ph.D. diss., Fordham University.

González Vales, Luis. 1983. "The Challenge to Colonialism." In *Puerto Rico: A Political and Cultural History*, ed. Arturo Morales Carrión. New York: W. W. Norton.

Gopin, Marc. 1997. "Religion, Violence, and Conflict Resolution." *Peace and Change* 22, no. 1: 1–31.

Gorenburg, Dmitry. 2000. "Not with One Voice: An Explanation of Intragroup Variation in Nationalist Sentiment." *World Politics* 53, no. 1: 115–42.

Gottlieb, Gidon. 1993. *Nation Against State: A New Approach to Ethnic Conflicts and the Decline of Sovereignty*. New York: Council on Foreign Relations Press.

Gould, Lyman J. 1975. *La ley Foraker: Raíces de la política colonial de los Estados Unidos* (The Foraker Act: Roots of United States colonial policy). 2nd ed. Río Piedras, P.R.: Editorial Universitaria.

Green, Kevin P. 2001. "Nuestra gran responsabilidad." Editorial. *El Nuevo Día*, San Juan (February 24): 112.

———. 2001. "Algo más que un cambio en un mapa." Editorial. *El Nuevo Día*, San Juan (May 15): 107.

Greenberg, Anna. 2000. "The Church and the Revitalization of Politics and Community." *Political Science Quarterly* 115, no. 3: 377–94.

Greenfeld, Liah. 1992. *Nationalism: Five Roads to Modernity*. Cambridge: Harvard University Press.

Grosfoguel, Ramón. 1997. "The Divorce of Nationalist Discourses from the Puerto Rican People: A Sociohistorical Perspective." In *Puerto Rican Jam: Rethinking Colonialism and Nationalism*, ed. Frances Negrón-Muntaner and Ramón Grosfoguel. Minneapolis: University of Minnesota Press.

———. 2000. "David Sanes y la puertorriqueñidad." Editorial. *El Nuevo Día*, San Juan (April 22): 112.

Grusky, Sara. 1991. "The U.S. Navy and Vieques, Puerto Rico: Conflict and Coexistence." *Canadian Journal of Latin American and Caribbean Studies* 16, no. 31: 105–22.

———. 1992. "The Navy as Social Provider in Vieques, Puerto Rico." *Armed Forces and Society* 18, no. 2: 215–30.

Guerra, Lillian. 1998. *Popular Expression and National Identity in Puerto Rico: The Struggle for Self, Community, and Nation*. Gainesville: University Press of Florida.

Guss, David. 2000. *The Festive State: Race, Ethnicity, and Nationalism as Cultural Performance*. Berkeley: University of California Press.

Gutiérrez, David G. 1995. *Walls and Mirrors: Mexican Americans, Mexican Immigrants, and the Politics of Ethnicity.* Berkeley: University of California Press.

Gutiérrez Olmedo, Luis. 1998. "Necesitamos reconciliación entre los puertorriqueños." *Claridad*, Santurce, P.R. (October 2–8): 32–33.

Guzmán, Pablo Y. 1996. "Puerto Rican Barrio Politics in the United States." In *Historical Perspectives on Puerto Rican Survival in the United States*, ed. Clara E. Rodríguez and Virginia Sánchez Korrol. Princeton, N.J.: Markus Wiener.

———. 1998. "La Vida Pura: A Lord of the Barrio." In *The Puerto Rican Movement: Voices from the Diaspora*, ed. Andrés Torres and José Velázquez. Philadelphia: Temple University Press.

Hamilton, Alexander, James Madison, and John Jay. 1961 [1788]. *The Federalist Papers*. Edited by Clinton Rossiter. New York: NAL Penguin.

Handler, Richard. 1988. *Nationalism and the Politics of Culture in Quebec*. Madison: University of Wisconsin Press.

Hardin, Russell. 1995. *One for All: The Logic of Group Conflict*. Princeton, N.J.: Princeton University Press.

Hardy-Fanta, Carol. 1993. *Latina Politics, Latino Politics: Gender, Culture, and Political Participation in Boston*. Philadelphia: Temple University Press.

Haslip-Viera, Gabriel. 1996. "The Evolution of the Latino Community in New York City: Early Nineteenth Century to the Present." In *Latinos in New York: Communities in Transition*, ed. Gabriel Haslip-Viera and Sherrie L. Baver. Notre Dame, Ind.: University of Notre Dame Press.

"Hawaii Gets Another Island." 1993. *New York Times* (October 24): 20.

Hechter, Michael. 1975. *Internal Colonialism: The Celtic Fringe in British National Development, 1536–1966*. Berkeley: University of California Press.

———. 2000. *Containing Nationalism*. New York: Oxford University Press.

Hernández, José. 1996. "The Identity and Culture of Latino College Students." In *Latinos in New York: Communities in Transition*, ed. Gabriel Haslip-Viera and Sherrie L. Baver. Notre Dame, Ind.: University of Notre Dame Press.

Hernández Colón, Rafael. 1999. "Presos políticos en U.S.A." Editorial. *El Nuevo Día*, San Juan (September 8): 133.

Hobsbawm, Eric. 1983. "Mass Producing Tradition: Europe, 1870–1914." In *The Invention of Tradition*, ed. Eric Hobsbawm and Terence Ranger. Cambridge: Cambridge University Press.

Huntington, Samuel P. 1968. *Political Order in Changing Societies*. New Haven, Conn.: Yale University Press.

"Indigna el 'robo' de agua por la Marina." 1999. *El Nuevo Día*, San Juan (July 8): 4.

"Intocable el líder del PIP." 1999. *El Nuevo Día*, San Juan (May 26): 38.

Ireland, Gordon. 1941. *Boundaries, Possessions, and Conflicts in Central and North America and the Caribbean*. Cambridge: Harvard University Press.

Irizarry Mora, Edwin. 1999. "Agenda para Vieques." Editorial. *El Nuevo Día*, San Juan (April 10): 108.

Janer, Zilkia. 1998. "Colonial Nationalism: The Nation Building Literary Field and Subaltern Intellectuals in Puerto Rico (1948–1952)." Ph.D. diss., Duke University.

Jennings, James. 1977. *Puerto Rican Politics in New York City*. Washington, D.C.: University Press of America.

———. 1984. "Introduction: The Emergence of Puerto Rican Electoral Activities in Urban America." In *Puerto Rican Politics in Urban America*, ed. James Jennings and Monte Rivera. Westport, Conn.: Greenwood Press.

Jiménez de Wagenheim, Olga. 1993. *Puerto Rico's Revolt for Independence: El Grito de Lares*. Princeton, N.J.: Markus Wiener.

Jones-Correa, Michael. 1998. *Between Two Nations: The Political Predicament of Latinos in New York City*. Ithaca, N.Y.: Cornell University Press.

Kaufmann, Eric. 1999. "American Exceptionalism Reconsidered: Anglo-Saxon Ethnogenesis in the 'Universal' Nation, 1776–1850." *Journal of American Studies* 33, no. 3: 437–57.

———. 2000. "Ethnic or Civic Nation?: Theorizing the American Case." *Canadian Review of Studies in Nationalism* 27: 133–54.

Kelly, Caroline, and John Kelly. 1994. "Who Gets Involved in Collective Action?: Social Psychological Determinants of Individual Participation in Trade Unions." *Human Relations* 47, no. 1: 63–88.

Kryukov, Michael V. 1996. "Self-determination from Marx to Mao." *Ethnic and Racial Studies* 19, no. 2: 352–78.

Lafaye, Jacques. 1976. *Quetzalcóatl and Guadalupe: The Formation of Mexican National Consciousness, 1531–1813*. Translated by Benjamin Keen. Chicago: University of Chicago Press.

Laitin, David D. 1986. *Hegemony and Culture: Politics and Religious Change among the Yorubas*. Chicago: University of Chicago Press.

———. 1999. "National Revivals and Violence." In *Critical Comparisons in Politics and Culture*, ed. John R. Bowen and Roger Petersen. Cambridge: Cambridge University Press.

Landau, Jacob M. 1986. "Diaspora and Language." In *Modern Diasporas in International Politics*, ed. Gabriel Sheffer. New York: St. Martin's Press.

Langhorne, Elizabeth. 1987. *Vieques: History of a Small Island*. Vieques, P.R.: Vieques Conservation and Historical Trust.

Langley, Lester D. 1985. "Roosevelt Roads, Puerto Rico, U.S. Naval Base, 1941–." In *United States Navy and Marine Corps Bases, Overseas*, ed. Paolo E. Coletta. Westport, Conn.: Greenwood Press.

Lao, Agustín. 1997. "Islands at the Crossroads: Puerto Ricanness Traveling Between the Translocal Nation and the Global City." In *Puerto Rican Jam: Rethinking Colonialism and Nationalism*, ed. Frances Negrón-Muntaner and Ramón Grosfoguel. Minneapolis: University of Minnesota Press.

Laponce, Jean A. 1987. *Languages and Their Territories*. Translated by Anthony Martin-Sperry. Toronto: University of Toronto Press.

Lebrón Velázquez, José R. 2000. "La marcha por la paz." Editorial. *El Nuevo Día*, San Juan (February 19): 129.

Leibowitz, Arnold H. 1989. *Defining Status: A Comprehensive Analysis of United States Territorial Relations*. Dordrecht, Netherlands: Martinus Nijhoff.

Lewis, Gordon. 1974. *Notes on the Puerto Rican Revolution: An Essay on American Dominance and Caribbean Resistance*. New York: Monthly Review Press.

Lichbach, Mark I. 1994. "What Makes Rational Peasants Revolutionary? Dilemmas, Paradox, and Irony in Peasant Collective Action." *World Politics* 46, no. 3: 383–418.

Lipset, Seymour M. 1990. *Continental Divide: The Values and Institutions of the United States and Canada*. London: Routledge.

Lleras Silva, Sylvia. 1999. "Defensa nacional mediante la resistencia civil." *Claridad*, Santurce, P.R. (May 14–20): 7.

———. 1999. "Defensa nacional mediante la resistencia civil II." *Claridad*, Santurce, P.R. (May 21–27): 7.

"Llevarían a la ONU el informe sobre Vieques." 1999. *El Nuevo Día*, San Juan (July 6): 5.

"Lo bueno y lo malo de tener bases militares en la isla." 1999. *El Nuevo Día*, San Juan (August 24): 5–6.

"Los 15 prisioneros." 1999. *El Nuevo Día*, San Juan (August 13): 30.

Lucas, Isidro. 1984. "Puerto Rican Politics in Chicago." In *Puerto Rican Politics in Urban America*, ed. James Jennings and Monte Rivera. Westport, Conn.: Greenwood Press.

Luciano, María J. 1999. "Lazo político al Instituto del Sida." *El Nuevo Día*, San Juan (March 12): 6.

———. 2000. "Calderón se lleva la mejor parte." *El Nuevo Día*, San Juan (October 19): 31.

"Luis A. Ferré: El defensor de la estadidad." 1999. *El diario/La prensa*. Special Supplement. New York (June 13): 8.

Lustick, Ian S. 1993. *Unsettled States, Disputed Lands: Britain and Ireland, France and Algeria, Israel and the West Bank-Gaza*. Ithaca, N.Y.: Cornell University Press.

Mahajani, Usha. 1971. *Philippine Nationalism: External Challenge and Filipino Response, 1565–1946*. St. Lucia, Australia: University of Queensland Press.

Mahan, Alfred T. 1975. *Letters and Papers of Alfred Thayer Mahan*. Vol. 1, *1847–1889*. Edited by Robert Seager and Doris D. Maguire. Annapolis, Md.: Naval Institute Press.

———. 1975. *Letters and Papers of Alfred Thayer Mahan*. Vol. 3, *1902–1914*. Edited by Robert Seager and Doris D. Maguire. Annapolis, Md.: Naval Institute Press.

Maldonado Arrigoitía, Wilma. 2000. "El paro llegó hasta Arecibo." *El Nuevo Día*, San Juan (May 5): 10.

Maldonado-Denis, Manuel. 1972. *Puerto Rico: A Socio-Historic Interpretation*. Translated by Elena Vialo. New York: Vintage Books.

———. 1976. "Prospects for Latin American Nationalism: The Case of Puerto Rico." *Latin American Perspectives* 3, no. 3: 36–45.

———. 1980 [1976]. *The Emigration Dialectic: Puerto Rico and the USA*. New York: International Publishers.

Mallon, Florencia E. 1995. *Peasant and Nation: The Making of Postcolonial Mexico and Peru*. Berkeley: University of California Press.

"Manifestación paralela de la Alizanza de Mujeres." 1999. *El Nuevo Día*, San Juan (June 21): 4.

"Marcha a favor del retiro de la Marina de Vieques." 1999. *El diario/La prensa*, New York (June 8): 7.

Mari Bras, Juan. 1984. *El independentismo en Puerto Rico: Su pasado, su presente y su porvenir* (The Independence Movement in Puerto Rico: Its past, present, and future). San Juan: Editorial CEPA.

Mari Narváez, Mari. 1999. "Rubén Berríos ve ventajas para Vieques." *Claridad*, Santurce, P.R. (July 2–8): 6.

Marquez, Benjamin, and James Jennings. 2000. "Representation by Other Means: Mexican American and Puerto Rican Social Movement Organizations." *Political Science and Politics* 23, no. 3: 541–46.

Martell, Esperanza. 1998. "In the Belly of the Beast: Beyond Survival." In *The Puerto Rican Movement: Voices from the Diaspora*, ed. Andrés Torres and José E. Velázquez. Philadelphia: Temple University Press.

Martínez, Andrea. 1999. "Freno a las maniobras." *El Nuevo Día*, San Juan (April 21): 5.

McCaffrey, Katherine T. 1998. "Forging Solidarity: Politics, Protest, and the Vieques Support Network." In *The Puerto Rican Movement: Voices from the Diaspora*, ed. Andrés Torres and José E. Velázquez. Philadelphia: Temple University Press.

———. 1999. "Culture, Power and Struggle: Anti-Military Protest in Vieques, Puerto Rico." Ph.D. diss., City University of New York.

McCoy, Kevin. 1999. "FALN Prisoners a Cause Celebre." *Daily News*, New York (August 18): 26.

McQuillan, Alice. 1999. "Terror Act an Explosive Issue '80s Cops Decry Move to Free 16." *Daily News*, New York (August 18): 27.

Meléndez, Edgardo. 1991. "The Politics of Puerto Rico's Plebiscite." *Caribbean Studies* 24: 117–50.

———. 1993. *Movimiento anexionista en Puerto Rico* (Annexationist movement in Puerto Rico). Río Piedras, P.R.: Editorial de la Universidad de Puerto Rico.

———. 1993. "Colonialism, Citizenship, and Contemporary Statehood." In *Colonial Dilemma: Critical Perspectives on Contemporary Puerto Rico*, ed. Edwin Meléndez and Edgardo Meléndez. Boston: South End Press.

———. 1995. "El estudio de los partidos políticos en Puerto Rico." *Revista de Ciencias Sociales* 30, nos. 3–4: 51–100.

Meléndez López, Arturo. 1989. *La batalla de Vieques* (The battle of Vieques). Río Piedras, P.R.: Editorial Edil.

"Mensaje del nuevo arzobispo." 1999. *El Visitante: Semanario católico de Puerto Rico*, San Juan (April 10): 1–2.

Merrill, Christopher. 1994. "Kaho'olawe Lives! A Little Justice in Hawai'i." *Nation* 259, no. 7 (September 5–12): 235–36.

Miles, William F. S. 1998. *Bridging Mental Boundaries in a Postcolonial Microcosm: Identity and Development in Vanuatu*. Honolulu: University of Hawai'i Press.

"Military Still Wants Access to Hawaiian Island." 1990. *New York Times* (December 20): B20.

Millar, Thomas B. 1984. ed. *Current International Treaties*. New York: New York University Press.

Mills, C. Wright. 1959. *The Power Elite*. New York: Oxford University Press.

Montano, Agnes J. 1999. "Multitudinario el recibimiento." *El Nuevo Día*, San Juan (September 11): 62.

Monteverde-Torres, Elliot, and Tania M. Frontera. 2000. "Puertorriqueños en EEUU también luchan contra la Marina en Vieques." Editorial. *El diario/La prensa*, New York (April 3): 18.

Morales, Ed. 1999. "El Grito de Lares." *Nation* 269, no. 13 (October 25): 9.

Morales, Iris. 1998. "¡Palante, Siempre Palante! (The Young Lords)." In *The Puerto Rican Movement: Voices from the Diaspora*, ed. Andrés Torres and José Velázquez. Philadelphia: Temple University Press.

Morales Meléndez, Benjamín. 1999. "Aglutina sus huestes el PIP." *El Nuevo Día*, San Juan (June 21): 5.

Morín, José L. 2000. "Indigenous Hawaiians Under Statehood: Lessons for Puerto Rico." *Centro Journal* 11, no. 2: 5–25.

Morris, Aldon D. 1993. "Birmingham Confrontation Reconsidered: An Analysis of the Dynamics and Tactics of Mobilization." *American Sociological Review* 54, no. 4: 621–36.

Morris, Nancy. 1995. *Puerto Rico: Culture, Politics, and Identity*. Westport, Conn.: Praeger.

Motley, James B. 1983. *U.S. Strategy to Counter Domestic Political Terrorism*. National Security Affairs Monograph Series 83–2. Washington, D.C.: National Defense University Press.

Movimiento Ecuménico Nacional de Puerto Rico. 1981. *Vieques and Christians*. Bayamón, P.R.: Movimiento Ecuménico Nacional de Puerto Rico.

———. 1984. "*. . . ni pa' coger impulso*": *Testimonio de mujeres de Vieques* (". . . not even to build up momentum": Women's testimony in Vieques). Bayamón, P.R.: Movimiento Ecuménico Nacional de Puerto Rico.

Moynihan, Daniel P. 1993. *Pandaemonium: Ethnicity in International Politics.* New York: Oxford University Press.

Mulero, Leonor. 1999. "Hastert necesita empaparse del asunto." *El Nuevo Día*, San Juan (May 1): 6.

———. 1999. "Considera Hastert que el plebiscito apoyó al ELA." *El Nuevo Día*, San Juan (May 1): 25.

———. 1999. "'Colgado' el status por el Senado." *El Nuevo Día*, San Juan (May 7): 27.

———. 1999. "Vista senatorial a la Marina." *El Nuevo Día*, San Juan (May 7): 28.

———. 1999. "Llamado al consenso para Vieques." *El Nuevo Día*, San Juan (May 8): 26.

———. 1999. "Recaban apoyo congresional." *El Nuevo Día*, San Juan (May 8): 26.

———. 1999. "Exigen en el Senado federal la salida de la Marina." *El Nuevo Día*, San Juan (May 10): 30.

———. 1999. "Temen más errores mortales." *El Nuevo Día*, San Juan (May 10): 30.

———. 1999. "Petición de amnistía incondicional." *El Nuevo Día*, San Juan (May 12): 28.

———. 1999. "La Marina no da un paso atrás." *El Nuevo Día*, San Juan (May 12): 29.

———. 1999. "Negociación antes que audiencias." *El Nuevo Día*, San Juan (May 13): 28.

———. 1999. "Cabildea la Marina por Vieques." *El Nuevo Día*, San Juan (May 13): 29.

———. 1999. "Decide la Marina seguir con los bombardeos." *El Nuevo Día*, San Juan (May 15): 5.

———. 1999. "Destaca CRB la defensa común." *El Nuevo Día*, San Juan (May 18): 34.

———. 1999. "Fuera de base la Marina." *El Nuevo Día*, San Juan (May 21): 4.

———. 1999. "No perdona al Comisionado." *El Nuevo Día*, San Juan (May 21): 4.

———. 1999. "Piden la mediación de Jackson." *El Nuevo Día*, San Juan (May 29): 4.

———. 1999. "Ascenso asombroso . . . precipitosa su caída." *El Nuevo Día*, San Juan (June 7): 4–5.

———. 1999. "Dan forma al Panel Especial." *El Nuevo Día*, San Juan (June 12): 5.

———. 1999. "Pesquisan el uso de material nuclear." *El Nuevo Día*, San Juan (June 19): 4.

———. 1999. "Despega el 'chantaje.'" *El Nuevo Día*, San Juan (June 24): 4.

———. 1999. "Se lava las manos la Marina por la muerte de Sanes." *El Nuevo Día*, San Juan (June 24): 4.

———. 1999. "Roto el diálogo entre Romero y Rosselló." *El Nuevo Día*, San Juan (July 5): 15.

———. 1999. "Revés para Rosselló." *El Nuevo Día*, San Juan (July 7): 4.

———. 1999. "'Tergiversada' la situación de la Isla Nena." *El Nuevo Día*, San Juan (July 10): 5.

———. 1999. "Ningún lugar como Vieques." *El Nuevo Día*, San Juan (July 16): 4.

———. 1999. "Mea culpa del Cuerpo de Marinos." *El Nuevo Día*, San Juan (July 22): 5.

———. 1999. "Gore con la mira en Vieques." *El Nuevo Día*, San Juan (July 28): 4.

———. 1999. "'Sí' a la liberación de 13 reos." *El Nuevo Día*, San Juan (August 10): 22.

———. 1999. "Consciente del daño de la Marina." *El Nuevo Día*, San Juan (August 11): 5.

———. 1999. "Firma Clinton la clemencia." *El Nuevo Día*, San Juan (August 12): 32.

———. 1999. "El dilema que enfrenta Vieques." *El Nuevo Día*, San Juan (August 27): 4.

———. 1999. "Una 'bomba de tiempo' la oferta de clemencia." *El Nuevo Día*, San Juan (September 1): 28.

———. 1999. "Callejón sin salida para los reos." *El Nuevo Día*, San Juan (September 6): 18.

———. 1999. "Firman los presos." *El Nuevo Día*, San Juan (September 7): 12.

———. 1999. "Dennis Rivera sigue con Hillary." *El Nuevo Día*, San Juan (September 7): 14.

———. 1999. "En libertad esta misma semana." *El Nuevo Día*, San Juan (September 8): 28.

———. 1999. "Firme el Gobierno contra la Marina." *El Nuevo Día*, San Juan (September 14): 6.

———. 1999. "No suelta prenda." *El Nuevo Día*, San Juan (September 17): 24.

———. 1999. "Polémico el voto del Panel." *El Nuevo Día*, San Juan (September 22): 4.

———. 1999. "Clinton confiesa por qué perdonó." *El Nuevo Día*, San Juan (September 22): 30.

———. 1999. "Serrano saca la cara por el PIP en el Congreso." *El Nuevo Día*, San Juan (October 16): 16.

———. 1999. "Propuestas desilusionantes." *El Nuevo Día*, San Juan (October 19): 5.

———. 1999. "Alto apoyo a las maniobras en la Isla Nena." *El Nuevo Día*, San Juan (October 22): 26.

———. 1999. "El status de la isla tendrá que esperar . . ." *El Nuevo Día*, San Juan (October 28): 42.

———. 1999. "Amenaza Lott con afectar a la isla." *El Nuevo Día*, San Juan (October 30): 8.

———. 1999. "Censura a Trent Lott." *El Nuevo Día*, San Juan (November 2): 5.

———. 1999. "Claman a Clinton por la Isla Nena en Hartford." *El Nuevo Día*, San Juan (November 6): 6.

———. 1999. "Desobediencia fuera de agenda." *El Nuevo Día*, San Juan (November 16): 10.

———. 1999. "Se queda la Marina cinco años más." *El Nuevo Día*, San Juan (December 4): 4.

———. 1999. "Censura el rol castrense en el diálogo." *El Nuevo Día*, San Juan (December 10): 5.

———. 2000. "Amplían la amenaza de cerrar las bases." *El Nuevo Día*, San Juan (January 26): 5.

———. 2000. "Gutiérrez ve a Clinton en papel de Pilatos." *El Nuevo Día*, San Juan (January 26): 5.

———. 2000. "Aplauso federal al acuerdo sobre Vieques." *El Nuevo Día*, San Juan (February 1): 5.

———. 2000. "Contento con la actitud de Rosselló." *El Nuevo Día*, San Juan (February 3): 5.

———. 2000. "Sin garras las órdenes ejecutivas." *El Nuevo Día*, San Juan (February 3): 8.

———. 2000. "Desmienten sacrificio de Vieques por la estadidad." *El Nuevo Día*, San Juan (February 4): 27.

———. 2000. "Clinton reta al Congreso por el status." *El Nuevo Día*, San Juan (February 15): 30.

———. 2000. "Pesquera advierte sobre los riesgos de la marcha pro Vieques." *El Nuevo Día*, San Juan (February 23): 5.

———. 2000. "Admite la persecución a independentistas el FBI." *El Nuevo Día*, San Juan (March 17): 30.

———. 2000. "Utilizan a Vieques para campaña contra estadidad." *El Nuevo Día*, San Juan (March 25): 34.

———. 2000. "Canta victoria Janet Reno." *El Nuevo Día*, San Juan (May 5): 19.

———. 2000. "FBI entregará todas las carpetas." *El Nuevo Día*, San Juan (May 18): 34.

———. "Urge Lott bala viva y comprar la Isla Nena." *El Nuevo Día*, San Juan (June 28): 10.

———. 2000. "Cambia Gore: Pide que la Marina deje de entrenar." *El Nuevo Día*, San Juan (July 7): 4.

———. 2000. "Inhofe insiste en no permitirlo. *El Nuevo Día*, San Juan (July 7): 8.

———. 2000. "Apoyo al plan de Vieques." *El Nuevo Día*, San Juan (August 3): 76.

———. 2000. "Ejercicios en Vieques." *El Nuevo Día*, San Juan (October 17): 4.

———. 2000. "Le ofrecen otra isla a la Marina por $35 millones." *El Nuevo Día*, San Juan (October 17): 5.

———. 2001. "Vieques antes que el status." *El Nuevo Día*, San Juan (February 21): 47.

———. 2001. "Senadores por Nueva York piden el cese inmediato de las bombas." *El Nuevo Día*, San Juan (March 14): 20.

———. 2001. "Suena Colombia como alternativa a Vieques." *El Nuevo Día*, San Juan (April 5): 30.

———. 2001. "Vía libre para los ejercicios navales." *El Nuevo Día*, San Juan (April 27): 4.

———. 2001. "Piden a Hansen no meterse en los fondos educativos para la isla." *El Nuevo Día*, San Juan (May 16): 14.

Mulero, Leonor, and Nilka Estrada Resto. 1999. "Responde Clinton al reclamo boricua." *El Nuevo Día*, San Juan (June 11): 5.

Mullenneaux, Lisa. 2000. *¡Ni una bomba más! Vieques vs. U.S. Navy*. New York: Pentagon Press.

Muriente Pérez, Julio. 1999. "Monseñor González y la nación espiritual." Editorial. *Claridad*, Santurce, P.R. (May 14–20): 10.

Murillo, Mario A. 2000. "The Value of Vieques." *NACLA Report on the Americas* 34, no. 3: 24–25.

———. 2001. "Puerto Rico in the U.S. News Media: There is Not Such a Thing as Colonialism." Paper presented at the symposium "None of the Above: Puerto Rican Politics and Culture in the New Millenium," Rutgers University, New Brunswick, N.J., April 10–12.

National Defense Research Institute. 1993. *Sexual Orientation and U.S. Military Personnel Policy: Options and Assessment*. Santa Monica, Calif.: Rand.

Negrón de Montilla, Aida. 1975. *Americanization in Puerto Rico and the Public School System, 1900–1930*. Río Piedras, P.R.: Editorial Universitaria.

Negrón-Muntaner, Frances. 1997. "English Only Jamas but Spanish Only Cuidado: Language and Nationalism in Contemporary Puerto Rico." In *Puerto Rican Jam: Rethinking Colonialism and Nationalism*, ed. Frances Negrón-Muntaner and Ramón Grosfoguel. Minneapolis: University of Minnesota Press.

Negrón-Portillo, Mariano. 1997. "Puerto Rico: Surviving Colonialism and Nationalism." In *Puerto Rican Jam: Rethinking Colonialism and Nationalism*, ed. Frances Negrón-Muntaner and Ramón Grosfoguel. Minneapolis: University of Minnesota Press.

Nieves Ramírez, Gladys. 2000. "Cierran filas el oeste con desobedientes." *El Nuevo Día*, San Juan (May 5): 14.

Noriega Rodríguez, David. 1999. "Seguridad nacional." Editorial. *El Nuevo Día*, San Juan (July 21): 128.

———. 2000. *El Instituto del SIDA: Historia de una investigación* (The AIDS Institute: History of an investigation). Río Piedras, P.R.: Editorial Cultural.

———. 2000. "Desobediencia religiosa." Editorial. *El Nuevo Día*, San Juan (February 16): 135.

———. 2000. "El día después." Editorial. *El Nuevo Día*, San Juan (May 10): 153.

"Nuevo alcalde de Vieques propone un referéndum." 2000. *El Nuevo Día*, San Juan (December 17): 24.

Oboler, Suzanne. 1995. *Ethnic Labels, Latino Lives: Identity and the Politics of (Re)Presentation in the United States*. Minneapolis: University of Minnesota Press.

O'Brien, Connor C. 1988. *God Land: Reflections on Religion and Nationalism*. Cambridge: Harvard University Press.

Olson, Mancur. 1971. *The Logic of Collective Action: Public Goods and the Theory of Groups*. Cambridge: Harvard University Press.

Omi, Michael, and Howard Winant. 1994. *Racial Formation in the United States: From the 1960s to the 1990s*. 2nd ed. New York: Routledge.

Ortiz Ramos, Pablo M. 2000. *Con Rubén en la playa: Un diario de Vieques* (On the beach with Rubén: A Vieques diary). San Juan: Pablo Marcial Ortiz Ramos.

Osuna, Juan J. 1975 [1949]. *A History of Education in Puerto Rico*. New York: Arno Press.

Pagán, Samuel. 2000. "Las iglesias, las desobediencias, la política y la moral." Editorial. *El Nuevo Día*, San Juan (March 8): 138.

Pantojas García, Emilio. 2000. "La noción de Pueblo y la política electoral en el 2000." *Diálogo* (April): 24–25.

Parés Arroyo, Marga. 1999. "Exonerada la víctima de faltar a su deber." *El Nuevo Día*, San Juan (August 3): 5.

———. 1999. "Decepción de Gutiérrez y Velázquez." *El Nuevo Día*, San Juan (August 13): 66.

———. 1999. "Consulta al pueblo viequense." *El Nuevo Día*, San Juan (November 15): 26.

Pastor Ruiz, Justo. 1947. *Vieques antiguo y moderno, 1493–1946* (Ancient and modern Vieques, 1493–1946). Yauco, P.R.: Tipografía Rodríguez Lugo.

"Pataki: No a bombardeos en Vieques." 2001. *El diario/La prensa*, New York (March 4): 2.

Pedreira, Antonio S. 1978 [1934]. *Insularismo* (Insularism). Río Piedras, P.R.: Editorial Edil.

Penchi, Luis. 1999. "En progreso las antenas de radar en Vieques." *El Nuevo Día*, San Juan (January 18): 34.

———. 1999. "Aconseja morir preso y no ceder." *El Nuevo Día*, San Juan (September 6): 21.

Pérez, José J. 1999. "Otorgan contrato para radar." *El Nuevo Día*, San Juan (August 11): 68.

Petrullo, Vincenzo. 1947. *Puerto Rican Paradox*. Philadelphia: University of Pennsylvania Press.

Picó, Fernando. 1986. *Historia general de Puerto Rico* (General history of Puerto Rico). Río Piedras, P.R.: Ediciones Huracán.

———. 1993. *Al filo del poder* (At power's edge). Río Piedras, P.R.: Editorial de la Universidad de Puerto Rico.

"Pide un regaño para los prelados." 2000. *El Nuevo Día*, San Juan (February 4): 10.

Pineda, Leoncio. 1999. "Pesa Vieques a la hora de votar en Nueva York." *El Nuevo Día*, San Juan (November 6): 35.

"Policía de Nueva York mutilado en atentado critica el indulto." 1999. *El Nuevo Día*, San Juan (August 13): 66.

Pratt, Julius W. 1955. *A History of United States Foreign Policy*. New York: Prentice Hall.

Pyle, Ricard. 1999. "Hillary reitera que no fue consultada." *El Nuevo Día*, San Juan (September 10): 25.

Quintero Rivera, Angel G. 1986. *Conflictos de clase y política en Puerto Rico*. 5th ed. Río Piedras, P.R.: Ediciones Huracán.

———. 1993. "La ideología populista y la institucionalización universitaria de las ciencias sociales." In *Del nacionalismo al populismo: Cultura y política en Puerto Rico* (From nationalism to populism: Culture and politics in Puerto Rico), ed. Silvia Alvarez-Curbelo and María E. Rodríguez Castro. Río Piedras, P.R.: Ediciones Huracán.

Rabin Siegal, Robert L. 1994. *Compendio de lecturas sobre la historia de Vieques* (Compendium of readings on the history of Vieques). Vieques, P.R.: Robert L. Rabin Siegal.

———. 1999. "El FBI toma Vieques." *Claridad*, Santurce, P.R. (February 12–18): 8.

———. 1999. "La batalla de Vieques continúa." *Claridad*, Santurce, P.R. (February 26–March 4): 8.

Ramírez Lavandero, Marcos, ed. 1988. *Documents on the Constitutional Relationship of Puerto Rico and the United States*. 3rd ed. Washington, D.C.: Puerto Rico Federal Affairs Administration.

Ramos Avalos, Jorge. 1999. "Vieques y el futuro de Puerto Rico." Editorial. *El Nuevo Día*, San Juan (August 5): 146.

———. 1999. "Puerto Rico: Independencia involuntaria." Editorial. *El Nuevo Día*, San Juan (October 9): 131.

Ramos de Santiago, Carmen. 1965. *El gobierno de Puerto Rico* (The government of Puerto Rico). Río Piedras, P.R.: Editorial de la Universidad de Puerto Rico.

Ramos-Zayas, Ana Y. 1997. "*La patria es valor y sacrificio*: Nationalist Ideologies, Cultural Authenticity, and Community Building among Puerto Ricans in Chicago." Ph.D. diss., Columbia University.

"Referendum en Vieques: El sentir del pueblo viequense luego de firmado el acuerdo." 2000. *El Nuevo Día*, San Juan (February 10): 4–5.

Ribes Tovar, Federico. 1975. *Albizu Campos: El Revolucionario* (Albizu Campos: The revolutionary). New York: Plus Ultra.

Rivas, Lilian. 1999. "Consejales de NY se unen por Vieques." *El diario/La prensa*, New York (September 18): 9.

———. 1999. "Boricuas son miopes e ingratos." *El diario/La prensa*, New York (October 23): 7.

Rivera, Angel I. 1996. *Puerto Rico: Ficción y mitología en sus alternativas de status* (Puerto Rico: Fiction and mythology in its status alternatives). San Juan: Nueva Aurora.

Rivera, Carmen V. 1998. "Our Movement: One Woman's Story." In *The Puerto Rican Movement: Voices from the Diaspora*, ed. Andrés Torres and José Velázquez. Philadelphia: Temple University Press.

Rivera, Geraldo. 1999. "Tras Vieques hay treinta millones de hispanos." *El diario/La prensa*, New York (November 19): 14.

Rivera, Manuel E. 1999. "Advertencia a Rubén Berríos." *El Nuevo Día*, San Juan (May 14): 33.

———. 1999. "Critican el vaivén de la Primera Dama." *El Nuevo Día*, San Juan (September 7): 15.

———. 2001. "Pide 'gobierno propio' para Vieques." *El Nuevo Día*, San Juan (February 9): 28.

Rivera, Mildred, and Leonor Mulero. 1999. "Se reúne hoy el PPD con Hastert." *El Nuevo Día*, San Juan (April 30): 29.

Rivera, Monte. 1984. "Organizational Politics of the East Harlem Barrio in the 1970s." In *Puerto Rican Politics in Urban America*, ed. James Jennings and Monte Rivera. Westport, Conn.: Greenwood Press.

Rivera Marrero, Mildred. 1999. "Anticipan cesantías en una fábrica en Vieques." *El Nuevo Día*, San Juan (February 9): 37.

———. 1999. "En oídos sordos los reclamos viequenses." *El Nuevo Día*, San Juan (March 22): 22.

———. 1999. "Fecha el PIP el incio de su desobediencia civil." *El Nuevo Día*, San Juan (April 30): 15.

———. 1999. "Ignorantes los congresistas de la realidad viequense." *El Nuevo Día*, San Juan (July 10): 4.

———. 1999. "Entusiasmo en las filas del PIP." *El Nuevo Día*, San Juan (July 12): 26.

———. 1999. "Respalda Manuela la desobediencia civil." *El Nuevo Día*, San Juan (July 17): 5.

———. 1999. "Acto de fe en la Isla Nena." *El Nuevo Día*, San Juan (July 17): 6.

———. 1999. "Prevalece el anhelo de la libertad completa." *El Nuevo Día*, San Juan (August 12): 33.

———. 1999. "Propone donar la compensación." *El Nuevo Día*, San Juan (December 15): 5.

———. 2000. "Inquietud partidista ante el juicio." *El Nuevo Día*, San Juan (January 10): 34.

———. 2000. "PPD se unirá a la apelación como amigo de la corte." *El Nuevo Día*, San Juan (September 12): 26.

———. 2000. "El PPD hará lo mismo que los pipilos." *El Nuevo Día*, San Juan (September 14): 30.

———. 2000. "'Sin voluntad' el PNP para defender la paz de la Isla Nena." *El Nuevo Día*, San Juan (November 1): 5.

———. 2000. "Calderón pide un voto contra la corrupción." *El Nuevo Día*, San Juan (November 6): 4–5.

———. 2001. "Rumsfeld no sorprende a Calderón." *El Nuevo Día*, San Juan (January 13): 5.

———. 2001. "Convencido Pataki de que hay que deterer el bombardeo." *El Nuevo Día*, San Juan (April 10): 5.

Rivera Renta, José. 1999. "Posible expulsión a Berríos." *El Nuevo Día*, San Juan (May 24): 22.

Rochon, Thomas R. 1990. "The West European Peace Movement and the Theory of New Social Movements." In *Challenging the Political Order: New Social and Political Movements in Western Democracies*, ed. Russell J. Dalton and Manfred Kuechler. New York: Oxford University Press.

Rodríguez, Clara E. 1996. "Racial Themes in the Literature: Puerto Ricans and Other Latinos." In *Latinos in New York: Communities in Transition*, ed. Gabriel Haslip-Viera and Sherrie L. Baver. Notre Dame, Ind.: University of Notre Dame Press.

Rodríguez, Israel. 2001. "Misla y McClintock desautorizan a Burgos." *El Nuevo Día*, San Juan (January 17): 31.

Rodríguez, Magdalys. 2001. "Radican ley para regular ruidos." *El Nuevo Día*, San Juan (April 19): 4.

Rodríguez, Víctor M. 1999. "Boricuas, African-Americans, and Chicanos in the 'Far West': Notes on the Puerto Rican Pro-Independence Movement in California, 1960s-1980s." In *Latino Social Movements: Historical and Theoretical Perspectives*, ed. Rodolfo D. Torres and George Katsiaficas. New York: Routledge.

Rodríguez Beruff, Jorge. 1988. *Política militar y dominación: Puerto Rico en el contexto latinoamericano* (Military policy and domination: Puerto Rico in the Latin American context). Río Piedras, P.R.: Ediciones Huracán.

———. 1995. "La cuestión estratégico militar y la libre determinación de Puerto Rico: el debate plebiscitario (1989–1993)." *Revista del Colegio de Abogados de Puerto Rico* 56, no. 1: 57–76.

———. 1999. "Guerra contra las drogas, militarización y democracia: Política y fuerzas de seguridad en Puerto Rico." In *Fronteras en conflicto: Guerra contra las drogas, militarización en el Caribe, Puerto Rico y Vieques* (Border conflicts: War against drugs, militarization in the Caribbean, Puerto Rico and Vieques), ed. Humberto García Muñiz and Jorge Rodríguez Beruff. San Juan: Red Caribeña de Geopolítica.

———. 2000. "Vieques y la construcción de un poder civil en Puerto Rico." *Nueva Sociedad* 168: 41–48.

Rodríguez Cotto, Sandra D. 1998. "Premio de derechos humanos para la Isla Nena." *El Nuevo Día*, San Juan (December 17): 5.

———. 1999. "Estrategia para mejorar la imagen de Puerto Rico." *El Nuevo Día*, San Juan (September 17): 25.

———. 1999. "Peña Clós truena contra el nacionalismo." *El Nuevo Día*, San Juan (September 22): 39.

———. 1999. "Organizan 'Marcha pro Americana.'" *El Nuevo Día*, San Juan (September 23): 35.

———. 1999. "Divide al PNP la desobediencia civil." *El Nuevo Día*, San Juan (October 4): 5.

———. 1999. "Ricky con los viequenses." *El Nuevo Día*, San Juan (December 9): 80.

———. 2000. "Nutrida la marcha de la ciudadanía." *El Nuevo Día*, San Juan (March 6): 20.

———. 2000. "Satisfecho con la Fiesta." *El Nuevo Día*, San Juan (March 7): 23.

———. 2000. "Líderes religiosos se reafirman en la vía de la resistencia pacífica." *El Nuevo Día*, San Juan (May 5): 18.

Rodríguez-Morazzani, Roberto P. 1998. "Political Cultures of the Puerto Rican Left in the United States." In *The Puerto Rican Movement: Voices from the Diaspora*, ed. Andrés Torres and José Velázquez. Philadelphia: Temple University Press.

Rodríguez Orellana, Manuel. 2001. "Puerto Rico: Political Status, Vieques, and the Island's Future." Forum at the Kennedy School of Government, Harvard University, Cambridge, May 9.

Rodríguez Sánchez, Israel. 2001. "Admite la senadora que Vieques le ha traído problemas." *El Nuevo Día*, San Juan (January 16): 31.

———. 2001. "Parga le aclara al Congreso que Isla Nena es parte del archipiélago boricua." *El Nuevo Día*, San Juan (March 6): 32.

Rogowski, Ronald. 1985. "Causes and Varieties of Nationalism: A Rationalist Account." In *New Nationalisms of the Developed West: Toward Explanation*, ed. Edward A. Tiryakian and Ronald Rogoswki. Boston: Allen and Unwin.

Roldán Soto, Camile. 2000. "Llama aguajeros a los que dijeron sí." *El Nuevo Día*, San Juan (February 2): 5.

———. 2000. "Ejército de paz." *El Nuevo Día*, San Juan (February 22): 5.

———. 2000. "Revalúa el PIP la estrategia de los 134 arrestados." *El Nuevo Día*, San Juan (June 29): 4.

———. 2000. "'Termina' el bombardeo." *El Nuevo Día*, San Juan (June 29): 4.

———. 2000. "Masivo apoyo del PIP a sus encarcelados." *El Nuevo Día*, San Juan (July 5): 6.

———. 2000. "Reitera su promesa de sacar a la Marina." *El Nuevo Día*, San Juan (November 9): 13.

Romero-Barceló, Carlos. 1978. *Statehood Is for the Poor*. San Juan: Romero-Barceló.

Romero-Barceló, Carlos, and James F. Goodrich. 1983. "Memorandum of Understanding Regarding the Island of Vieques." San Juan: Commonwealth of Puerto Rico.

Roosens, Eugeen E. 1989. *Creating Ethnicity: The Process of Ethnogenesis*. Newbury Park, Calif.: Sage Publications.

Roosevelt, Franklin D. 1938. *The Public Papers and Addresses of Franklin D. Roosevelt with a Special Introduction and Explanatory Notes by President Roosevelt*. Vol. 3, *The Advance of Recovery and Reform, 1934*. New York: MacMillan.

———. 1941. *The Public Papers and Addresses of Franklin D. Roosevelt with a Special Introduction and Explanatory Notes by President Roosevelt*. 1937 volume, *The Constitution Prevails*. New York: MacMillan.

Rosario, Frances. 2001. "Al Capitolio una réplica de la capilla ecuménica." *El Nuevo Día*, San Juan (February 6): 14.

Rosario Natal, Carmelo. 1970. "El debate sobre el origen de la actual Bandera Puertorriqueña." *Revista del Instituto de Cultura Puertorriqueña* 46: 44–49.

"Rosselló mantiene buenas notas, pero pedería la Gobernación." 1999. *El Nuevo Día*, San Juan (March 29): 22–25.

Rozell, Mark J., and Clyde Wilcox. 1999. *Interest Groups in American Campaigns: The New Face of Electioneering*. Washington, D.C.: Congressional Quarterly.

Rudé, George. 1995. *Ideology and Popular Protest*. Chapel Hill: University of North Carolina Press.

Rüdig, Wolfgang. 1988. "Peace and Ecology Movements in Western Europe." *West European Politics* 11, no. 1: 26–39.

Ruiz Marrero, Carmelo. 1999. "Condenan tragedia en Vieques." *Claridad*, Santurce, P.R. (April 23–29): 3.

Said, Edward W. 1979. *Orientalism*. New York: Vintage Books.

"Saint Kitts por Vieques." 2001. *El Nuevo Día*, San Juan (March 20): 28.

Samoiloff, L. Cripps. 1987. *Calamity in the Caribbean: Puerto Rico and the Bomb*. Cambridge, Mass.: Schenkman Books.

Sánchez, José R. 1996. "Puerto Rican Politics in New York: Beyond 'Secondhand' Theory." In *Latinos in New York: Communities in Transition*, ed. Gabriel Haslip-Viera and Sherrie L. Baver. Notre Dame, Ind.: University of Notre Dame Press.

Sánchez Korrol, Virginia. 1994. *From Colonia to Community: The History of Puerto Ricans in New York City*. Berkeley: University of California Press.

Santana, Arturo. 1983. "Puerto Rico in a Revolutionary World." In *Puerto Rico: A Political and Cultural History*, ed. Arturo Morales Carrión. New York: W. W. Norton.

Santana, Mario. 1999. "Esperan por Clinton." *El Nuevo Día*, San Juan (June 9): 4.

———. 2000. "Hasta hoy la protesta en el recinto ponceño." *El Nuevo Día*, San Juan (May 5): 8.

———. 2000. "Marchan más de 8 mil en Ponce." *El Nuevo Día*, San Juan (July 5): 8.

Santori, Fufi. 2001. "La bastilla federal." Editorial. *El Nuevo Día*, San Juan (May 14): 103.

Scarano, Francisco A. 1996. "The *Jíbaro* Masquerade and the Subaltern Politics of Creole Identity Formation in Puerto Rico, 1745–1823." *American Historical Review* 101, no. 5: 1398–431.

Schneider, Jo A. 1990. "Defining Boundaries, Creating Contacts: Puerto Rican and Polish Presentations of Group Identity through Ethnic Parades." *Journal of Ethnic Studies* 18, no. 1: 33–57.

Serrano, Basilio. 1998. "¡Rifle, Cañón, y Escopeta! A Chronicle of the Puerto Rican Student Union." In *The Puerto Rican Movement: Voices from the Diaspora*, ed. Andrés Torres and José Velázquez. Philadelphia: Temple University Press.

Serrano, José E. 1999. "Se abre el diálogo sobre las carpetas y el FBI." Editorial. *El diario/La prensa*, New York (April 10): 16.

———. 1999. "Sin condiciones para la libertad." *Claridad*, Santurce, P.R. (August 20–26): 6.

Sheheane, Mike. 2000. "Depleted Uranium—The Truth and Nothing but the Truth." *Armor* 109, no. 4 (July–August): 32–33, 48.

"La situación de Vieques: el sentir de Puerto Rico." 1999. *El Nuevo Día*, San Juan (November 19): 4–5.

"Situación de Vieques después del desalojo." 2000. *El Nuevo Día*, San Juan (June 6): 5–6.

Smith, Anthony D. 1981. *The Ethnic Revival*. Cambridge: Cambridge University Press.

Smith, Robert C. 1996. "Mexicans in New York: Membership and Incorporation in a New Immigrant Community." In *Latinos in New York: Communities in Transition*, ed. Gabriel Haslip-Viera and Sherrie L. Baver. Notre Dame, Ind.: University of Notre Dame Press.

Sosa Pascual, Omaya. 2001. "Reafirma la Marina que no entregará las tierras." *El Nuevo Día*, San Juan (January 2): 16.

Sprout, Harold, and Margaret Sprout. 1946. *Toward a New Order of Sea Power: American Naval Policy and the World Scene, 1918–1922*. Princeton, N.J.: Princeton University Press.

"The State; Also . . ." 1997. *Los Angeles Times* (July 31).

Stavans, Ilan. 1995. *The Hispanic Condition: Reflections on Culture and Identity in America*. New York: Harper Collins.

Steinberg, Stephen. 1989. *The Ethnic Myth: Race, Ethnicity and Class in America*. Boston: Beacon Press.

Stephen, Lynn. 1996. "The Creation and Re-creation of Ethnicity: Lessons from the Zapotec and Mixtec of Oaxaca." *Latin American Perspectives* 23, no. 2: 17–37.

Tió, Elsa. 2000. "Vieques a cambio de . . ." Editorial. *El Nuevo Día*, San Juan (January 7): 133.

Tocqueville, Alexis de. 1969 [1848]. *Democracy in America*. Translated by George Lawrence; edited by J. P. Mayer. New York: Harper and Row.

Toland, Judith D. 1993. "Introduction: Dialogue of Self and Other: Ethnicity and the Statehood Process." In *Ethnicity and the State*. Political Anthropology Series, ed. Judith D. Toland. Vol. 9. New Brunswick, N.J.: Transaction Publishers.

Torres, Andrés. 1995. *Between Melting Pot and Mosaic: African Americans and Puerto Ricans in the New York Political Economy*. Philadelphia: Temple University Press.

———. 1998. "Introduction: Political Radicalism in the Diaspora—The Puerto Rican Experience." In *The Puerto Rican Movement: Voices from the Diaspora*, ed. Andrés Torres and José Velázquez. Philadelphia: Temple University Press.

Torres, Benjamín. 2000. "Vuelve a tirar la Marina." *El Nuevo Día*, San Juan (May 11): 6.

Torres, Chegüí. 2001. "Vieques y 'los americanos.'" *El diario/La prensa*, New York (February 20): 5.

Torres, Ismael. 2000. "Expresión de un cambio político el caso viequense." *El Nuevo Día*, San Juan (April 24): 8.

———. 2000. "Ya es ley votar por el presidente." *El Nuevo Día*, San Juan (September 11): 22.

Torres Gotay, Benjamín. 1999. "'Conviente' el subdesarrollo." *El Nuevo Día*, San Juan (May 10): 12.

———. 1999. "Esperan el arresto." *El Nuevo Día*, San Juan (May 10): 14.

———. 1999. "Conmociona a Vieques el hallazgo de un torpedo." *El Nuevo Día*, San Juan (May 13): 6.

———. 1999. "Listos para la confrontación." *El Nuevo Día*, San Juan (June 9): 5.

———. 1999. "A sopesar el futuro de Vieques." *El Nuevo Día*, San Juan (June 16): 4.

———. 1999. "A repeler las maniobras bélicas." *El Nuevo Día*, San Juan (June 21): 4.

———. 1999. "Al desnudo las tácticas de la Marina." *El Nuevo Día*, San Juan (June 25): 5.

———. 1999. "No baja la guardia el PIP." *El Nuevo Día*, San Juan (July 2): 4.

———. 1999. "Unidos por la paz de la Isla Nena." *El Nuevo Día*, San Juan (July 5): 4.

———. 1999. "Vieques sorprende al congresista." *El Nuevo Día*, San Juan (July 9): 5.

———. 1999. "La Marina defiende un tóxico." *El Nuevo Día*, San Juan (August 17): 4.

———. 1999. "Ceiba con Vieques aunque se afecte." *El Nuevo Día*, San Juan (August 17): 6.

———. 1999. "Sobrepasa la marcha las expectativas." *El Nuevo Día*, San Juan (August 30): 18–19.

———. 1999. "Pasan un susto los desobedientes." *El Nuevo Día*, San Juan (November 19): 14.

———. 2000. "El PIP planta al Gobernador." *El Nuevo Día*, San Juan (February 1): 8.

———. 2000. "Un abuso de poder el trato sobre Vieques, según Jorge Raschke." *El Nuevo Día*, San Juan (February 5): 6.

———. 2000. "Histeria anexionista la conspiración." *El Nuevo Día*, San Juan (February 25): 29.

———. 2000. "Reforzado el mollero militar." *El Nuevo Día*, San Juan (May 2): 4.

———. 2000. "Pide Berríos apoyar a Calderón." *El Nuevo Día*, San Juan (December 15): 6.

———. 2001. "Golpea la tragedia de nuevo." *El Nuevo Día*, San Juan (April 20): 4.

———. 2001. "Consiguen detener las prácticas militares." *El Nuevo Día*, San Juan (April 29): 4.

———. 2001. "17 vertederos tóxicos en las tierras entregadas." *El Nuevo Día*, San Juan (May 18): 6.

Torres Gotay, Benjamín, and Leonor Mulero. 1999. "Unidos contra la Marina." *El Nuevo Día*, San Juan (April 21): 4.

———. 1999. "Pide perdón la Marina de Guerra estadounidense." *El Nuevo Día*, San Juan (April 21): 8.

Torres Rivera, Alejandro. 1999. *Militarismo y descolonización: Puerto Rico ante el siglo 21* (Militarism and decolonization: Puerto Rico before the twenty-first century). San Juan: Congreso Nacional Hostosiano.

———. 1999. "Puerto Rico, el Comando Sur y la militarización de Colombia." *Revista del Colegio de Abogados de Puerto Rico* 60, no. 4: 45–58.

Trask, Haunani-Kay. 1993. *From a Native Daughter: Colonialism and Sovereignty in Hawai'i*. Monroe, Maine: Common Courage Press.

Trías Monge, José. 1980. *Historia constitucional de Puerto Rico* (Constitutional history of Puerto Rico). Vol. 1. Río Piedras, P.R.: Editorial Universitaria.

———. 1981. *Historia constitucional de Puerto Rico* (Constitutional history of Puerto Rico). Vol. 2. Río Piedras, P.R.: Editorial Universitaria.

———. 1997. *Puerto Rico: The Trials of the Oldest Colony in the World*. New Haven, Conn.: Yale University Press.

———. 1999. "La Marina en Vieques." Editorial. *El Nuevo Día*, San Juan (July 10): 116.

Trigo, Benigno. 1999. "Anemia and Vampires: Figures to Govern the Colony, Puerto Rico, 1880 to 1904." *Comparative Study of Society and History* 41, no. 1: 104–23.

Tugwell, Rexford G. 1968 [1946]. *The Stricken Land: The Story of Puerto Rico*. New York: Greenwood.

Ture, Kwame, and Charles V. Hamilton. 1992 [1967]. *Black Power: The Politics of Liberation*. New York: Vintage Books.

Udovički, Jaminka. 1995. "Nationalism, Ethnic Conflict, and Self-Determination in the Former Yugoslavia." In *The National Question: Nationalism, Ethnic Conflict, and Self-Determination in the 20th Century*, ed. Berch Berberoglu. Philadelphia: Temple University Press.

United States House of Representatives. 1980. *Naval Training Activities on the Island of Vieques, Puerto Rico*. Hearings before the Panel to Review the Status of Navy Training Activities on the Island of Vieques of the Committee on Armed Services (H.A.S.C. 96–66). Washington, D.C.: Government Printing Office (May 28, 29; July 10, 11; and September 24).

———. 1980. *Report on the Inspection of U.S. Military Bases in Puerto Rico, Cuba and the Panama Canal Zone*. Report of the Committee on Armed Services (96–25). Washington, D.C.: Governing Printing Office (March 20).

———. 1981. *Naval Training Activities on the Island of Vieques, Puerto Rico*. Report of the Panel to Review the Status of Navy Training Activities on the Island of Vieques of the Committee on Armed Services (96–31). Washington, D.C.: Government Printing Office (February 3).

———. 1994. *Vieques Lands Transfer Act of 1994*. Hearing before the Subcommittee on Insular and International Affairs of the Committee on Natural Resources (103–114). Washington, D.C.: Government Printing Office (October 4).

United States Navy. 1979. *Continued Use of the Atlantic Fleet Weapons Training Facility Inner Range (Vieques): Draft Environmental Impact Statement*. Vol. 1. Tippetts-Abbett- McCarthy-Stratton; Ecology and Environment.

Urciuoli, Bonnie. 1998. *Exposing Prejudice: Puerto Rican Experiences of Language, Race, and Class*. Boulder, Colo.: Westview.

Valdés-Pizzini, Manuel. 1990. "Fisherman Associations in Puerto Rico: Praxis and Discourse in the Politics of Fishing." *Human Organization* 49, no. 2: 164–73.

Valdivia, Yadira. 1999. "Llegó el Obispo." *El Nuevo Día*, San Juan (March 27): 4.

———. 1999. "Da la bienvenida a acción presidencial." *El Nuevo Día*, San Juan (June 12): 6.

———. 2000. "No cede la alta incidencia de cáncer en la Isla Nena." *El Nuevo Día*, San Juan (March 7): 8.

———. 2000. "Confirmado: hay más cáncer en Vieques." *El Nuevo Día*, San Juan (March 8): 73.

———. 2000. "Destaca el Arzobispo la cohesión del pueblo." *El Nuevo Día*, San Juan (April 20): 5.

———. 2000. "Protesta y palos frente al Fuerte Buchanan." *El Nuevo Día*, San Juan (May 5): 6.

———. 2000. "Nombran a Corrada como obispo de Tyler, Texas." *El Nuevo Día*, San Juan (December 5): 12.

———. 2000. "Compromiso con Vieques del sucesor de Corrada." *El Nuevo Día*, San Juan (December 13): 24.

———. 2001. "Mensaje papal de fe al pueblo boricua." *El Nuevo Día*, San Juan (May 1): 16.

Valentín, Dorcas. 1999. "José Celso Barbosa: Un hombre del pueblo." *El diario/La prensa*. Special Supplement. New York (June 13): 12.

Varela, Luis R. 1999. "Rivera, hijo, apoya a Berríos." *El Nuevo Día*, San Juan (May 31): 16.

Vázquez, Marcherie. 1999. "Denuncian ante la Casa Blanca situación de Vieques." *El diario/La prensa*, New York (August 6): 3.

———. 1999. "No apoyo el voto del boricua ausente." *El diario/La prensa*, New York (August 28): 2.

———. 1999. "Funcionarios electos volverán a Vieques." *El diario/La prensa*, New York (November 4): 4.

Veaz, Maribel. 1995. "Las expropiaciones de la década del cuarenta en Vieques." *Revista del Colegio de Abogados de Puerto Rico* 56, no. 2: 159–213.

Vega, Bernardo. 1984. *Memoirs of Bernardo Vega: A Contribution to the History of the Puerto Rican Community in New York*. Translated by Juan Flores; edited by César Andreu Iglesias. New York: Monthly Press.

Vega, María. 1999. "Liberación incondicional de los presos políticos." *El diario/La prensa*, New York (August 14): 3.

———. 1999. "¿Cuál es su posición sobre los presos políticos puertorriqueños?" *El diario/La prensa*, New York (August 21): 2.

Velázquez, José E. 1998. "Another West Side Story: An Interview with Members of El Comité-MINP." In *The Puerto Rican Movement: Voices from the Diaspora*, ed. Andrés Torres and José Velázquez. Philadelphia: Temple University Press.

———. 1998. "Coming Full Circle: The Puerto Rican Socialist Party, U.S. Branch." In *The Puerto Rican Movement: Voices from the Diaspora*, ed. Andrés Torres and José Velázquez. Philadelphia: Temple University Press.

Verrill, A. Hyatt. 1914. *Porto Rico Past and Present and San Domingo of To-Day*. New York: Dodd, Mead.

"Vieques and Albizu Hold a Place in History." 2000. Editorial, Special Supplement. *El diario/La prensa*, New York (June 11): 6.

"Vieques une; el status divide." 1999. *El Nuevo Día*, San Juan (August 24): 4–5.

Villanueva, Eduardo. 1999. "El consenso como instrumento de lucha en el reclamo de derechos humanos por Vieques." *Revista del Colegio de Abogados de Puerto Rico* 60, no. 3: 98–111.

Villarreal, Sandra I. 2000. "Toledo señala vínculos del FBI con el carpeteo." *El Nuevo Día*, San Juan (January 16): 64.

Vinicio, Marco. 2000. "'Viento en popa' las protestas por la salida de la Marina en Vieques." *El diario/La prensa*, New York (July 5): 3.

———. 2000. "Vieques, decisivo en las elecciones." *El diario/La prensa*, New York (October 22): 3.

Waters, Mary C. 1990. *Ethnic Options: Choosing Identities in America*. Berkeley: University of California Press.

Weinstein, Brian. 1993. *The Civic Tongue: Political Consequences of Language Choice*. New York: Longman.

Weisskoff, Richard. 1985. *Factories and Food Stamps: The Puerto Rican Model of Development*. Baltimore: Johns Hopkins University Press.

Wells, Henry. 1979. *La modernización de Puerto Rico: Un análisis político de valores e instituciones en proceso de cambio* (The modernization of Puerto Rico: A political analysis of values and institutions undergoing change). Translated by Pedro G. Salazar. Río Piedras, P.R.: Editorial Universitaria.

Whalen, Carmen T. 1998. "Bridging Homeland and Barrio Politics: The Young Lords in Philadelphia." In *The Puerto Rican Movement: Voices from the Diaspora*, ed. Andrés Torres and José Velázquez. Philadelphia: Temple University Press.

White, Trumbull. 1975 [1938]. *Puerto Rico and Its People*. New York: Arno Press.

Wong, Timothy K., and Milan T. Sun. 1998. "Dissolution and Reconstruction of National Identity: The Experience of Subjectivity in Taiwan." *Nations and Nationalism* 4, no. 2: 247–72.

X, Malcolm. 1990 [1965]. *Malcolm X Speaks: Selected Speeches and Statements*. New York: Grove Weidenfeld.

Young Lords Party. 1972. *Resolutions and Speeches: Puerto Rican Revolutionary Workers Organization*. New York: Young Lords Party.

Index

Adams, John Q., 8
Agricultural Adjustment Administration, 23
AIDS Hospital inquiry, 38, 47, 51, 60
Albandoz, Dulce M., 67
Albizu Campos, Pedro: and Gesta de Jayuya (1950), 76; and Grito de Lares commemoration, 17, 90; as nationalist icon, 17, 19, 76, 79–80, 84–85, 100; as Nationalist Party leader, 17–18, 24; and Puerto Rican Day Parade, 84–85; trial of, 18, 109n.110; in U.S. Army, 108n.105; on Vieques, 24
American Federation of Labor, 73
American identity, 13, 15, 16, 75–77, 101, 121n.39, 121n.49
Americanization, 15, 44–45, 62
American Labor Party, 74
Aponte Martínez, Luis, 45
Aristegui, Rafael, 8
Armey, Dick, 55
Aspin, Les, 34
Atlantic Fleet, 22, 24, 25

Badillo, Herman, 78
Barbey, Daniel E., 27
Barbosa, José C., 84
Barrios, Luis, 82
Bastille, Federal, 64
Bate, William B., 15
Berríos Martínez, Rubén, 19, 46, 60, 61, 66–67, 70
Betances, Ramón E., 17, 90
Biblical Society of Puerto Rico, 64
Black Panther Party, 79, 99
Bolívar, Simón, 7
British Royal Navy, 22, 27
British Virgin Islands, 7

Brown, Henry, 15
Bulter, Hugh M., 27
Burgos, Norma, 46, 48, 68
Bush, George, 33, 40
Bush, George W., 65, 68, 69, 102, 103

Calderón, Sila M., 39, 46, 61, 62, 66–67
Camacho Negrón, Antonio, 55
Carr, Raymond, 30
Carrión, Adolfo, 82
Carroll, Henry, 14, 20
Carter, Jimmy, 54
Ceiba, 21, 49
Charter of Autonomy (1897), 13, 16
Chávez, César, 79
Chávez, Linda, 76
Chicano movement, 79
Christensen, Ernest E., 35
Christian, Pepe, 29
Churches, and Vieques movement, 30, 43–46, 62–63, 67–68, 82
Clemency debate, 38, 52, 54–57, 79
Clinton, Hillary R., 47, 54–57, 69, 82
Clinton, William J.: and clemency issue, 54–56; and Kaho'olawe, 40; and Pedro Rosselló, 42, 61, 102; and Puerto Rico's status, 60, 61; and U.S. armed forces, 34, 59, 103; and Vieques crisis, 47–48, 60, 103; Vieques plan, 57, 60–61, 63, 66
Club Boriquen, 73
Coalición Ecuménica pro Vieques, 68
Cohen, Richard, 48
Colombia, 13, 68
Comité Pro Rescate y Desarrollo de Vieques, 34–35, 43
Commonwealth government. *See* Puerto Rican government

Commonwealth movement: and Puerto Rican culture, 122n.72; view of U.S. Navy, 51–52
Commonwealth party. *See* Partido Popular Democrático
Concepción de Gracia, Gilberto, 19
Congreso Nacional Hostosiano, 43
Congress: debate on Puerto Rico's status, 60, 63, 69, 83, 112n.103
Corrada del Río, Alvaro, 45, 61, 67
Cortés, Edwin, 55
Crab Island. *See* Vieques (history)
Cruz, Gerardo, 49
Cruzada Pro Rescate de Vieques, 31
Cuba: Bay of Pigs, 27; and Cold War, 20, 88; Grito de Yara (1868), 9; Guantánamo, 25; independence movement, 7, 9, 107n.62; missile crisis, 25; under Spanish rule, 6; U.S. invasion of, 12; U.S. territorial ambitions in, 8
Culebra: military lands in, 16, 22, 24, 30; movement, 42; municipal government, 29; and Roosevelt Roads, 24; settlement, 8; target practice, 17, 29, 49

Dandie Co., 34
Danzig, Richard, 43
Davis, James P., 62
Decolonization Committee. *See* United Nations
Defense industry. *See* individual companies and political action committees
De la Torre, Miguel, 8
Dellums, Ronald, 32
Democratic Party (U.S.), 73–74, 77
Depleted uranium. *See* Uranium
Dracula Plan, 28
Duany, Jorge, 93

Eastern Sugar Associates Co., 23
Edison, Charles, 22
Eisenhower, Dwight D., 58
El Comité-MINP, 81, 92
Elections (2000), 65–67
Elective Governor Act (1947), 27
Encarnación, Alba, 40, 57, 62

Environmental devastation, 27, 48, 114n.110
Escobar, Elizam, 55
Estadidad jíbara, 90
Estrada, Wilfredo, 64–65
Ethnicity: and collective action, 96–97; and elites, 93–94; formation of, 10, 93–94; and intellectuals, 10, 30, 93–94; iron law of, 89; and nationalist icons, 123n.100; and separatism, 89–90; territoriality and, 88–89, 91, 93
Evangelical churches and Vieques movement, 30, 43–44, 62–63, 82
Evangelical Foundation, 63

Farinacci, Jorge, 71
Feder, Don, 76
Federación Universitaria Pro Independencia, 81
Federal Bureau of Investigation, 59–60
Ferré, Luis A., 30, 62, 84
Fishermen associations: in Hawaii, 40; in Puerto Rico, 29, 31, 32, 106n.47
Flores, Juan, 72, 92, 93
Foraker Act (1900), 16
Fortín Accord (1983), 32, 33, 35, 47, 60, 98–99
Freeh, Louis, 59–60
Fuerzas Armadas de Liberación Nacional, 53–55, 81, 95

García Rivera, Oscar, 74
García San Inocencio, Víctor, 41
Géigel Polanco, Vincente, 26
General Dynamics Co., 33
General Electric Co., 33, 40
Germany, 12, 21–22, 24, 109n.2
Gesta de Jayuya (1950), 76
Giuliani, Rudolph, 55
Glazer, Nathan, 75
González, Efraín, 82
González, José, 91
González Medina, Rubén, 67
González Nieves, Roberto, 45, 46, 61, 63
Goodrich, James, 33
Gore, Al, 47, 54, 65, 82, 103
Gramm, Phil, 55

Granados Navedo, José, 60
Gran familia puertorriqueña, 10
Green, Kevin, 68, 70
Grito de Lares (1868), 9, 10 17, 58; annual commemoration, 17, 58, 60; role in nationalist folklore, 90, 124n.20
Grosfoguel, Ramón, 93
Grumman Aerospace Co., 33
Guadalpe, Ismael, 82
Guss, David, 85
Gutiérrez, Luis, 42, 47, 59, 82

Hamilton, Alexander, 8
Hamilton, Lee, 48
Hansen, James, 68–69
Hawaii, 15, 39–40. *See also* Kaho'olawe
Hechter, Michael, 94
Helm, George, 40
Hepburn, Arthur J., 22
Hernández, Diego, 48
Hernández Colón, Rafael, 54
Hidalgo, Edward, 24, 30

Iglesias, Roger, 41
Independence movement: and clemency issue, 38; and federal policy, 57; and intellectuals, 29–30, 111n.60; and mainland Puerto Ricans, 72–73, 78, 80–81, 85, 87; persecution under Spanish rule, 9; persecution under U.S. rule, 18, 19, 59–60; and Vieques movement, 30, 31, 42–43; view of U.S. Navy, 51–52
Independence party. *See* Partido Independentista Puertorriqueño; Partido Nacionalista; Partido Socialista Puertorriqueño
Independentistas. *See* Independence movement
Inhofe, James, 56, 61, 65, 76
International Cigar Makers Union, 73
Isabel Segunda. *See* Vieques (history)
Isla Grande, 22
Isla Nena. *See* Vieques (history)

Jayuya uprising. *See* Gesta de Jayuya (1950)
Jefferson, Thomas, 8

Jíbaros, 11, 94
Jiménez, Ricardo, 55
Johnson, Lyndon B., 79
Jones Act (1917), 16, 26, 72

Kaho'olawe, 39–40, 49
Kennedy, John F., 28
Kennedy, Robert, Jr., 66
Knoizen, Arthur, 30, 32, 49
Kouri, Yamil, 39
Kuhn, Robert, 32

La Guardia, Fiorello, 74
Lao, Agustín, 93
Laponce, Jean, 91
Lares. *See* Grito de Lares (1868)
Leahy, William D., 22, 23
Lebrón, José, 63
Leguillou, Teófilo, 8, 105n.17
Lewis, Gordon, 26, 35, 92
Liga Antillana, 73
Liga de Artesanos, 73
Lindsay, John, 78
Lockheed Co., 33
Lodge, Henry C., 12
López, Margarita, 82
López de Baños, Miguel, 105n.22
López Rivera, Oscar, 55
Lott, Trent, 56–57, 65

Macheteros, 31, 53–54, 81
Madison, James, 8
Mahan, Alfred T., 12, 15
Mainland Puerto Ricans. *See* Puerto Ricans, mainland
Marcantonio, Vito, 74
Mari Bras, Juan, 19, 43
Martínez, Gaspar, 7
Matos, Adolfo, 55
McCaffrey, Katherine, 29
McCarthy, Joseph, 121n.49
McDonnell Douglas Co., 33
McManus, James E., 62
Memorandum of Understanding. *See* Fortín Accord (1983)
Migration, Puerto Rican, 72, 79
Miles, William, 94

Military installations (British), 22, 24
Military installations (U.S.): in British colonies, 109n.4; in Cuba, 25; in Culebra, 16, 30; expropriations in Vieques, 23, 24, 27, 28; in Hawaii, 21, 22, 24, 39; Roosevelt Roads, 22, 24, 27, 28, 33, 49; in San Juan, 16, 22; in Vieques, 16, 23–26, 41
Misla Aldarondo, Edison, 57
Mitchell, Kimo, 40
Monroe Doctrine, 8, 12
Monte David, 42, 59, 91. *See also* Sanes Rodríguez, David
Morris, Dick, 55
Movement for National Liberation, 81
Movimiento Pro Independencia, 81, 83. *See also* Partido Socialista Puertorriqueño
Moynihan, Daniel P., 47, 75
Muñiz Air National Guard Base, 53
Muñoz Marín, Luis, 18, 19, 27, 28, 62, 74, 124n.136
Muriente, Julio, 50

Napalm, 27, 48
National Council of Churches, 39
National Guard. *See* Muñiz Air National Guard Base
Nationalist party. *See* Partido Nacionalista
Navy. *See* U.S. Navy
Navy League, 31, 32
Neal, Richard, 48
New York, Puerto Rican community in, 54, 55, 66, 69, 71
Ninguna de las anteriores, 38, 60
Nixon, Richard, 30
"None of the Above." *See Ninguna de las anteriores*
Noriega Rodríguez, David, 39, 63, 64
Nuclear weapons, 28. *See also* Uranium
Nuevo Movimiento Independentista Puertorriqueño, 50
Núñez, José, 62

O'Connor, John, 54
Office of Economic Adjustment, 33

Pacific Fleet, 39–40
Pagán, Dylcia N., 55
Pagán, Samuel, 63
Palacio González, Romualdo, 9
Panama, 13, 25, 27, 68
Panama Canal, 12, 15, 22, 107n.54
Parga, Orlando, 58
Partido Acción Cristiana, 62
Partido Independentista Puertorriqueño, 19, 30, 38, 41–42, 50, 61, 66, 83, 91
Partido Nacionalista, 17–18, 83
Partido Nuevo Progresista, 30, 38, 41, 47, 68
Partido Popular Democrático, 19, 27, 38, 62, 66, 74
Partido Republicano, 26
Partido Socialista, 26, 110n.36
Partido Socialista Puertorriqueño, 30, 79, 81, 83, 92, 110n.36
Pataki, George, 69
Paz para Vieques, 66–67, 70
Pearl Harbor, 21, 22, 24
Pedreira, Antonio S., 91
Pentagon. *See* U.S. Defense Department
Peña Clos, Sergio, 46
Pesquera, Carlos, 66–67, 83
Philippines, 12, 15, 16, 18
Pieras, Jaime, 66–67
Piñero, Jesús T., 27
PIP. *See* Partido Independentista Puertorriqueño
Political action committees, 58
Political persecution in Puerto Rico: under Spanish rule, 9; under U.S. rule, 18, 19, 59–60
Political prisoners. *See* Clemency debate
PPD. *See* Partido Popular Democrático
Presidential vote in Puerto Rico, 66–67
Prim y Prats, Juan, 8–9
Pro-American demonstrations, 58, 63, 118n.110
Project Kaho'olawe Ohana, 40
Pro Libertad, 53
Puerto Rican Day Parade, 84–85, 123n.125
Puerto Rican government: Charter of

Autonomy (1897), 13, 16; Commonwealth, 14, 27; Elective Governor Act (1947), 27; Foraker Act (1900), 16; Jones Act (1917), 16, 27, 72; military government, 16; offices on U.S. mainland, 77–78; persecution of *independentistas*, 60; Supreme Court of, 67; territorial status, 107n.66; 108n.86; Vieques resolutions, 42, 69

Puerto Rican identity: and Americanization, 15, 44–45; and criollos, 10–11, 93, 91; and flag, 84–85, 95, 124n.136; genesis of, 9–11, 106n.28; and the *gran familia puertorriqueña*, 10; impact on status debate in U.S., 63–64; and *jíbaros*, 11, 94; and Pedro Albizu Campos, 19, 100; and race, 11, 77, 91, 106n.46; and Roman Catholicism, 44–45, 62; and Spanish language, 15, 77; and territoriality, 45, 72, 79, 89–94, 100, 125n.57; in U.S., 75; Vieques in, 88, 95. *See also* Puerto Rican nationalism

Puerto Rican nationalism: and autonomism, 17, 90; cultural, 46, 122n.72; and Pedro Albizu Campos, 17, 19, 76, 79–80, 84–85, 100; and separatism, 17, 90; and violence, 76. *See also* Puerto Rican identity

Puerto Ricans, mainland: African-American influence on, 78–80, 84, 92, 99–100; and clemency debate, 54, 55, 56; and independence movement, 72–73, 78–81, 85, 87; marginalization in U.S., 80, 87, 88, 99; and migration, 72, 79; political leaders, 42, 46, 55, 74, 81; solidarity with Vieques, 66, 69, 79, 81–83, 91, 95, 123n.124; and statehood movement, 83–84; and status plebiscite, 83

Puerto Rican Student Union, 81, 83

Puerto Rico: and Caribbean Basin Initiative, 32; centennial of U.S. rule, 37–38; consensus on Vieques, 51–52, 65, 66, 67; dependency on federal funds, 48–49; environmental devastation, 27, 48; political persecution under Spain, 9; political persecution under U.S., 18, 19, 59–60; public opinion, 51–52, 59, 65; and status debate, 51, 69, 83; strategic value of, 12–13, 33; U.S. invasion of, 11, 12, 13, 107n.66; U.S. territorial ambitions in, 8

Puertorriqueñidad. *See* Puerto Rican identity

Punta Borinquen, 22

Rabin, Robert, 40, 57
Race: and American identity, 13–15, 76, 101, 121n.39; and Puerto Rican identity, 11, 77, 91, 106n.46
Radical statehooders, 38, 49, 61
Ramírez, Roberto, 82
Ramos, Jorge, 57–58
Raschke, Jorge, 62–63
Raytheon Co., 50
Reagan, Ronald, 32
Relocatable-Over-The-Horizon-Radar, 50
Reno, Janet, 56, 64
Republican Party (U.S.), 74
Reynolds, Thomas, 55
Riggs, Francis E., 18
Rivera, Dennis, 55, 66
Rivera, José, 54, 55, 82
Rivera Cruz, Ramón, 46
Rivera Guishard, Juana, 67
Rivera Morales, Severino, 44
Rodham Clinton, Hillary. *See* Clinton, Hillary R.
Rodríguez, Alberto, 55
Rodríguez, Alicia, 55
Rodríguez, Carlos M., 70
Rodríguez, Charlie, 46
Rodríguez, Ida L., 55
Rodríguez Cristóbal, Angel, 31
Roman Catholic Church, 43–46, 62, 63, 121n.49
Romero-Barceló, Carlos, 33, 35, 43, 47, 49, 55, 68, 112n.99
Romero Donnelly, Melinda, 68
Roosevelt, Eleanor, 76
Roosevelt, Franklin D., 15, 18, 21, 22, 112n.3
Roosevelt, Theodore, 12

166 | Index

Roosevelt Roads Naval Base, 22–24, 27–28, 30, 33, 48, 49, 109n.23
Rosa, Luis, 55
Rosselló, Pedro: and Al Gore, 47; and centennial of U.S. rule, 37; and clemency debate, 54; and Clinton administration, 42, 47, 54, 102; and Clinton plan, 57, 60–61; and peace demonstrations, 63–64; and plebiscites, 38, 58, 60–61, 112n.3; and presidential vote, 67; promoting English language, 36; promoting statehood, 36; and Puerto Rican Day Parade, 84; and Puerto Rican nationalism, 58, 60; and radical statehooders, 61; reelection, 61; and Trent Lott, 56–57; and U.N., 50; and U.S. Navy, 43, 47; and Vieques Commission, 46, 49, 50
Royal Navy. *See* British Royal Navy
Rumsfeld, Donald, 68, 69

Said, Edward, 14
Saiki, Patricia, 40
Sánchez, Luis, 69
Sanes Rodríguez, David: death of, 41–42, 47; death, anniversary of, 63, 69, 120n.176; as martyr, 50, 97, 98; Monte David, 42, 59, 91; Navy report on, 50
Santiago, Manuela, 46, 50
Schumer, Charles, 69
Segarra, Juan E., 55
Serrano, Dámaso, 67
Serrano, José, 42, 54, 56, 58, 59–60
Sessions, Jeff, 55
Socialist Party (U.S.), 73
South Bronx Greenhouse Co., 34
Spain, 6–9, 13
Spanish-American War (1898), 12, 13
Spanish Civil War, 75
Special commission. *See* Vieques commission
St. Croix, 8, 23, 28
St. John, 6
St. Kitts, 68
St. Thomas, 6, 8, 105n.11
Statehood movement: and *estadidad jíbara*, 90; and independence movement, 57–58; and mainland Puerto Ricans, 83–84; and peace demonstrations, 63, 68; popular support of, 38; and Puerto Rican culture, 122n.72; and radical statehooders, 38, 49, 61; and Roman Catholic Church, 62; and Vieques movement, 47, 49; view of U.S. Navy, 51–52, 65
Statehood party. *See* Partido Nuevo Progresista; Partido Republicano; Partido Socialista
Status plebiscites, 38
Steinberg, Stephen, 89
Student Nonviolent Coordinating Committee, 79
Susoni, Francisco, 26
Swope, Guy, 18, 19

Tabaqueros, 73, 74–75
Tió, Juan A., 23
Tobacco workers. *See Tabaqueros*
"Todo Puerto Rico con Vieques," 50
Toqueville, Alexis de, 8
Torres, Alejandrina, 55
Torres, Carlos A., 55
Treaty of Paris (1898), 13
Treaty of Tlateloco (1967), 28
Trías Monge, José, 13, 107n.66
Truman, Harry S., 18, 27, 76
Tugwell, Rexford, 18, 19
Tutu, Desmond, 54

Unificación Puertorriqueña Tripartita, 26
United Farm Workers Union, 45
United Kingdom, 6, 12, 22, 28
United Nations, 50, 83
United States: citizenship, 16, 108n.86; invasion of Puerto Rico, 11, 12, 107n.66; and Panama Canal, 12; territorial ambitions in Puerto Rico, 8
United Technologies Co., 33
Uranium, 48, 114n.110
U.S. Defense Department: and Clinton administration, 34, 40, 59; and Dracula Plan, 28; nuclear policy in Puerto Rico, 28; Office of Economic Adjustment, 33; and Puerto Rico's status, 112n.103; September 11 aftermath, 103. *See also* Military installations (U.S.)

U.S. House of Representatives: Armed Services Committee, 28, 32; Subcommittee on Insular and International Affairs, 35. *See also* Congress

U.S. Navy: Atlantic Fleet, 22, 24, 25; economic development of Vieques, 28–29, 33, 34, 39, 40, 59; enlarging Vieques landholdings, 28; Pacific Fleet, 39–40; public support in Puerto Rico, 51–52, 65; report on Sanes Rodríguez death, 50; and Rosselló administration, 47; target practice in Culebra, 17, 29, 49; and Vieques civilians, 29, 32, 41, 43, 48–50; and Vieques movement, 31; and Vieques plebiscite, 59, 60–61. *See also* U.S. Defense Department; Military installations (U.S.)

U.S. Senate: Armed Services Committee, 56, 58. *See also* Congress

U.S. Southern Command, 25, 40

U.S. Virgin Islands, 6, 7, 15, 23, 28

Valentín, Carmen, 55

Vanguardia Pro-Navy, 31

Vega, Bernardo, 74, 76, 85

Velázquez, Nydia, 55, 82

Ventura, Carlos, 40, 61–62

Vera, Juan, 63

Viequenses Pro Marina, 69

Viequenses Unidos, 31

Vieques (history): Bieque, 7, 105n.3; Crab Island, 7, 105n.3; Fortín, 8, 16, 106n.23; geography, 6–7; governors, 8; Isabel Segunda, 25, 106n.23; Isla Nena, 7; military role under Spain, 7; military role under U.S., 17; name, 105n.3; and Pedro Albizu Campos, 18, 24; as Puerto Rican municipality, 8; sea wall, 24; settlement, 7, 8, 105n.22; and Simón Bolívar, 7; union activism, 17; U.S. invasion of, 12, 13; and U.S. Navy personnel, 29; U.S. territorial ambitions in, 8; and World War II, 25–26

Vieques (land and economy): agriculture, 8, 16; civilian relocation, 27; economic development, 29, 39, 59; expropriations, 23, 24, 27, 28; fishing, 29; industrialization, 33–34, 40; military lands transfer, 35, 66; sugar plantations, 23, 24; target areas, 110n.25; tourism development, 28; U.S. military installations in, 16, 23–26

Vieques (people and politics): American expatriates in, 34; and Clinton administration, 47–48, 56, 57, 59, 62, 103; and Cold War, 25, 27, 32, 34; consensus in Puerto Rico, 51–52, 65, 66, 67; and depleted uranium, 48, 114n.110; and environmental devastation, 48; fishermen associations, 31, 32; independence from Puerto Rico, 69; local identity, 31; as metaphor, 82, 99; plebiscite, 58–59, 102; public opinion, 59, 61; and Puerto Rican identity, 88; Santa María community, 35; War on Drugs, 30, 41, 50

Vieques commission: federal, 48; in Puerto Rico 46, 49, 50

Vieques Graphics Co., 34

Vieques movement: and churches, 30, 39, 43–46, 62–63, 67–68, 82; and clemency debate, 54–56, 79; and Federal Bastille, 64; and fishermen associations, 31, 32, 40; and independence organizations, 30, 31, 42–43, 47, 50; and mainland movements, 80, 84; and mainland Puerto Rican leaders, 42, 46, 54–56, 66, 69, 81–85; perception in the U.S., 57, 63, 64, 68–69, 79, 85; protests, 50, 63–64, 69, 70, 82, 83, 96; and U.N., 50, 83; and U.S. Navy, 31. *See also* individual activists and organizations

Vieques Solidarity Group, 84

Warner, John, 58

Winship, Blanton, 22

Woolnor Co., 28

X, Malcolm, 80, 100

Young, Don, 60

Young Lords Party, 79–81, 83, 92, 95, 99

Amílcar Antonio Barreto is assistant professor of political science at Northeastern University. He is the author of *Language, Elites, and the State: Nationalism in Puerto Rico and Quebec* (1998) and *The Politics of Language in Puerto Rico* (2001).